CITIZENS OF THE WORLD

BOOKS BY STRINGFELLOW BARR

CITIZENS OF THE WORLD

MAZZINI: PORTRAIT OF AN EXILE

THE PILGRIMAGE OF WESTERN MAN

LET'S JOIN THE HUMAN RACE

Stringfellow Barr

Citizens of the World

BY STRINGFELLOW BARR

PREFACE BY JUSTICE WILLIAM O. DOUGLAS

1953

DOUBLEDAY & COMPANY, INC.

GARDEN CITY, NEW YORK

To those that hunger

ACKNOWLEDGMENTS

I could not have written this book without the help of scores of persons in my own and many other countries. I cannot mention them all here. But the following persons have been of especial help, even though none of them can be blamed for the defects in this book: my colleagues, Scott Buchanan, Clifford Dancer, Germaine Moncayo, Peter Weiss, Barbara Witt, and Harris Wofford; also Gladys Baldwin Barr, Ruth Dancer, Adolfo Dorfman, Arthur Fletcher, Jack Goodman, Robert W. Hudgens, Arno Mayer, Leon and Sonia Mohill, Karen Rye, Robert Sarrazac, Timothy Seldes, and Palmer Weber.

Stringfellow Barr

CHARLOTTESVILLE, VIRGINIA

7

PREFACE

*L*et's Join the Human Race by Stringfellow Barr
was one of the most important political tracts of our time. The
present volume is an expansion and extension of it. Dr. Barr puts
himself to the task of formulating a whole new approach to our
problems of foreign policy. There is nothing staid nor orthodox
about his thinking. He has a fresh viewpoint. He is at home in the
world of ideas; he prefers ideas to dollars and bombs and guns
as answers to the fix we are in. He is at home with Dr. A. Powell
Davies (*Man's Vast Future*), Robert Brittain (*Let There Be
Bread*), and Josué de Castro (*The Geography of Hunger*).

The power of ideas is tremendous. The ideas of freedom, justice, and equality, loosed in the world, have made up into powerful revolutions. The Declaration of Independence, drafted as a
charter of freedom for Americans, works today in Asia as an
inspiration to millions who seek their place in the sun. A part
of this struggle is for independence—independence from Soviet,
French, Dutch, and British empires. A part of this struggle is for
equality. The peoples of Asia want social justice, economic opportunity, and a fair share of the riches of the world. They want that,

9

but they want more. The great quest is for equality of status; the great rebellion is against inequality of status. The important aspect of the problem of equality is racial equality.

For centuries the East believed it was doomed to be subservient to the West. It accepted that condition with the fatalism that has fashioned the religion of the renunciation of life. The influence of renunciation of life is strong in the East today. But the East has awakened.

The Russian Revolution was one influence that gave encouragement to the idea that men could cast off their yokes. Woodrow Wilson's Fourteen Points was another. The teachings and example of Gandhi made a powerful contribution. So did the Atlantic Charter. Fast communication facilities, increased movements of peoples, the intensified tempo of propaganda all played a part. The causes were many; and they varied from country to country. But they built up into a demand for independence and equality that produced a great variety of political programs. Color consciousness was pushed to the forefront. Land reforms were demanded. Medical care was promoted as a public cause. Socialism was embraced, primarily as a revolt against the sweatshops of private capital and as an assurance that the people, rather than some promoter, would get the dividends from the new wealth.

Political organization in Asia is very immature. There are few countries on that continent where there are political parties as we know them. The paucity of political parties is due to the lack of opportunity over the centuries for the people to develop political traditions. The subservient peoples of the East were subservient in the political as well as in the economic sense. Political traditions are the product of experience. The empires that ruled Asia (and Africa) for so long developed none of them. The sudden necessity to be an independent nation thrust political responsibility on a people who never had political experience.

To the outside world these new aggregations of political forces often seem to be irresponsible and inefficient. To the Communist elements they present unique opportunities to organize and promote the cause of the Kremlin.

The problem of America as respects these revolutionary situations is, I think, a simple one. Many times in the past a great power has had one policy at home, another policy abroad. England, meticulous to respect every minority at home, has promoted repressive policies abroad. France, whose proudest boast was liberty, equality, and fraternity, has squandered those ideals in her colonial policy. America, proud of her standards of freedom and justice at home, has in recent years been too often associated not with the forces of liberation, but with the forces of repression.

As a result of these and other influences, there is a political vacuum in the world. The struggle for independence and equality has created difficult problems. People need moral leadership. There is a hunger for sympathetic guidance and direction.

There is no way for America to maintain her moral leadership other than to be faithful abroad, as well as at home, to her principles. The best possible politics for America in the foreign field is to be true to her ideals of freedom, justice, and equality. If the voice of America is always heard on the side of the weak and the oppressed, if America in the councils of nations is always looking for a way to help the underprivileged help themselves, if America is against exploitation whoever the exploiter is and whoever the exploited are, then America becomes strong in the hearts of people the world around. Then Soviet Russia has competition at the political level. Then Soviet Russia has competition so powerful that the purveyors of the Communist creed will go begging.

If America is true to her principles, there will be a vast change in the world. The Red tide of Communism will ebb. There will be renewed hopes among all nations. If we keep America's ideals in the forefront of every domestic and foreign program, the victory of civilization will be easy.

11

If we are afraid of free speech at home, we will be frightened abroad. If we adopt repressive policies at home—curbing speech, persecuting people for their political creeds, being suspicious of anyone who is not thoroughly orthodox in his views—then we are in for trouble abroad. If we are fearful of new ideas at home, we will be startled in Asia.

Asia will not be remade in the image of America. All the money, all the atomic bombs in the world could not force it. Asia will evolve differently. She will use some borrowed ideas; she will make many political inventions. Her industrial revolution will have a stronger flavor of socialism than ours ever knew.

The truth is that Asia (and Africa too) is seething with ideas that are not orthodox. If we are congenial only to the orthodox, if we are afraid to explore ideas to the periphery, if we do not encourage experimental attitudes, then we will be alarmed, confused, and bewildered abroad. Then every socialist, every rebel, every unorthodox political leader in Asia will look like a dangerous undercover man for the Kremlin. If we have that attitude, we will miss opportunities for warm and enduring political alliances that could build for friendship and peace, rather than for tensions and doubts.

While this is not the theme of this book, it is a starting point for the analysis of world problems which Stringfellow Barr presents. His presentation will stir old prejudices; it will provoke many. There is great resistance these days to looking at the world problems primarily as political rather than as military. This volume presents the problems at the political level. That to me is the correct approach. The book contains what the Great Debate of 1952 should have been about.

Once we start with the political approach there will be much room for disagreement on specific measures. But the country will flourish better on disagreement than on billingsgate. Moreover, there is the possibility, though slight, that our present military strategy will succeed in saving Asia from Communism. If it does, we will be desperately unprepared to handle the revolutions that will continue unless we come full face with the political problems that this volume presents.

William O. Douglas

CITIZENS OF THE WORLD

CHAPTER I

WARNING TO THE READER

This book involves a critical attack on America's present foreign policy. But since this policy is "our" policy, this book is bound to irritate or anger many Americans. I am sorry this must be the case. I myself believe deeply that it is only through undergoing critical attacks that human policies are likely to become good policies.

American foreign policy is today being attacked all over the world, both for good reasons and bad ones. I have tried here to attack it for good ones. It is being attacked with peculiar ferocity by the Russian Government and by the Communist parties of the world. Given the temper of our times, this fact immediately places me with Russians and Communists. Since they and I agree that America has a bad foreign policy, many readers will not bother to find out whether we agree for the same reasons.

I shall therefore be classified by some readers as a pro-Russian or a Communist or a fellow-traveler, or at least a dupe of the Kremlin. I know of no honorable way of avoiding this unpleasant experience. I could of course lie or keep silent. But I happen to believe that the citizen of a self-governing democracy is heavily

15

obligated to speak his mind on matters of public concern, including the foreign policy of his government. Especially when speaking his mind will make him unpopular.

It may reassure you personally if I report that I am not a Communist, have never been one, and have no plans for joining the Communist Party. I disagree with Communists on too many vital matters to make even a good fellow-traveler, although I made up my mind several years ago to avoid becoming what many of my friends have, alas, become: a fellow-traveler-by-opposition, that is, an anti-Communist ready to dislike anything Communists like or to like anything Communists dislike. For this is to be dominated by the Kremlin. I am an American, by birth and by preference. I am immensely proud of my country and intensely ashamed of some of its present policies, not because I consider them malicious but because I consider them foolish. I think there can be little doubt of the verdict of history.

This book is concerned with our relation to some two billion human beings who are neither Russian nor American. It is concerned with how we lost touch with them and how we might find them again and join with them in attacking our common problems. This book is not directly concerned with our relations with Russia. During the Second World War, I expected that these relations would be bad and I have not been disappointed.

This book discusses, however inadequately, problems of life-and-death importance to every living American as well as to Americans yet unborn. I wish I could have discussed these problems better. Perhaps this book will provoke others to discuss them better. In case you feel impelled by my words to dislike me personally, it will be worth remembering that whether my character or general political views are good, bad, or middling can neither validate nor invalidate the arguments I have advanced. Therefore, if what I have said, particularly in the early pages, angers you, I would ask you to skip it and listen to the argument that follows. My literary awkwardness, or plain bad manners, can be of little importance to our country. The matters touched on later are of the most tragic importance. Two billion people are watching us.

CHAPTER II

For several years now, the government of the United States has had one basic foreign policy: stop Russia, and stop Communism. During that time Russia has steadily expanded her sphere of influence; the number of persons governed by Communists has increased by hundreds of millions; the American people have suffered more than a hundred thousand casualties in Korea; and the arms race threatens us and our allies with a galloping inflation that should greatly aid the Communists. This is not a handsome record for a foreign policy, not even a bi-partisan policy.

The government of the United States has awarded itself the leadership of "the free world"; and, although that term has never been very tightly defined, it apparently refers to all governments not dominated by Russia or Communism, the two things our government is out to "stop."

Now that our policy has failed us, we can see clearly enough why: it is purely negative. This is what has left us with that most useless of instruments, a foreign policy that does not appeal to foreigners. It not only does not attract them, it does not even make sense to them. Since it never has made too much sense to the American, this is a good time for inventory.

The best way to take stock, since we admit we are the leaders of the free world, would be to have another look at the free world. We have been staring with such breathless horror at the Kremlin for so long that we have forgotten the two billion men and women on this planet who are neither Russian nor American and who are a little skeptical of both Moscow and Washington. A realistic foreign policy would have to be positive, not negative, and it would have to be based on the actual facts about all those two billion human beings whom an inscrutable Providence placed somewhere else than in America or Russia. No foreign policy that made sense could afford to ignore what those two billion foreigners think, feel, want, or intend to do. We have been counting them only to see how many of them could and would carry a rifle and help "contain" Russia. Let's take our eyes off Russia just long enough to listen to these two billion men and women, or even just look at them.

They will be hard for us to see. For America today is like a rich suburb surrounded almost entirely by slums, and rich suburbanites always find it hard to put themselves in the place of a man who lives in a slum. Perhaps that is why, when we talk about Asia, we use expressions like "teeming millions"—anonymous, inhuman phrases, phrases that reduce men to statistics, that rob men of their faces. If Asians have no faces, you and I don't have to look in their eyes.

But a few American economists and engineers, and a lot of American G.I.'s, have seen at firsthand the unspeakable human misery of Asia, of Africa, of Latin America. The rest of us had better find some way to imagine it, if we possibly can. Otherwise we will go on as we are going, cut off from the bulk of the human race, ignorant of its real problems, and therefore unable to insist that our foreign policy be realistic. Until we Americans see our new neighbors in that Mighty Neighborhood which modern techniques have created, we will go on tolerating an American foreign policy which has not enough to do with the real facts of life—of life and of death. The gold curtain that separates our comfort-loving land from the bulk of the human race will go on glittering, will go on reflecting an imaginary free world—the one that exists only in our own minds and on that smooth gold curtain that contains us now.

"I believe there is a trick by which we Americans can understand these two billion men, women, and children scattered all over the globe. Will the reader play 'Let's pretend' with me, the way children do? Let's pretend that you have not yet been born but will be born this year, somewhere on the planet, somewhere in this Mighty Neighborhood. And let's try to estimate your chances of living a happy, healthy, decent, and useful life.

"If you are born this year, then on the same day more than 200,000 other babies will be born, all over the world.

"You will have less than one chance in twenty of being born in the United States. Your chance of being born in the Soviet Union will be not much better. These countries may be heavily armed, but most people just don't live in them.

"You will probably be colored. Remember that you and the 200,000 other squawking brats who will be the day's baby crop are going to be born all over the planet and that there are just not many openings in the places where the white race lives. You must take your chances with the other babies. And the chances are, you will be colored—colored black, or colored brown, or colored yellow.

"Your chances of being born white this year are not more than one in three. Your chances of being Chinese are one in four; of being born in India, better than one in nine.

21

"If you are born colored, you will probably be born either among people who have recently revolted and thrown out the white folks who used to govern them or else in a country that is still trying to throw the white folks out. If you are born in Africa, you are likely to learn the maxim: 'Never trust a white man.'

"You have only about one chance in four of being born a Christian. It is far more likely that you will be born a Confucian or a Buddhist, a Mohammedan or a Taoist.

"If you are born in the United States—and, remember, that's quite an *if*—you will probably live longer than a year. But if you are born in India, which is more likely, you have only a little better than a one-to-four chance of living more than a year. But cheer up! your chances in some places would be worse; and, besides, even if you survive babyhood in India, you have only a fifty-fifty chance of growing to maturity.

"If you are born colored, the chances are overwhelming that you will be chronically sick all your life—from malaria, or intestinal parasites, or tuberculosis, or maybe even leprosy. And even if you are not chronically sick, you are likely to be weak from hunger. You have about a two-to-one chance of suffering from malnutrition, either from too little food or from food that is not a balanced or nourishing diet. You have a reasonably good chance of experiencing real famine—to the point where you will be glad to eat the bark off a tree. But this chance is extremely hard to calculate.

"Again, if you are born colored, you have only a one-to-four chance of learning to read. And since you almost certainly will not own a radio, you will be pretty well cut off from that part of the human family that has enough to eat and that is reasonably healthy. You will most likely live in a mud hut, with a dirt floor and no chimney, its roof thatched with straw. You will almost certainly work on the land, and most of what you raise will go to the landlord. In addition, you are likely to be deeply in debt to

22

the local moneylender, and you may have to pay him annual interest of anywhere from 30 to 100 per cent."*

This is a picture of the actual condition of man in the mid-twentieth century. The statistics in it are not precise. How could they be? It takes money, and lots of it, to hold a modern census. But these statistics have at least the merit of being conservative; and really accurate ones could not change the total picture.

These are the free nations, or a good part of them, which we propose to lead in a crusade against the Russians, if the Russians are not more careful, and in defense of the American way of life. We hope these free nations prove enthusiastic and dependable allies.

Meanwhile, our government, our press (and particularly the advertising matter printed by our press), our radio commentators (and particularly our commercial and patriotic plugs), our office seekers and commencement orators, and even the preachers in many of our churches have created a quite different picture of the world, an American picture. It is a jingoistic picture and a narcissistic one. And it is a picture charged with violence, with the appeal to force. It is composed of clichés and slogans. In it the United States stands firm and tight-lipped, surrounded by scheming enemies and by weak-kneed, confused allies. In such a world, the U.S.—regretfully—gets tough, demands a showdown, with no holds barred, tit for tat, and insists that its allies put it on the line, that they put up or shut up. It works through total diplomacy and hopes to achieve situations of strength. Until then, any negotiation with the Kremlin, no matter how hard the bargaining, would be appeasement. And we all know about Munich. We are deeply realistic and follow only enlightened self-interest. When our statesmen speak, they speak tersely; and if the Russians sneer at them, they sneer back. (In fact, considering how much less

*Let's Join the Human Race. By Stringfellow Barr. Copyright by The University of Chicago Press, 1950; pp. 3 and 4.

23

practice we have had at diplomatic billingsgate than the Russians, our diplomats deserve a lot of credit for the way they dish it out.) Our generals are grim-faced. Our political leaders publicly estimate flying distances to various Russian cities, and a Secretary of the Navy publicly suggests attacking Russia. For force is all the Russians understand. We have been repeatedly assured by speakers from the President down that this was the gravest hour of peril in our history (which should put Gettysburg in its place once for all). With the Red hordes poised and ready to sweep to the Atlantic, we desperately try to persuade those of our allies who live in the horde's path to arm against aggression. We ourselves make every sacrifice: we offer to rearm the Germans, we go easy on the Japanese, we back Chiang Kai-shek, and we stand shoulder to shoulder with Franco. If our allies object, it is because they lack moral principles; but who can blame them, considering the danger they are in? We may have to tighten our belts still farther: to date the problem of guns or butter has been met with the hopeful slogan: Guns and the whole cow. But at least we put up signs directing our citizens to the nearest bomb shelter, which is more than our allies do. They are horrified by what sounds like an argument here over whether to fight in Europe or Asia; but to us, because of our moral principles, it is a Great Debate, with capital letters.

We are not engaged in a power struggle with Russia, as some people in the free world seem to believe. On the contrary we are fighting for the minds and hearts of men and calling on all men everywhere to stand firm against the Godless atheists in the Kremlin. That the words Godless and atheist are synonymous will not deter us. Part of our job is to stop the Big Lie, borrowed from Hitler, by repeating the same idea in different words. We would be justified even if we called the Russians Godless, atheistic, irreligious opponents of Divinity. For it is moral principles we are fighting for: freedom, liberty (another case of a wisely chosen synonym), and perhaps free enterprise, which many of our business leaders hold to be the true basis of our Bill of Rights. The Bill of Rights itself is slipping a little, according to two justices of the U. S. Supreme Court; but we are willing to sacrifice even freedom and liberty, though perhaps not free enterprise, to stop Russia. And we will stop them, even if—in General MacArthur's celebrated phrase—we have to go it alone; even if we have to take the wraps off our air force (only a shoestring air force in any case), take the wraps off Chiang Kai-shek, off Franco, off Hitler, if he should unexpectedly show up. We have steeled ourselves to fight the devil with fire, since force is all the Russians understand; and we would thank our allies not to get queasy in an hour like the present—the gravest in our national history. Besides, granted that they are about to be overrun by Russian armies and don't know it, our peril is just as grave and we do know it: General MacArthur has told us we must hold Formosa, or California might be in danger.[1]

Luckily, we are fortified by our moral principles, and even more by religion. Before the threat of Russia, we had almost forgotten what an invaluable ally religion is. God is on our side, not only in our dealings with Russia but even in our dealings with our allies. On Sunday, August 12, 1951, in St. Patrick's Cathedral in New York, after a reading from the Gospel of how Christ healed ten lepers and only one returned to thank him, the preacher of the day asserted that about the same percentage of the nations America has helped through Lend-Lease have bothered to thank us. Next day a headline in the New York *Times* read: "Thankless Allies Likened to Lepers." The sermon was not unique: for, at long last, in this gravest hour of peril in our national history, we Americans remind ourselves of Jesus Christ, and our allies through no fault of ours remind us of lepers. Greatness was ever lonely.

Happily, we know our enemy. It is not the Russian people, to whom we send balloons loaded with greetings. It is the cunning

25

men in the Kremlin, who run a police state and thereby control
absolutely hundreds of millions of wretched men and women.
They press a button, and North Korea springs to arms. They have
other buttons they may yet press. Some day they will press the
wrong button and our whole stock pile will fall down their necks!
Meanwhile, they keep us guessing. On the one hand, they have
piled up the most formidable armaments in history for their mad
career of world conquest. Yet, according to the same newspapers,
their factories either fail to make their quotas or simply refuse to
run at all. So they are not easy to size up. What we do know is
that if they speak words of violence, then they mean what they
say; while, if they speak words of peace, they are trying to deceive
us, or to weaken the spiritual resistance of our allies. In the long
run, our industrial know-how will defeat them, certainly after our
industrial show-how has armed our allies to the teeth and inspired
them with our own moral principles in our fight for the minds and
hearts of men.

The flood of clichés, slogans, threats, recriminations, and self-
congratulations which I have just repeated is, unhappily, the
daily fare of the American newspaper reader, and has been these
many, many months. Most of it was presumably written by public
relations experts with an extremely low opinion of the intelligence
of the American people. I do not share that low opinion. Moreover, I have ample evidence that countless Americans are as much
disgusted by it as I am, even when it has driven them to admit
sadly that war with Russia is probably inevitable and they wish
we could get it over with. It is this nonsense which has left the
American people confused, frightened, and depressed: and, because that is all it has achieved, the military draft and Universal
Military Training have remained unpopular and Civilian Defense
a farce. But these clichés and slogans, taken together, make up the
Big Myth on which our cold-war foreign policy rests.

The Big Myth is no good for export. Wherever it goes—and it

goes lots of places—it hurts America. It has, after all, so little to do with facts. It goes lots of places, because, whereas before World War I, European newspaper readers had little cause to want American news, since World War II what we Americans do is literally a matter of life or death to them. If a member of the Congress discusses Europe now, even in a whisper, his whisper is likely to reverberate through Europe as a shout. And many members of Congress, especially around election time, are not in the first place given to whispering. Asia and Africa are listening, too; and, for a long time now, Latin America has had to listen.

Europe emerged from the second war a wreck, its cities laid waste, its industrial plant impaired, its peoples demoralized and scattered, its social fabric torn, its governments unstable. We emerged a great deal stronger than when we entered, with a vast new industrial plant built in large part by the taxpayers, our cities unbombed, our people well-fed, our one fear the fear of massive unemployment in the postwar slump that our best economists freely predicted, our one desire to forget the war and enjoy our vast new prosperity in peace.

Would we promptly "pull out," as we had pulled out after the first war over Woodrow Wilson's objections? It looked to Europe as if we would. Without waiting for a peace settlement, we started frantically demobilizing. Since the shooting had stopped, we decided the war was "over," and President Truman canceled Lend-Lease. We did join the United Nations, whereas after the first war we had refused to join the League of Nations. But the forces of isolationism were far from sleeping.

Then, with Europe threatening to collapse economically, and perhaps to go Communist politically, we acted. General Marshall, then Secretary of State, proposed what Europeans came to call "the Marshall Plan," by which we would aid Europe financially to rebuild its shattered productive plant. It was the most statesmanlike action our government has taken since the war. It was a simultaneous attack on two grave problems. It more than restored Europe's prewar production, and, by acting as a gigantic PWA, it absorbed America's surplus product and pump-primed us right out of a threatened depression. Both things were worth doing. Unhappily, since it was done by Washington bilaterally, and not by the United Nations, in accordance with its Charter, as a venture in mutual aid, it forced Washington willy-nilly into the position of Europe's paymaster; and the Congress can scarcely be blamed if it showed a growing determination to call the tune.

Meanwhile, America's relations with Russia deteriorated, and the two military giants glared at each other across the still prostrate form of a convalescent Europe. Washington's emphasis shifted from repairing the wreckage of World War II to arming all possible allies against, or if necessary for, World War III. Washington offered Western Europe the Atlantic Pact, and Western Europe hesitantly and unhappily accepted. True, the American press at this time pictured our European cousins as holding out to us imploring hands as the Reds prepared for a Hitlerian drive for the sea. But anybody who was in Europe at that time and could read some language other than English knows that this was a patriotic American fiction. Europeans generally took no stock in the Red-horde story. What they did take stock in was the speed with which local Communist parties, notably in such countries as France and Italy, could gather strength whenever Europe's growing production appeared to lack orderly means of distributing its product. In short, Europe's recipe for defense was prosperity; more and more often our recipe was weapons. Maybe we were right and Europe was wrong. For the purposes of the present discussion, it does not matter. The point is that we and our military allies differed deeply and fundamentally in our assessment of "the Communist Menace." We still differ.

Until the summer of 1950, the average American believed that the average non-Communist European thought as he did: that the danger of Communism was a military danger. But in that summer, at a diplomatic meeting in New York, Secretary Acheson suddenly proposed the rearming of Germany. The reaction of Western Europe was so violent that not even the American press, dominated as it was by the Big Myth, could ignore the fact that, although Washington could carry the governments it subsidized pretty far, it was not necessarily carrying with them the peoples they governed. American opinion was shocked. It need not have been, if our press had been reporting European currents of opinion more competently and with less attention to the Big Myth it had helped create. But, while Communism could be freely and dispassionately discussed in Europe, it had become a highly charged word in our country; and any discussion here of the European attitude would have sounded like "fellow-traveler talk." Doubtless it would have cleared the air if Americans generally could have learned that most Europeans were "fellow-travelers"— in the present American epithet sense, not at all in the European sense. That is, most Europeans rejected the Communist solution for the problems which beset them. But they did not, as so many Americans did, consider Democratic Socialism as a stage toward Communism; or a jealous governmental concern for the general welfare the last step ("the welfare state") toward Democratic Socialism. Most of them not only rejected Russian Communism because it denied the civil rights for which Western Europe had fought and bled in numerous revolutions: they also rejected as irrelevant for them what the American business world extols as "free enterprise." One should add that many of them knew enough about the rapidly increasing concentration of industrial power in America to doubt that business competition was the chief characteristic of the American system anyhow. Nor did they believe that the American system had solved the economic problem, as many Americans did. They were quite aware that the Marshall Plan provided us with a temporary solution and that our massive rearmament was an even vaster **PWA** than the Marshall Plan had been.

I am not talking here about European Communists: what they said was in large part Moscow speaking. And Moscow, like Washington, was using words chiefly as weapons. I am talking here about the European non-Communists. And by the summer of 1951 their views on American foreign policy, as distinguished from the American people, were pretty emphatic. They did not want a remilitarized Germany, particularly a Germany which was far from having been de-Nazified—thanks largely to American Occupation policies. Thousands upon thousands of them, it may be worth our recalling, had known the inside of a Nazi concentration camp for political prisoners. How many native-born Americans had? It made a difference. To be "against Communism" was no guarantee of virtue to a European. The Nazis were conspicuously against Communism.

To Europeans it seemed obvious that China, though not the island of Formosa, was governed by the Chinese Communist Party; and equally obvious that Chiang Kai-shek was through, no matter how many weapons Washington continued to send him. They could see no practical gain in Washington's victory when it persuaded the majority of governments in the United Nations to brand China an aggressor in Korea. They were much more interested in helping the Chinese Government to be independent of Russian influence.

They objected strenuously to bringing Franco into the European defense system. His entry would spell an important victory for Communist propaganda in every country of Europe. We Americans chose to believe that they opposed our flirtations with Franco because of fear—fear that in a pinch we would withdraw our forces behind the Pyrenees if we and Russia fell to blows, and leave our sworn allies to a Russian occupation. Undoubtedly that entered in; but an equally grave reason was that partnership with

Franco would wreck the morale of any European army. Non-Communist Europeans had fought shoulder to shoulder with Communist Europeans against all that Franco represents—and bunked beside them in the same concentration camps and undergone the same tortures. If we asked them to forget it, they could not forget it.

A Congressional bill to cut off all economic assistance to any country that might sell critical materials to Russia or her allies might seem wise and reasonable enough to an American riding an armaments boom, fearing nothing but war with Russia. It seemed unwise and unreasonable to Europeans, who were not in a boom, who badly needed—as they always had—the goods that Eastern Europe has wanted ever since the war to sell them; and who badly needed—as they always had—a market for their own goods, which the United States steadfastly refused to open to them here.

The treaty with Japan which we were preparing to ram down their throats alarmed them less than it did Asia, but it accentuated our growing affection for countries with a strong fascist tradition. It therefore fed Communist propaganda in Europe. Even the staid London *Times*, no anti-American organ, spoke of our take-it-or-leave-it policy in inviting delegates to San Francisco not to discuss a treaty, but to sign one.

To Europeans in general, Americans seemed to have forgotten the art of negotiation—the only alternative for a sovereign state to the art of war. In a world of sovereign states, hard bargaining and horse trading were quite obviously the only alternative to shooting. Europe wondered whether, having decided to create situations of strength that would enable us to negotiate successfully, we had not forgotten our original purpose for creating such situations and had decided just to go on creating them. Meanwhile, public protests were deceptively rare, and Americans were told by their press that we must be patient: Europe would come along.

31

When our Secretary of State turned historian and reminded us publicly how in a few short centuries the Grand Duchy of Moscow expanded clear to the Pacific, Europeans must have grinned sheepishly. For in less time than that little Portugal, Spain, little Holland, France, and little England built, or lost, or rebuilt world empires. The Muscovites, with their perpetual desire for warm-water ports and egress to the ocean, were perhaps unfashionable in making their expansion continental, but they were no more unfashionable than the Secretary of State's own country. Russia expanded across Asia to the Pacific and we expanded from Jamestown and Plymouth to the same Pacific. As for the Poles and Czechs being governed from Moscow—well, the West European feels he cannot exactly ignore Washington. And he notes with interest that American air bases and naval bases are rapidly girdling the globe. And, like most human beings, he hates cant and hypocrisy.

If Washington challenges Moscow to open Russia to American visitors, to prove it wants peace, then the West European grins again. For years he has been reading newspaper stories about our immigration controls against Communists, and he wonders whether we might not be rather embarrassed if the Russians started trying to visit us.

And yet, he is basically on our side. That is why he finds our frequent sermons so embarrassing.

The Korean War was our show. It was we who rounded up the votes in the U.N., and it was we who with far greater difficulty rounded up token military forces from fellow-members. Early in the discussions an American orator at Lake Success, whose speech was heard on American radios, suffered an interesting slip of the tongue: he spoke of the United Stations. It is possible that many American listeners failed to detect the slip for the same psychological reasons that caused the American diplomat to make it. Shortly after the Chinese intervened in Korea, the New York

Times announced unsmilingly that as soon as Washington had decided what was to be done, it would be done through the United Nations.[2] The statement doubtless struck many American readers as both accurate and natural. But Senator Flanders, in view of the new situation the Chinese had created, judged that we should make up our minds who was fighting the Korean War, the United States or the United Nations.[3] It was hard to tell by reading the newspapers. Perhaps it was being fought by the United Stations.

We are fond now of demonstrating that there was no alternative for the U.N. but to defend South Korea from imperialist aggression, a phrase we have borrowed from Russian propaganda and now throw in their teeth. But if this is so obvious as we claim it is, how can we explain the fact that Washington's first reaction, freely expressed by both press and radio, was that Korea was none of our business? A good case can, I think, be made for the action we persuaded the U.N. to take. How good, depends largely on what else the U.S. and the U.N. do. But we Americans are in no position to doubt the morals of anybody who questions the action.

When General MacArthur had cleared South Korea of invaders, he started for the Chinese border. The Chinese Communists protested. India advised against it. We angrily shouted India down. Our allies began to suspect that General MacArthur wanted to provoke a war with China, a war which could quickly become the third world war. Many of his public statements supported this view. They also suspected that for political reasons President Truman had lost control of his military subordinate; they were horrified when the President went all the way to Wake Island to consult him, and when the President and the General gave different accounts of what happened there. At last, European opinion became so disturbed by the apparent growth of General MacArthur's policy that Prime Minister Attlee raced to Washington, with the backing of the French, to clarify what was supposed to be a joint policy.

Why does not Western Europe openly rebel against a leadership in which they have lost confidence? For many reasons. Basically, most West Europeans agree with our political principles rather than with Russia's. But they are conscious that they are powerless and that Washington is not much interested in what they think should be done. In large degree they are now governed from Washington, although they have no right to elect members of Congress. This is why a witty Paris journalist long ago declared that he planned to take out American citizenship so as to have some influence on French affairs. This is why the French Ministry of Finance submitted the national budget of France to the American Government before submitting it to the National Assembly of France, an act unique in modern history.[4]

European "neutralists" have tried to formulate a program that would build a Third Force, independent of both Eastern Giant and Western Giant. They have failed. More and more, events are forcing Europeans to take sides for the Big Showdown, a showdown which the Europeans feel may well wreck civilization but will settle nothing, regardless of who "wins." They are horrified by public statements in America that imply a war may be the way to settle things. "We Europeans," remarked one of my French friends, "naturally feel closer to you Americans than to the Russians. We share with you the same political traditions, the same institutions. But there is one thing we share with Russia that we do not share with you: we know what war is."

There is no use answering that we Americans helped win both world wars. This Frenchman is not talking of battlefields. He is talking of bombed cities, of wasted fields, of millions of displaced persons, of torture, of hunger, and of the complete human demoralization, that now follow total war. And these things we cannot claim to share. He is right that the Russians can. Since our public statements have been systematically bellicose, Russia's peace propaganda has done very well. She has shoved us into the role of reckless adolescents. She secured a copyright on the word peace—a precious word in Europe—so that Americans cannot use it without raising doubts as to their "loyalty." She had already taken out a Communist copyright on the word justice, once so precious in America. That left us with only liberty, freedom, and free enterprise to use as shibboleths. For most of the world, these words without the other two are simply not good enough.

Finally, although most Europeans think the Marshall Plan was both wise and generous, that is not all they think about it. To a considerable extent, it has made the rich richer, and left the poor in the lurch. This is largely the fault of the economic systems of certain European countries, such as the French and Italian, a fact that has been recognized by American administrators. The Plan has certainly helped, as the Communists ceaselessly predicted it would, to establish American corporations in strong positions in Europe. It has vastly strengthened production without answering adequately the problem of distribution—either to workers at home or to foreign markets abroad. Intelligent Europeans are too sensible to blame this on us; but neither do they accept, any more than President Roosevelt did, the opinion, so popular in the American business community, that if you take care of production, distribution will take care of itself. They admire Adam Smith as a writer, but they know he lived in the eighteenth, not the twentieth, century.

All of this boils down to saying that, among the European peoples whose governments are allied with ours and financially propped up by ours, neither the U.S. military policy nor the U.S. economic policies command support. Despite this fact there is a great deal of friendliness toward the American people, and a sympathetic awareness that they are for the moment caught in a wave of political reaction of the sort Europeans themselves have only too often experienced. Meanwhile, the Europeans are trying to learn how to live in a world they no longer govern.

CHAPTER III

We have been talking in this book about the actual condition of mankind today; about what the Big Myth in America makes us think it is; and about how the world, and particularly America's Big-Myth policies, look to the Europeans. But how do these same things look to the rest of the free world we are trying to lead—to the non-Communist peoples of Asia, of Africa, of the Near East, of Latin America? It might matter. In fact, Europe is learning slowly, and we are learning even more slowly, that it does matter, profoundly.

Well, these peoples see things in various ways, naturally, according to their traditions, their social organization, and whether they are still colonial possessions of Europe, or have recently won independence from the white man who was their burden, or whether their colonial status is disguised by words like trusteeship, or whether their own flag flies high while the fruits of their labor inexorably flow to Europe or the United States. But they hold some views in common; and those views may give us the key to what an intelligent American policy might look like if we found it—for it is they who most feel the unbearable pressures of a world

37

with no common government. We Americans are perhaps too rich and powerful to think. Europe, stunned by her fall from wealth and power, is perhaps too dazed to think well, and too disillusioned. But the colonial areas are poor enough to have to think, weak enough to have to think, and have been disillusioned so long that they are used to it. Let us include in these colonial areas every country that is outside Europe and is not industrialized. By that definition, the colonial world includes some 1,600,000,000 persons, about two thirds of the human race. And it receives about one sixth of the world's income.[5] In the City of Man, this area is the slum, while Western Europe is merely threatened with becoming a slum. Several centuries before Christ, Plato wrote that most cities were actually two cities parading as one: the City of the Rich and the City of the Poor. A century ago a Conservative British Prime Minister wrote a novel with the subtitle *The Two Nations*—the rich and the poor. Today, in the new world community which the airplane, the radio, and modern technology have brought for the first time into existence—today, in this Mighty Neighborhood, the colonial areas we are talking about make up the City of the Poor.

The City of the Poor is too poor to have gone in for very much education. Those men and women in it who did get educated were educated in large part in either Europe or the United States. They know our City, as well as theirs. We know ours too, but few of us know theirs. They are doing the thinking for their City now, the speaking for it, and in many places the governing of it. They are very vocal. But when they speak for it, we have a tendency to tell them to sit down. Our recent altercations with Prime Minister Nehru will illustrate this point.

What they could tell us if we cared to listen is that there is a world revolution going on, and that it is taking many forms in different parts of the world. In Russia it has taken the form of Communism; and those who govern Russia are doing all they can to make it take that form throughout the world. In Asia it is taking the form of a revolt against the landlord, the usurer, and foreign white domination.

The outstanding physical fact about Asia is its unspeakable misery: its ghastly poverty, its famines, its endemic diseases, its illiteracy. The outstanding spiritual fact about Asia is its torrential longing to escape from this misery. Nowhere else on the planet is the world revolution for equality more obvious and more impossible to stem. The "unchanging East" is changing at an appalling rate. Neither Chiang Kai-shek nor Syngman Rhee nor Bao Dai can stop that change. Not even if a remilitarized Japan, a remilitarized and re-Nazified Germany, and a subsidized Franco help. Not even if Washington holds Formosa in order to protect California. Russian Communists did not start that revolution, although they have shown more skill than anybody else has in capturing and directing it. The Kremlin could not stop it if it wanted to. But Washington has been trying to. A few Americans have stated why Washington's policy must fail. They have also stated why every good American ought to want the Asian Revolution to succeed: the Asians are basically out to get the rights we Americans won long ago—freedom from foreign domination, from colonial exploitation, and freedom for a man to earn a living by the sweat of his face. But since Communist Russia has sided with that revolution, and since Communists have in many areas captured the leadership of it, we have regularly fought it. Is not our basic policy to stop Communism? A few Americans have urged us to stop bucking Asia's overdue revolt, and start backing it, and guiding it.

This is what Jefferson would doubtless propose; but for several reasons it is hard for us to hear distinctly what Jefferson is saying. In the first place, a powerful group in America is determined that we shall see in Asia's revolt nothing but another wing of the Kremlin's world-wide conspiracy, indeed nothing but the spread of a vast Russian empire. In the second place, many of us were raised on Rudyard Kipling and, like General MacArthur, we know the Oriental mind. As children we had comfortably identified ourselves with the European rulers of these teeming millions, all of whom—in India, at least—addressed white persons like ourselves as sahibs; all of whom, as lesser breeds without the law, must be duly grateful for the gift of civilization which white men were bringing them. This slightly dated view of the Orient was surely back of General Marshall's remark to American reporters in Tokyo that in judging the actions of the Chinese in Korea, we must remember the Oriental had to save face, a fact, he went on to observe, which Americans found it difficult to understand. But there was another fact—this one hard for Americans to remember —that many of our most important actions for months had been dictated by considerations of national prestige, always important considerations for Occidental powers. The difference between us and the Orientals would seem to be a difference in vocabulary. It is Hollywood clichés of this type which are making it hard for us to hear what Jefferson is saying. No doubt Hollywood also complicates the Asian's view of us.

But to the Asian, his basic problems seem easy enough to grasp. So do his basic views on the rest of the world, including American foreign policy. By and large, Asia is agricultural and feudal. Its workers are therefore mostly farmers. They are tenant farmers. They are at the mercy of their landlords, and they are therefore compelled to pay rents that would scandalize Americans. They are therefore deeply in debt, and they have to pay interest on their loans at rates that are prohibited here by law. Neither their landlord nor their creditor is interested in helping them build up production. In much of Asia farm production is steadily falling. The landlord and usurer are merely riding piggyback. And the peasant has grown tired of the game. He has started to write new rules, or to support Communists who write them. In any case, basic agrarian reform is an issue all over Asia.

The grip the landlord held on the peasant, and indirectly the grip the usurer held, was supported for centuries by European conquerors. The colonial administrator counted on the landlord class to hold the cow steady while the European merchant or planter milked her. Moreover, the European merchant did not want native businessmen cutting in and the colonial administrator therefore made it tough for native businessmen. This explains why Chinese businessmen, for example, have sided with Chinese Communists as a means of throwing out any Chinese elements that Europeans or Americans backed.

Asians are sick of being despised by white people. For centuries they have been held down by force, and Europeans added insult to injury by telling them it was done for their own good. They suffered daily and highly personal humiliations at the hands of white men and women, and not always the best examples of the white peoples at that. They remember, sometimes with violent hate, and sometimes only with sorrow. But they do not want armed white men in Asia, whether in Malaya, French Indo-China, Japan, Formosa, or Korea. They do not want them even as liberators. It is interesting that they do not even like to be called Asiatics, because centuries of European scorn or patronage spoiled the word for men who have now tasted independence and are determined to achieve equality. They prefer to be called Asians. American armed forces call them neither: they call them gooks. Asians are quite aware that the word expresses scorn and derision. Our habit of using it has therefore proved of the greatest value to Communists everywhere.

Inevitably, the self-respect Asians have won sometimes takes the form of pride and touchiness. We cannot cure that touchiness by using force in Asia. Presumably it will be cured when Asia's achievements compel the respect of both the Asians themselves and the white races which have habitually scorned Asia. Meanwhile, no American foreign policy which ignores that touchiness

41

will succeed. It is true that not all the white men and women who went to Asia during her years of white bondage went there to oppress, exploit, get rich. Some went to teach, to heal, to succor, and to love. At the moment Asians are tempted to forget those exceptions, and this may strike us as cruel ingratitude. For the moment we had better not dwell on the West's gifts to Asia. Gratitude is something that is not very easy to exact.

Finally, Asians want to industrialize their countries. Those who studied in Europe or in America frequently studied economics. And where young Americans studied Adam Smith or those who wrote in the Smith tradition, Asians were strongly drawn to Karl Marx. They did not necessarily become Communists, or even Socialists. But the methods by which financial capital can be used to exploit human labor were so nakedly exemplified in Asia that the writings of Marx were peculiarly relevant and luminous for Asian students. In contrast to the average American, the average Asian tends to use Marxist terms of analysis when he thinks about economic problems. In Europe, the capitalist system was often propped up by drastic police action. In Asia, it was propped up by foreign bayonets, and nobody could miss the gleam.

When the Asian looks out at the Mighty Neighborhood, he sees a Europe, weakened it is true, but clutching hard at its remaining possessions in Asia. He sees two world wars which resulted from European greed and European faith in military force. And he remembers that one of the chief causes for those wars was rivalry over who should exploit Asia. The wreckage they left in their wake in Europe may cause him the grim satisfaction that all human beings take when Nineveh falls.

He looks toward America with somewhat different emotions. The Americans were the first to revolt against European colonial exploitation. Jefferson and Lincoln are heroes in Asia. But America humiliates men and women daily because of color. America's atomic bomb is the perfect symbol of the Occident's love of physical power and the Occident's Faustian lust to conquer nature, to rape the earth rather than husband her. And the Asian remembers that Americans are the only nation ever to drop atomic bombs on cities full of men, women, and children. Moreover, he remembers that the cities were in Asia, and he doubts whether the bombs would have been dropped on cities of Europeans. Americans, despite their efforts for Indonesian independence, back up the British in Malaya and the French in Indo-China. Indeed, it just so happened that for a period America's Marshall Plan aid to France approximately equaled what it cost France to shoot Indo-Chinese. Was America purposely subsidizing white imperialism in Asia? Asians were not enthusiastic about our intervention in Korea. When we answered that we were defending the cause of the United Nations, Asians noted that we were busily building air and naval bases on their side of the world's widest ocean, that we apparently intended to hold bases in Japan. As for the United Nations, isn't it basically an Occidental club organized on caste lines? Five members only, out of sixty, enjoy the first-class citizenship of permanent seats in the Security Council. Only one of these, China, is truly Asian; and it is interesting to note that China's seat is held by what looks to Asians like an American puppet in Formosa.

Although the Charter of the United Nations seems to promise Asia the economic aid it so desperately requires, it is to Europe, not to Asia, that real economic aid has gone. To Europe, which despite the wreckage of World War II was an earthly paradise compared with the conditions most Asians faced. Meanwhile, America urges Asia to fight for freedom, not against France in Indo-China, but against Russia if and when Russian armies should invade an Asian country. And when Indians were falling in the street from want of bread, and the Indian Government requested the sale or loan of surplus wheat we could not use, Washington demanded to know what team India would be fighting on if war came. However it sounded here, to Asia this question suggested blackmail. When a dying man asks for bread, you do not ask him first to tell you how he expects to vote in November. Unless, perhaps, the dying man is an Asian. The fact that Washington ultimately sent the wheat did not answer these questions in Asia's mind.

To such an Asia as really exists, American foreign propaganda has had too much to do with automobiles and electric refrigerators to be more than a Hollywood product. You do not propose electric candles on a man's next birthday cake when he is frantically seeking not cake, but bread. American talk expounds too much the high standard of living which free enterprise brings. Asia wants bread.

She wants bread and she wants machines. Whether informed by Karl Marx, or Stalin, or just daily observation, she believes she knows what fate awaits any purely agricultural country that trades with an industrial one. For the City of the Rich is the City with the Machines, and the City of the Poor is the City without the Machines. Asia and Africa and South America alike have learned this lesson. It is a lesson we Americans should appreciate. We learned it during the period when England alone had machines. And the Americans in southern and western states had to learn it again when New England alone, inside our tariff walls, had the machines. Today, not only does the City of the Poor desire passionately racial equality and mutual human respect, but it is determined to have something approaching equality in the area of economic productivity. It is sometimes naïve in its expression of this determination. It sometimes asks for complicated gadgets that come later, not at the beginning, in the difficult and dangerous process of industrialization. But it does not propose to accept the role of country cousin, or to grow groundnuts for Europe, or to mine its soil for the food and metals industrial

44

Europe and America demand. It wants to trade, but on equal, not on "cheap labor," coolie terms.

People who live in industrial communities wonder nostalgically why agricultural communities are not overjoyed to retain their bucolic flavor. The answer is simple. Their flavor is no longer bucolic. The North Dakota wheat farmer depends on Detroit for spare parts for his tractor, not his ox. Spare parts cost money. As a general tendency, it has cost more and more bushels of wheat to buy spare parts. The same thing is increasingly true in Asia, Africa, and Latin America. Native women still carry water on their heads, but more and more they prefer oilcans to homemade clay jars. They are lighter and they don't break. More and more, their mud shacks are roofed with corrugated aluminum rather than with picturesque thatch. Aluminum reflects tropical heat, it is more permanent than thatch, it is tighter than thatch, and— believe it or not—it looks prettier. The adobe walls that used to keep the poultry in may now be replaced by a hastily built fence, constructed of flattened-out oilcans. The products of industrial lands have flooded in and destroyed ancient handicrafts and cottage industries. And the net effect seems to be to hoist the standard of living in industrial lands and to lower it, or leave it, or raise it very slightly, in lands that merely farm and mine and lumber. All these phenomena ought to be familiar to Americans who saw the old Cotton Kingdom in our southern states. The economy of the "backward" countries has been integrated into the new, world community which science and the machine have created. Ancient folkways are vanishing. The backward countries are becoming merely the backyard, not the garden, of the factory countries. They believe their real choice is not to be bucolic or like us. They believe their real choice is to be like us or our slum. To be at our mercy, economically and militarily, or independent neighbors.

The City of the Rich knows that when you clean up a slum, the servant problem gets tough. This stimulates the City of the Rich to expatiate on the joys of the simple life, and the division of labor. Nobody is listening. Everybody is too busy looking for capital to develop industry and buy some servants of his own— that is, some machines. They don't want to rent the servants. That is, they don't want machines owned by foreign investors. They want their own.

If we refuse the machines—that is, if we refuse the credits or even outright grants—that will enable our slum-dwellers to rescue themselves, then they will probably have to accumulate the capital themselves, the way the Russians did when we refused it to them in the twenties. They will have to squeeze it out of human labor; that is, they will have to make "slave labor" produce the needed capital goods rather than the consumer goods people would like to enjoy. Can any government weaker than a Communist dictatorship put that squeeze on? Many Asians say no. If they go Communist, will we say Russia is spreading her empire? Will we start shooting, to defend the democratic way of life? It might cost a lot less to advance the capital to the countries that want to industrialize. And since the vast wealth of Europe and America was built largely out of cheap raw materials—that is, out of sweated coolie labor—from Asia and Africa and Latin America, there might be a certain poetic justice in sending some capital back to them. There was certainly that kind of justice when New Yorkers put more tax money into TVA than Tennesseans did.

The World Slum is going to rescue itself, either the TVA way or the Communist way. If we decline to help make the TVA way possible and continue to devote all our resources and energies to "containing" Communism, we shall place ourselves in the unattractive posture of containing the world revolution. In fact, we are in that posture already, so far as Asia is concerned, and the problem is to find another and more realistic posture. If we do not want the world revolution to turn to the Communists for leadership, then we will just have to furnish alternative leadership. The bulk of the planet's population is in the position of a sick man visited by two doctors. One doctor offers him a pill, a Red one, which he claims can cure him. The other doctor is looking not at the dying man but at his rival, and is shouting: "Don't trust that man! He's a quack!" These exclamations do not constitute a medical prescription. Which doctor is the dying man likely to choose?

In the Near East, we find, of course, the same basic problem, but with important complications: water is scarcer, oil is more plentiful, and Russia is nearer. Water is so scarce that the average Occidental can see little hope of a healthy agriculture even if he got rid of those piggyback partners, the landlord and the usurer. But since Roman engineers found the Roman know-how and the capital to make gardens of the Near East and North Africa, it would seem premature for us to go on claiming the climate has changed. Fortunately, archaeologists are beginning to help modern know-how and capital catch up with ancient Rome by recovering the ancient irrigation systems. Thousands of years before the Romans were heard from, Babylonian technology and capital made what is now Iraq a paradise of productive farmland. We may yet catch up with the Babylonians. The misery of Iraq is quite unnecessary. Iraq can supply not only oil for the cars on U.S. Route One; it could even furnish food instead of malaria to its own people, if life-giving irrigation canals again took the place of death-dealing swamps. That it supplies oil for Americans is pleasant for Americans. That it could supply food and health for the Iraquis could be even more pleasant for the Iraquis. We already have a good deal of oil in Texas. They have a good deal of food—nowhere.

At the other end of the ancient Romans' Africa lies South Africa, which has the honor to be the only country in the world with a worse world-wide reputation for race discrimination than we Americans have. South Africa is very much on the minds of the majority of mankind, because the vast majority of mankind are colored and are sick of being treated by the white minority as untouchables.

In between South African segregation and the sand-choked cisterns of Roman Africa lies Black Africa, where the natives are beginning to ask: "What are white people doing here in Africa?" Independence movements are younger than in Asia, are weaker than in Asia, and are growing stronger by the year. Africans are acutely conscious that, as the Europeans get thrown out of more and more sections of Asia, they get more and more interested in "developing" Africa: that is, in making arrangements to have Africa yield Europe food for Europeans to eat and raw materials for Europe's factories to process and sell, in Africa and elsewhere. But Africa, too, has begun to dream of owning its own machines.

South America is in many ways a more raped continent than either Asia or Africa. She learned about absentee landlords and giant land holdings early, from Spain. She revolted against Spain; but she did not get rid of the grosser forms of exploitation that many American travelers have witnessed. It is an exploitation that has produced countless revolutions and is likely to produce a few more. But the thing South Americans are increasingly vocal about is the undeveloped state of their industries, a state that condemns their countries to be economic colonies of the United States. Their Communists are vocal but not numerically strong in most countries. But the people who agree with the Communists on the evils of economic colonialism are numerically strong and increasingly vocal. Venezuela, one of the richest oil-producing countries on the planet, with mountains of iron that have recently drawn American capital like magnets, has millions of acres potentially able to produce food, and an undernourished population, and imports more than half its food from the United States. The shopwindows in its cities contain practically everything that failed to sell on Main Street, and at fancy prices. It will either industrialize or go on as it is going. Naturally, it takes a military junta to hold things steady. No invasion is expected, but there are a great many soldiers. Their weapons and uniforms were made in U.S.A.

These weapons and uniforms are symbolic of our present policies. Our interest is security. Things have to be kept steady. We are opposed to violence, whether riot, rebellion, or invasion. We want "world law" and perhaps a world police force. Force will bring stability, and stability will bring prosperity. But is this true? Does force ever make more than a very minor contribution to stability? Would not bread bring it faster? Well, we reply, what kind of prosperity would the United States have if it were not for its police? It might be useful to ask: What kind of police would it have if it were not for its prosperity? And how many? Hunger breeds violence, partly because the body craves food, and partly because the soul demands justice. The Communist believes that bread and justice can be secured only through Communism. I believe that both can be secured through what we Americans call the democratic system—but only if we use the democratic system aggressively and realistically and purposively to get them. Bread and justice are desperately needed over most of our planet. There is nothing in American foreign policy today that will help get them for those who need them most. They ask for bread and we are giving them law and order.

But what about Point Four? What about technical assistance for underdeveloped areas? What about the International Bank? The Marshall Plan? For years now, we American taxpayers have been digging deep into our pockets because our government has told us that other peoples need our help. We have put up billions of dollars and are still putting them up. Our own national debt has reached astronomical figures. Our tax load is enough to make a less patient people revolt. Our cost of living soars. Inflation threatens to wipe out our personal savings. And now we are told that America's popularity, which had reached an all-time high at the end of the last war, is plummeting all over the world. Asia

fears us. South America grumbles. Our own military allies in
Europe criticize our policies and complain about arming, as if it
were our country and not theirs that was in danger! Through the
Truman Doctrine we have publicly offered to help any country on
earth against Communist imperialism. And we get nothing but
unfriendly and carping criticism for our pains. After World War I
they blamed us for withdrawing and minding our business. Now,
after World War II, must they blame us for meddling in theirs?
I have heard these questions asked in many states of the Union,
both from angry people and from people who merely feel hurt.
That the questions are being asked is a good sign. They merit
better answers than the State Department has been giving. And
infinitely better ones than the Department's Congressional critics
have furnished.

But it is hard to give the real answers in the midst of the cold
war. The cold war has caught us in a vicious circle. It took very
few years of the cold war to liquidate the American liberal, so far
as his political usefulness was concerned, and to turn America
over to those elements whom the liberal, in the days of Roosevelt,
had considered dangerously reactionary or frankly fascist. Under
Roosevelt, the American liberal, along with the bulk of the human
race, had urged many of the same things the Communists claimed
to want also. Since the Communist Party, weak as it was, now
appeared to take its orders from the Kremlin, and since the
Kremlin was America's greatest threat, the Red hunt was on. Since
Socialists seemed to want at least some of the things that Communists wanted, the reactionary bracketed the two. And since the
liberal wanted some of the things the Socialists wanted, the reactionary could throw him in for good measure unless he vigorously
helped hunt the Reds—which many "liberals" promptly did. European observers were horrified. They instantly recognized the old
Nazi game of: Gang up on the extreme left. And they knew by
bitter experience the likely sequel: when the extreme left has

been eliminated, the next man becomes the extreme left and the game goes on until none but the extreme right survives. To play the game, it is necessary to terrify everybody into refusing to help the extreme left under threat of being called a fellow-traveler. By the time the American liberal caught on to the rules of the game he was too demoralized to demand new rules.

The fear of the unknown had seized the country. Nobody knew how many Communists there were in America or which of his neighbors was included, and for these two dread unknowns the secrecy of the Communists was responsible. But there was a worse unknown. Few Americans could have passed a grade-school examination in what doctrines Communism taught—in short, in what a Communist was. And for this they had their own political illiteracy to thank. This innocence of the average American was based on the fact that Communist doctrine has had so much less relevance to America than to Europe that we have never had much incentive to inform ourselves. But since the number of Communists was unknown, since their names were unknown, and since what a Communist is was unknown, there were three good unknowns for fear to feed on, and it fed. Like Jacobinism in the eighteenth century, Communism was thought of as "catching," and analogies to contagious diseases multiplied, in the press, in the radio, and in Congressional debate. Most political terms ceased to denote ideas and became charged with political passions instead. The theme of diplomacy became the famous rejoinder, "So's your old man." Political morals grew easy, since the only real crime now was "disloyalty." The press, and not merely the Hearst press either, whooped it up. Reporters soon learned not to submit stories that cast doubt on some of our wilder accusations against the Communists. An orgy of clichés ensued and a murderous assault against ideas in general. Was not Communism an idea, among other things? The American vocabulary grew noticeably more violent. Humor flagged and failed. An idea or two might have come from the universities, but the reactionaries were taking advantage of the change of political climate to hound faculties; and college courses, especially in dangerous areas like economics, were growing more and more innocuous. Hollywood became so frightened that it lost its grip on its small remaining store of ideas; and the intellectually adult started hunting for foreign films. The voices of radio commentators grew ominous and stern, and many of those with gentle voices and a taste for the analytical could find no sponsors and disappeared from the air.

Whence came this Great Fear, this great folly, that led one wit to remark, parodying Vice-President Marshall's remark about the cigar, that what America needs is a good five-cent psychiatrist? When the shameful history of this Great Fear comes to be written, future historians will be puzzled. But certain features stand out clear, and are not irrelevant to the present discussion. This was the herd fright of a largely collectivized society. A farmer can stand slander if his feed and hay hold out. He may even survive a burned barn or two. But in the mid-twentieth century a large fraction of Americans found themselves working for very large organizations, organizations whose profits depended on the good will of a huge and often distant public. These organizations, whether manufacturers, newspapers, film producers, or broadcasting companies, simply felt unable to stand up financially under a smear—that is, under slander. It was a problem in public relations. Innocence was no help. Proof of innocence always came too late, and always made less interesting reading than the accusation and slander had made.

Moreover, although informers plied a lucrative trade as long ago as ancient Rome, and although Aretino in the Renaissance could blackmail cash out of his victim by merely threatening him with a satire, modern America put its characteristic twist on slander as a profession. Groups organized themselves for systematic slander, not to get money out of the victim, but with the hope of extracting it from reactionary business executives. These could be readily coaxed or frightened into subscribing funds for "patriotic" groups to use in cleansing the land of "subversives." True, it was necessary to produce an occasional head, in order to keep the subscription list alive. But the victim was merely a casualty in a deal between organized slanderers and their conservative clients.

These groups were not Nazis, and did not call before dawn. Some of the liberals who cried fascism may have been as guilty of thinking by epithet as were those who charged guilt by association. The penalty was rarely prison; it was loss of a job. As some wag put it: "In Russia, if you disagree, they send you to a camp and make you work. In America, if you disagree, they won't let you work." But in addition to the economic sanction, the loss of work, the privation for dependents, there was a vaguer social penalty that most Americans could not face: the shame of belonging to an ill-defined but despised group of those who presumably served Stalin. The fear of that label held most Americans in line, and left their tongues with too little saliva to speak the truth as they saw it.

This is a sad and shameful tale, and an all too familiar one. It would not have had to be told here except that it had a sharp incidence on our foreign policy. The tendency to agree with most of the human race on certain vital policies now brought down the charge of disloyalty. The Red hunt at home rendered it practically impossible to make peace—that is, to conclude the second world war. In July 1951, an American radio broadcaster, speaking from London, reported that Europeans were afraid that, having decided to rearm in order to negotiate with Russia from situations of strength, we might have forgotten our original end and redoubled our means. Scarcely a week later, the *United States News* observed unconcernedly:

"*Unanswered question* is how strong U.S. must get before it can negotiate on even terms with Stalin. Officials don't seem to know. Nor do they know what U.S. and Stalin can negotiate about, when the time comes. Eastern Europe? China, say? Issues like these can't be negotiated now. So it's possible, after U.S. builds up its strength, it may discover U.S. and Stalin can't usefully talk at all."[6]

That was a good deal not to know, for a government that was seeking allies among postwar Europeans.

If the Red hunt at home made it practically impossible to negotiate peace, by shutting the mouths of nearly all the Americans who agreed with Europe that peace was both possible and necessary, the reverse was equally obvious: that it was precisely the refusal to negotiate, the speeding of rearmament, and the whole cold-war policy that kept it open season for the Reds, and for those who agreed with the Reds on at least one thing, that peace was possible—for they could be smeared as peacemongers. This was the circle in which America was caught.

It is often asserted that we cannot get a good foreign policy until we have cleaned up at home: in short, that the domestic front is where the circle must be broken. I suggest that the opposite tactic would be more fruitful. I admit that it is of the first importance that the American citizen demand his customary rights: the right to hear ideas expounded, even dangerous ones; the right to expound any ideas that he has himself, or thinks he has; the right to elect anybody he pleases to head his labor union, regardless of his political ideas; the right to cross his own frontier when the fancy strikes him without pleading for a passport as a special favor from a benign government; the right to build the roads and schools and river dams and even dwellings which he so badly needs without pouring his taxes and strategic materials into a foreign policy that has already failed. But I believe that long before those demands could be met, our present foreign policy would spawn a third world war, and a war that would bring most unpleasant surprises for the millions of Americans who have been fooled into thinking that most of mankind is on our side. It would be a war which most of mankind would most likely judge had been provoked by us, not by Russia, out of blind hate, or white anger, or reckless folly, or economic necessity. For the ugly fact is that our present economy rests in large measure on our rearmament program. That is why Wall Street is thrown into a panic whenever it fears "peace may break out." The Kremlin talks as if that proves Wall Street is trying to start a war. All the evidence suggests that Wall Street is more afraid of a war than most parts of the country are. But the brokers in Wall Street, whatever their professional defects, know enough to wonder what would happen to our economy if our preparation for war stopped short or even tapered off too sharply. And an economic collapse in this country would spell sorrow not only for America but for most of the world.

Non-Communists in Europe know that we share one thing with Nazi Germany from which Communist Russia is free. Our economy is a war economy now, as Hitler's was. To some extent, like him, we are caught. Russia's economy does not depend on war. Because this is a Marxist point, we Americans do not like to hear it. Non-Communists in Europe also hate to think about it—not because it is Marxist, but because it is true. The point is, if we stop arming, we are going to find some other use for our excess production—or else. If the Kremlin really wants, at least for the present, to avoid war (as even we Americans are beginning to suspect) then it would be a smart thing for the Kremlin to consult the holy Communist scriptures for the answer to one question: "What can America do with its industrial surplus?" But consulting the scriptures will not be enough. The Marxist answer that if we socialized our production, then all Americans could live in ease, lacks political realism. Before we will do that, we will probably go to war. I can imagine a long-drawn-out war with Russia that might result in the overthrow, or pretty complete

55

erosion, of capitalist production in America. But does the Kremlin ask us to believe that America would go Communist, or even Socialist, to avoid war?

Moreover, although my knowledge of Marx is somewhat amateurish, I would suggest to our neighbors in the Kremlin that the development of technology since Marx may pose an interesting problem—can even the whole American people absorb our surplus? Unless, that is, we break all records for plowing under little pigs. To our neighbors in Washington I would suggest that there is a limit to how many little pigs a hungry world will watch plowed under. Our system for pumping blue dye into surplus potatoes to render them unfit for future consumption has already shaken our prestige.

CHAPTER IV

V-E Day, when Hitler's Germany quit, came on May 7, 1945. V-J Day, when Japan quit, came on September 2, 1945. The shooting was scarcely over when somebody handed President Truman a paper canceling Lend-Lease and President Truman signed.[7] He has since that time had the manliness to declare publicly that, when he signed, he made a mistake. Unhappily, that signature marked an important departure from the realistic foreign policy of President Roosevelt. Mr. Roosevelt's Lend-Lease was soundly based on fact: if Europe were to be liberated, the Nazis' frank bid for world conquest and a world governed by the master race could be met only by a common effort. That this common effort called for West-East delivery was obvious since America was considerably richer than any other great power and was likely to suffer considerably less. Lend-Lease was a joint, international effort. When it was canceled, our relations with Russia—or so we certainly claim now—were not bad.

Those relations were, of course, ambiguous. They had always been ambiguous. Many Americans sincerely hoped that the Russians and Germans would kill each other off to a point where we and the British could pretty well organize the peace. It was also obvious before Stalin's pact with Hitler that Russia would have been delighted if we and the British had fought Germany to a standstill and she could make the peace. Germany first hoped that the West would stand by until she had attacked and destroyed Russia, leaving her free to subjugate the West later. When Britain and France came to Poland's rescue, they forced Hitler to fight the West first. Hitler hoped to force peace on the West first and then assault Russia. From the start, this triangle existed. It was based on several political realities. We and the Russians alike feared Hitler's plans for world conquest. We and Hitler alike feared Communism. Hitler and Stalin alike were aware of Western enmity. But Roosevelt's program called for a common assault on German militarism, and negotiation with Russia in the context of general international co-operation for peace and prosperity. Lend-Lease was one of the expressions of that purpose. Its cancellation was in the direction of each nation going it alone.

Nevertheless, there was still UNRRA—the United Nations Relief and Rehabilitation Administration—to carry the ball for a common international purpose. It was set up even before the present United Nations Organization was created in San Francisco. When the U.N. did come into being, its Charter explicitly provided not merely for joint efforts to prevent military aggression, a function assigned particularly to the Security Council, but for joint efforts to promote full employment and economic development, a function assigned to the Economic and Social Council.

UNRRA saved the lives of millions by outright relief and helped many more millions to save their own. In 1946, its American director, Fiorello La Guardia, reported to the U.N. General Assembly and recommended a smaller agency to finish the job. The Economic and Social Council backed him up. Russia backed him up. But the United States opposed, and the British supported its opposition. The Americans and British wanted "to be free to judge on their own when and where relief was needed."[8] A desperate world problem would no longer be handled as a world problem; it would be handled by separate national governments, each with its own foreign policy. La Guardia, not noted for pulling his punches, was indignant. "Does the government of the United States," he demanded, "intend to adopt a policy which will make innocent men, women and children suffer because of some political situation which makes their government unacceptable to the United States?" The answer to that question was Yes, it did. For it was already beginning to go it alone, in matters touching the world economy. UNRRA was the last organization in which Americans worked beside men of all races to attack the common economic perils of the human race, on anything like an adequate scale. The next year U.N. records would register sharply the shift in American policy. American aid, except for a share in the U.N. Children's Fund, was going not where the suffering was most acute, but where cold-war politics directed it. This shift in policy amounted to a kind of secession from the human race.

From that day to this, Washington's recipe for handling the ghastly problem of world misery that confronts us was nationalist solutions and "enlightened self-interest." Once we declined to pool our resources with our neighbors', once we decided to act nationally on what are problems not of a nation, least of all of a government, but of the human race, our programs of economic aid, technical assistance, or whatever they might at any given moment be called, were doomed to become one facet of our foreign policy. The military purposes of our government took over; and any economic aid that could not be fitted into our military policies became either a pittance or an immoral handout. American public interest focused on the Security Council, and the Economic and Social Council was all but forgotten. Moreover, since we stopped thinking in terms of a world community acting for itself and began thinking in terms of American resources to be used only to defend America, we began to think not only of feeding probable allies in war and neglecting to feed potential enemies; we began also to think of "strengthening" America by strengthening free enterprise and business profits. Our recipe, therefore, for human misery came more and more to be "the revival of normal trade"—except, of course, with Russia and her satellites. And direct attack on the problem of mass misery took on the now dubious aspect of a world New Deal, the very sort of thing Roosevelt's death had rid us of at home. It was not practicable to unharness the Tennessee River, of course, but we would willingly see the whole Mississippi Valley in flood before we would harness the Missouri too. To our neighbors of every political persuasion, our chief interests seemed to be profits at home and weapons abroad. With the decline in international co-operation, and with a world in revolution, a revolution that took many forms in many countries but that could always be diagnosed as Communist and hence as manipulated by the Kremlin, we threw rearmament into high gear, as if you could shoot a world revolution and kill it. In any case, we no longer saw the world as our neighbors saw it. And our allies dragged their feet accordingly.

But, unknown to most Americans, an argument has raged for five years in the Economic and Social Council which is ever so much closer to the real problem than we are. The countries represented in ECOSOC, like the countries in the whole U.N. General Assembly, can be grouped in various ways: those who favor us against Russia, those who favor Russia against us, those who are sick of both of us and hope to stay dry when the storm breaks. But, in terms of the problem this book is about, they can be divided quite simply into rich countries and poor countries. There are, of course, poor countries which are not members of U.N. at all, because each of them is still the colonial possession

of one of the rich countries. But enough of the poor are present
to permit certain very interesting debates. These debates, largely
unknown to the American people, have revolved around one burning issue: whether the United Nations should set up an International Development Authority, like the Tennessee Valley Authority the American Congress once set up in an underdeveloped
part of the United States. The poor countries want it set up. The
rich countries, led by the United States, do not. Another way of
stating what happens in ECOSOC is that the unindustrialized
countries, the countries without machines, want a development
authority to help them industrialize; the industrialized countries,
the countries that have a near monopoly of machines, do not want
it. They want to go on buying raw materials from the poor countries and selling them finished goods. The poor countries, many
of which are politically colonial and all of which are economically
colonial, are rapidly coming to the kind of boil that the Bostonians
had reached when they held a certain famous tea party. The poor
countries are sick of laying golden eggs for other people to sell.
The most interesting detail of the fight is that one of the few
things on which the United States and the Soviet Union now vote
the same way is an International Development Authority; they
both refuse it, although for different reasons.[9]

The go-it-alone policy, in the matter of world starvation, world
disease, and world misery, inevitably subordinated American
economic aid to military considerations. But since no other people, not even the French or British, have believed at any time
since World War II that the Communist danger was primarily a
military danger, our efforts to "lead the free world" have involved
using some pretty heavy economic pressure to persuade them to
follow. This was extremely evident in the French press, for example, all the way from right to left, at the time when we were
busy persuading the French to sign the Atlantic Pact. Yet, at that
time the average American (who did not read the French press)

61

was led by his own press to regard the Atlantic Pact as something Europeans earnestly desired as a protection against what our press called the Red hordes and their plan to occupy Western Europe. We drew our analogies from Hitler and his Nazis; but Europe never accepted those analogies. Nevertheless, the French Government signed. The average Frenchman shrugged his shoulders, since he realized that America was picking up the check. Some Frenchmen may have foreseen that we would have to pick up a good many more checks than we then planned to pick up. If they did, it was an excellent prediction.

That our foreign policy appealed less and less to foreigners was owing to a very simple fact: the human race that our policy was designed to befriend, rescue, inspire, and lead did not exist on our planet. A very different human race did, a race I attempted early in this book to describe. This fatal mistake led us to base our foreign policy on at least five fundamentally false assumptions:

First False Assumption: That Russia is all that stands between mankind and a stable peace.

Second False Assumption: That American "know-how" and American money can rebuild the world economy, or at least enough of it to stop Russia.

Third False Assumption: That "free enterprise" (what most non-Communists in the world still call "private enterprise") can do the job even better than government.

Fourth False Assumption: That, even if we allow the United Nations to do a small fraction of the job, it can best do it on small yearly appropriations.

Fifth False Assumption: That America can best preserve freedom by backing any anti-Communists she can find anywhere, including reactionaries and even fascists.

These basic assumptions of our postwar foreign policy are worth examining with great care. I believe it is true that the

American people are the only people in the world today who accept these assumptions. And I believe most Americans reject most of them once they are clearly and simply stated. Yet on these assumptions our policy has rested.

"That Russia is all that stands between mankind and a stable peace." One glance at the actual condition of mankind today will convince us that this doctrine is not for export. For if all the Russians in the world obligingly blew out their brains tomorrow at noon, it might rejoice some Americans, but it could mean little to most of the men and women on this planet, who dwell in hunger, in poverty, in sickness, and in ignorance. They simply cannot view Russia or Communism as the world's chief problem. Communism is Russia's answer to the problems that interest them the most acutely. Is any other solution possible? Yes, say the underdeveloped countries through their delegates in ECO-SOC. Yes, there is the solution you applied to the Tennessee Valley with brilliant success. What we want is an International Development Authority. You don't approve of Russia's solution. We don't either, if an alternative can be found. Isn't the American-invented TVA, which is now being imitated in many countries though not in the Missouri Valley, the proper model for the international agency we need? No, says Russia.[10] And then— believe it or not—no, says America too.

Then has the American Government any other method to propose? Yes, it has:

"That American 'know-how' and American money can rebuild the world economy, or at least enough of it to stop Russia."

Let us first recognize that the world's hungry men and women do not want to eat just enough to stop Russia. They know that Americans are not eating just enough to stop Russia. They know, in fact, that when we sit down to a good meal, we are not sitting down for the purpose of stopping Russia, but to enjoy the food our body needs. They would like to sit down for the same sensible reason.

This distinction between eating to stop the gnawings of hunger and eating to stop Communism explains the dangerous gulf between American foreign policy and the opinion of the majority of mankind. The gulf is even more dangerous both to our people and to mankind than the gulf between Russians and Americans. But the first gulf appears in ECOSOC and the average American knows nothing about it. The second appears in the Security Council and makes the headlines in forty-eight states. The average American does not know that his government sabotaged UNRRA, the last great postwar effort at an international assault on world misery. For that matter, the average American may never have heard of UNRRA itself. He does not know that his President considers we made a mistake in sabotaging Lend-Lease. And he certainly does not know that in ECOSOC we have steadily sabotaged efforts to set up alternative machinery. Yet the documents prove conclusively that we have.[11] The documents would horrify the average American. For, despite his own government's apparent belief that the only excuse for a starving foreigner to eat is so he can become a strong ally of America in the third world war, the average American would assume that a hungry foreigner's best reason for eating would be that he was hungry.

What I have called the Second False Assumption on which our government's foreign policy rests, "That American money and American 'know-how' can do the job, or at least enough of it to stop Russia," would have to be cleansed of that last brutal and shortsighted phrase if the American people ever learned the facts. But even without that phrase, it remains false, chiefly because of misunderstandings about our know-how and about money. It is worth inquiring why we substituted the cliché "know-how" for what we had always called in plain English "skill." Skill is shorter, older, more eloquent, less farfetched, and less boastful. I suspect that when the national advertising campaigns of American industrial corporations popularized "know-how," they were congratulating the reader on having access to American industrial products even at inflationary prices and flattering him into supposing that only Americans "know how" to make things and do things. I suspect that we Americans enjoyed learning that the reason we are the richest nation in history is that we are the smartest, not just the luckiest or the most blessed by God. I suppose rich nations, like rich individuals, would always rather ascribe their wealth to their own wisdom than to good luck. It furnishes a firmer title and it earns more respect from the neighbors.

But the implication that industrial and scientific techniques are peculiar to Americans insults the intelligence of every American who knows a little history, and every foreigner as well. It omits the fact that American techniques originated in Europe, have always leaned heavily on Europe, and have often fallen short of the techniques in Europe. What we did develop here, and spread to other countries, was the assembly line; and, though it has often led to abuses, it was an important contribution. But know-how exists not only in Europe. It exists, in lesser quantity, in the other continents. The "backward" countries contain many first-class scientists—often, it is true, trained in Europe or America. What they lack is an adequate number of them, and even more an adequate amount of investment capital ready to put to use the knowledge their scientists possess. If they are colonial countries, they are likely to lack also the freedom of action that we won in the American Revolution against colonial exploitation by our imperialistic mother country.

All of which brings us to our own current misunderstanding about money. The same two world wars that smashed Europe's economy enormously strengthened our American economy. When the second war ended, America was one of the few places to which Europeans could turn for an emergency supply of food;

and American industry was the only source they could turn to for replenishing their own supply of machines. At the same moment we were haunted by the specter of surpluses and another great depression. The economic blood of the world had run out of the vein called Europe and formed a clot in the vein called America. Our goods flowed to Europe. Europe had as yet few goods to send back in payment and some of those she could have sent collided with our tariff wall—a wall we had wisely lowered but not yet made low enough. The result was the great dollar gap. To that gap we replied with the Marshall Plan. We had sabotaged the U.N. as a common international device for handling a world economic problem, but we did the next most intelligent thing, in fact the only sensible thing left to do. We made the rehabilitation of Europe an American project.

The dollar gap convinced the average American that the only money that seemed to do anybody any good was our money. Some American tourists between the two world wars had already suspected this was the case and the least tactful of them had publicly lighted their cigars with local currencies. But fortunately every currency is current somewhere. The postwar problem has been that so many currencies were "soft" once they crossed their own frontiers. The apparent fact that only the dollar could buy the things mankind needed, we were tempted to ascribe to our superior economic system and superior economic beliefs rather than to our good fortune in escaping invasion, occupation, and devastation. That made it a slightly flattering position to be left holding the bag. And it was also gratifying that the Marshall Plan of aid for Europe was extremely stimulating to American prosperity. It is important that all these aspects of it were familiar to our friends in Europe and would have been familiar to them even if the Communists had not pointed them out and harped upon them.

But by this time our foreign policy was dominated by its First—

and most basic—False Assumption: that the cause of the world's ills was Russia. Our fatal choice of Washington rather than the United Nations as the place to direct the rehabilitation of Europe (Where else could you find the know-how? Where else, the real money?) meant that you could not get the necessary funds from Congress without defining the rehabilitation of Europe as an aspect of our power struggle with Russia. Since most Europeans have never believed that the problem was fundamentally a military problem, we found ourselves paymaster to allies who would not have gone along with our policies had they not needed our aid. So they dragged their feet. So members of Congress sometimes made destructively bitter observations about their morals, about their political systems, about their economic methods. American liberals shuddered at these remarks. But if you accept the assumptions of our foreign policy, were these Congressmen wrong? What business had the Senator from Ohio to vote subsidies to foreign governments unless those governments gave the American people a quid pro quo, and what quid was wanted so much as a promise to help if we had war with Russia? Could he reasonably demand less for the hard-earned dollars his constituents had paid to the tax collector?

If the United Nations had remained the chosen instrument of all its members, including the United States, for getting a sick world economy on its feet, the senator from Ohio could reasonably have demanded only that we put in the common kitty no more than our fair share, although even then some of his constituents would have objected. For the plain fact is that the American Government is an agency of the American people to secure, among other things, the general welfare of the American people, and has no direct responsibility for the more than two billion non-Americans on this planet who neither obey its laws nor elect its officers nor pay their salaries. The only agency that all men everywhere have at the moment, which sixty governments have agreed to support and use, is the United Nations. They explicitly charged it in its Charter with looking to the general welfare of the world community.

Those who wanted to keep control of what would have been America's contribution to the United Nations assured us that the U.N. was too weak to do the job, so Washington would have to. But the only way the U.N. could ever become strong would be for it to tackle those jobs assigned to it. Instead, in the economic area, the U.N. defaulted for lack of funds to national governments, concerned by definition with local national problems and particularly with local national defense. Then Washington tried to make the United Nations assume its police functions, its law-and-order functions, its military functions, which for some reason it was considered strong enough to assume. But the police of any agency, normally of government, derive their moral authority from the fact that the government that uses them faces courageously the whole problem of justice in the community, including economic justice. Otherwise, the police are condemned to be the instrument of tyranny.

This is why our efforts in Korea to punish international invasion have been so unfruitful. Although we were able to round up enough votes to secure U.N. sanction to drive the Communist invaders back, we have never been able to get more than token participation from most of them. For they do not share our first premise, that Russian imperialism, not human misery, is the basic problem. Could we have secured even their formal votes, had we not already worked ourselves unintentionally into the position of paymaster?

I can see no escape from these ambiguous positions so long as we decline to participate financially in a genuine attack by the United Nations on what is a U.N., not a U.S., problem. In the fall of 1950 both President Truman and Secretary Acheson, in speeches to the U.N. General Assembly, predicted such participa-

tion to rehabilitate ravaged Korea. But the sums we have subscribed to U.N. are ludicrous when viewed in the light of the
world's desperate economic plight, even though our share is always, for obvious reasons, the biggest share. In January 1949,
President Truman presented as "Point Four" of his inaugural
address a "bold, new program for making the benefits of our
scientific advances and industrial progress available for the im-
provement and growth of underdeveloped areas." It is perhaps
no exaggeration to say that Point Four got a warmer reception
from the American press and the American people than any other
policy President Truman has ever enunciated. Eleven months
later, the late Brien McMahon proposed in the Senate that
America subscribe ten billion dollars a year for five years as
her share toward a joint international fund to tackle the problem.
His speech met with an enthusiastic reception. Five months later
a Senate committee examined a House bill providing a total of
thirty-five million and tried to whittle it to ten million. That
happens to be less than New York City had spent in the previous
year to clean its streets and empty its garbage. A few days later
Walter Reuther, President of the United Automobile Workers,
proposed thirteen billions a year for a hundred years, totaling
over one trillion dollars.

Senator McMahon had suggested one thousand times as much
money per year as the Senate committee thought right; and Mr.
Reuther suggested a third more than that for twenty times as
long. Senator McMahon and Mr. Reuther were of course speaking
of an alternative to war and knew that World War II cost the
United States alone more than three hundred billion. Just as
obviously, the Senate committee that bid ten million was not
talking about an alternative to war, but about a possibly useful
gimmick in the cold war, and it is doubtful whether a single
gimmick in a still cold war was worth more than ten million, if
that. Most of the discussion of Point Four in America has been

based on the gimmick theory. Consequently most of it sounds bitterly humorous to the millions of human beings in the world who are trying to solve a problem far more desperate for them than the cold war is for us. They are convinced that neither a cold war nor a hot one can solve that problem. Yet, so long as the richest nation in the community insists on handling a sick world economy, an economy that breeds wars and revolutions, as one aspect of the military defense of one nation—itself—just so long Point Four will remain a gimmick, bought at the price of a gimmick. Which means that the only serious bid to handle the real problem will remain Russia's bid, Communism. In such conditions, Communism will continue to spread through the world community, by simple default—because America lacks a foreign policy based on fact instead of fancy. There is a paradox in this business: the only way to "stop Communism" is to stop considering it the source of all the world's ills and to understand why our neighbors are more interested in its cause, human misery. The only way to stop it is to remove its cause—in short, to treat the disease, and not merely the symptom.

The middle world between Russia and America, comprising a modest two billion people, tells in this regard an anecdote that makes them chuckle. We in America must discover why they are amused, and learn to share their amusement. The story goes that a certain Asian government cabled a Latin-American government: "Send us two Communists at once." The Latin Americans were puzzled and cabled back: "Why?" "Because," came the reply, "we have no Communists, and we will never get American economic aid until we have some."

Farfetched? I'm not so sure. They say that when the Pakistani delegate Zafrulla Khan, was asked at a press conference how many Communists there were in Pakistan, he replied: "Please do not press me, gentlemen. If I told you there were many, I should be lying to you, and if I told you how few there are, America would lose interest in us."

It does not greatly matter whether these are true stories. What matters is that their significance is instantly recognized by people all over the world: that Washington will not handle mankind's worst problem unless the problem can be disguised as the Communist problem—which Washington mistakes for mankind's worst problem.

If, through a miracle, the American Congress began to vote the billions, not the millions, that this job requires, it would quite properly keep a close eye on how it was spent. Whatever agency tackles the job will have to keep a close eye on expenditure. But if the close eye is an American eye, then from all over the world will arise angry shouts of American imperialism. And the cries will be justified. If this gigantic problem is assigned to Washington, if it is approached with funds collected by Washington from American taxpayers, history will inexorably require that Washington build a world empire and administer it. For those who assume the responsibility must inevitably be free to make the necessary decisions. In such event, the Russians will not be the only people to resent the concentration in Washington not only of economic power, but now of political power as well. There will be struggles against that power, and Washington will have to call out the marines. To recognize these forces is to reflect no discredit on either the American government or the American people. There are merely some laws of history and of empire from which not even we Americans are exempt. That such laws exist is known already to men in many countries: hence the cries of "Cocacolonization" from Marshall Plan countries and from many European non-Communists. They would prefer us to the Russians, but they want neither; and they know that America could not possibly assume unilaterally so much responsibility for the economic welfare of the people of Western Europe without acquiring some measure of political control of Europe.

Most of us Americans know that this is the way life works when it comes to relations between private individuals, but we have had too little experience of international politics to realize that this is the way life works there, too. And when non-Communists in Marshall Plan countries display fear of American political control, our feelings get hurt. We sense that those we have helped are suspecting our moral intentions. But it is not our moral intentions that they suspect, it is our political procedures, procedures which through many centuries have provided a greased track to empire.

Actually, some of our best American administrators abroad are so conscious that our procedures look suspect—and therefore furnish our opponents and critics with constant ammunition—that they are constantly forced to lean over backward in order not to appear as foreign meddlers, as Yankee imperialists. This is an awkward posture for a man with work to do. Yet in the case of labor policies in France, or land reform in Italy, or marketing problems in Greece, American administrators of the Marshall Plan have been in this situation. Had these administrators been the nationals of many countries, working for an international development authority financed by the United Nations, they could have been firmer where the job called for firmness.

The long and short of it is that it it quite unfair to expect either the American voter or his representatives in Congress to do a job that only an international agency can do. The frustration of trying to do it has driven us to depend more and more on an arms program, on weapons, and on force, rather than on international co-operation. We excuse ourselves by saying that Russia has rendered international co-operation impossible. But most of mankind instinctively knows that true co-operation has been abandoned for an arms race. And a good many of them know who killed Cock Robin. Most Americans do not know; nor do they know the catastrophic consequences of Cock Robin's death for most of the peoples on this planet.

CHAPTER V

The international job ahead called for the joint effort of many governments and their peoples. Our foreign policy loaded it onto one government, ours, and onto one people, ourselves. The failures and frustrations that were bound to result have tended to support the clamor of those who hold a Third False Assumption: "That private enterprise can do the job even better than government." This quite unfairly shifts the burden from the American taxpayer and his government, who cannot bear it without building an empire which nobody wants, to the shoulders of the American businessman, who cannot bear it, no matter what he does. It is true that this crucifixion of the businessman has been attempted not so much by foreigners, or by American politicians or even by the average American taxpayer, as by the public relations man and advertising copywriter whom the businessman has hired. This point of view has been vociferously expressed by the National Association of Manufacturers in repeated Congressional hearings on Point Four. The N.A.M. has thereby done the businessman a grave disservice, by grossly overestimating his resources and knowledge. American business, as

73

many businessmen know from travel and observation, could not possibly raise the capital this job demands nor are our businessmen sufficiently familiar with the peculiar conditions, both political and economic, which they would have to face. As a result, in the period since World War II, they have wisely refrained from heavy capital investment in distant and troubled spots. When they have invested, it has been chiefly in oil, an investment that scarcely touches the problem we are talking about here.

But ever since the early days of Franklin Roosevelt, the chief spokesmen of American business have been trying to "keep government out of business," except where government could supply services or markets or tax concessions that would obviously bring quick profits to business. Thus, the chief voices of the business world were opposed to economic developments like the TVA as "competing with business"; even though many businessmen knew individually that the Federal Government was undertaking in the Tennessee Valley what neither our great industrial corporations nor our principal banks nor any other agency could or would do, and even though many businessmen knew, or shortly learned, that the TVA created a vast new market and unheard-of opportunities for private enterprise. In brief, American business has remained predominantly opposed to New Deals, Fair Deals, public works. It certainly wants no "World New Deal." Even in the case of the Marshall Plan, it favored restrictions that forced the recipient country to buy the things that it needed from America, not elsewhere; although an elementary knowledge of foreign trade would have made it clear that a dollar let loose in Europe would inevitably find its way back to the counters of American business, by no matter what circuitous and fertilizing route.

The paid spokesmen of American business, who thoughtlessly tried to saddle their employers with this incredible task, had a powerful myth to work with. During World War II, American industry faced a problem unique in history. It possessed a productive plant exceeding any other in human history, capable of stupendous profits but also capable of tremendous losses if it collided with the postwar depression that nearly everybody expected. This vast plant was growing, as government stimulated productive expansion with huge tax concessions. Meanwhile, this plant was in many cases forbidden to produce civilian goods. Advertisements for refrigerators could scarcely urge the reader to buy one when none was available. Yet, in terms of postwar competition, it was important to keep this particular brand of refrigerator in the public mind. Moreover, war profits before taxes were exceedingly high, and so were taxes. These profits could go to the tax collector or to the advertising budget. So advertising budgets were very large. The business corporation often faced, therefore, the curious combination of huge funds for advertising but nothing to sell. In this situation, the corporation was forced to confine itself to "institutional advertising"—that is, to advertisements written not to get the customer to act now, but to remember a trademark so that he could act when the war was over. There followed a flood of homily, intimate chats, and political advice unique in the history of American advertising. Since Communism was a growing phenomenon in the world, since democratic socialism was also spreading, and since the depression had developed in most American voters a pardonable interest in the general welfare, in full employment, and in social security, the favorite theme of institutional advertising during the war became a passionate defense of capitalism, now called "free enterprise," with the implication that all our other "freedoms" sprang basically from this one, and that the search for security was a kind of cowardice unworthy of a nation in arms.

To what extent the American people have been persuaded by this advertising is, I think, highly debatable. Many of them probably agree with Arnold Toynbee that the issue before our generation is not so simple or doctrinaire as a choice between socialism

75

and capitalism, and certainly not a choice between atheistic totalitarian Communism and American free enterprise. Most of them
probably agree with Toynbee that the real problem is to discover
in each society what functions can best be performed by private
agencies and what functions had best be socialized, since nearly
every country is, and has for a long time been, a mixed economy.
This problem calls, of course, for more intelligence and more
effort and a cooler head than the excitingly passionate defense
of either "Communism" or "free enterprise." It is a problem which
cannot be solved with either slogans or billingsgate or slander.

Whatever the reaction of most Americans to this advertising
campaign may be—and perhaps only a sizable depression would
disclose their answer—it is certain that billions of dollars have
been spent on propaganda written to convince them that the
extreme forms of free enterprise are best for their freedom and
happiness. It is understandable that organizations like the N.A.M.,
operating in such an atmosphere, should have wistfully assigned
to free enterprise a job which under no conceivable circumstances American business could do. They were victims of their
own propaganda. They tried to make the job sound reasonable
by urging Washington to protect American investors against so-
cialization in foreign countries, as in the case of Iran's recent
nationalization of a British oil company; to grant tax rebates to
the American who invested abroad; and to secure for him special
rights to convert foreign profits into dollars. These special privileges look both realistic and moderate not only to the N.A.M.,
but to the average American. Unhappily, they look like imperialism to most of the people of the world, and like the colonialism
against which there is swelling up nothing short of a world revolution.

Yet, without these guarantees, American business management
hesitates to make foreign investments. I do not blame the American business manager. The investors he represents would hesitate,

76

too. If I had invested in an oil company, I would be horrified to learn that my money was being used not to drill for oil, process it, sell it, and bring me dividends, but to build a primary road system, or finance public sanitation, or build schools, in a country I had never heard of. Yet it is precisely things like roads, malarial control, and schools that are needed. We got them here not from free enterprise, but from public funds—indeed from none other than government, whether national, state, or local. If we had waited for free enterprise to provide these things, we would have had to wait a long time. And this is nothing against free enterprise. There never was any good reason for Standard Oil to build U.S. Route One, and it never built it. True, a lot of Esso is sold along Route One. But so is a lot of Texaco and a lot of Amoco and a lot of other brands of gas and oil. Why should Esso build a highway so that Esso *and* Amoco *and* Texaco can sell their stuff? We Americans followed the wiser course and let government build the highway, which may be a little socialistic but certainly made things simpler for free enterprise with gas and oil to sell. One of our leading historians pointed out two years ago that this has always been the pattern of American development[12]—and TVA is in the great American tradition, along with U.S. Route One: massive capital investment by government, followed by a vast expansion of private business.

Part of the New Myth which several billion dollars' worth of advertising have spread is that the businessman created America. He did, along with government, farmers, professional men, soldiers, workers, foreigners, women, children, and mules. All of us should be congratulated. None of us should be rewarded by having a job dropped in our laps that we cannot possibly do and that, in fact, all of us taken together cannot do. This, the investor is smart enough to know. Like the American voter, the American investor is not prepared to take on the world. When they are forced to look as if they wanted to, one votes peanuts and one invests peanuts, and the world remains where it was. Meanwhile, the New Myth is a dangerous ingredient for our foreign policy. When Egyptians or Iranians scream in the streets, "Down with Britain! Down with America!", it is our New Myth coming home to roost. And calling out the Marines would be a mere headache pill that would not touch the disease of which the headache is a symptom. The disease is going-it-alone in handling a problem that will be solved only by the joint action of ourselves and our neighbors. Maybe we had better abandon going-it-alone and call in the neighbors. In any case there is no use picking on the American businessman, or trying to make him do what he has not done, is not doing, and cannot do. There is no use picking on him even if the N.A.M. begs us to.

A Fourth False Assumption is steadily confusing our foreign policy. This is the assumption that even if the United Nations and not the United States did the big job, the U.N. could do it with small annual appropriations. For, despite our steadfast refusal to join the rest of the human race in defining and solving a problem that is human, not merely American, we do go through the motions of working "through the United Nations" too. Our last budget included over four and a half billions for military aid to our potential allies against Russia, and under two billions for economic aid to weaken local Communist movements, keep our Allies strong enough to fight, or coax them into letting us have raw materials in short supply so we can carry out our own arms program; but it also included under nine *millions* as our contribution to the U.N.'s own "Point Four."[13] Going through the motions is usually an expensive activity, precisely because it is basically futile, and our appropriation to the U.N. for technical assistance is no exception.

Our appropriation is, of course, too minute to enable the United Nations to face the real problem.[14] To which we reply that in the initial stages of the U.N. program it is study that is needed, and

78

that the U.N. has been given adequate funds with which to study and lay plans. Until recently, that was partly true. Only the uninformed romantic supposes that an agency, whether the U.N. or the U.S., can rush out and spend many billions of dollars intelligently without long and careful planning first. True, the U.S. and the Marshall Plan governments rushed out and spent several billions pretty quickly. But that was to rebuild the economies of highly developed countries, which possessed abundant information on their own needs and great numbers of trained personnel.

It was only partly true that the United Nations could not profitably accept larger funds for development work, and it is becoming less true by the week. Our policy has kept the U.N.'s Technical Assistance Administration on a hand-to-mouth basis. It has never been able to make long-term plans because it has never known whether there would be any appropriation at all, three years later. This has precluded it from offering a career to the sort of personnel this job calls for. It has kept its operations tentative. It has given no guarantee to underdeveloped countries that the job would ever be tackled at all in any serious and determined fashion. The excuse we give is that the U.N. is still young, still a child, and has not learned to walk yet. But can you teach children to walk by confining them year after year to a play pen? It is interesting that the U.S. never uses this argument about the U.N.'s military problem, about the necessity to have in being an international police force. There, we are all for getting the child out of the play pen and giving him a hand until he can walk for himself. Other peoples reasonably deduce that the military functions of the Security Council interest us, while the full-employment and economic-development functions of the Economic and Social Council leave us cold. Noting that we are rich, well-fed, and comfortable but at the same time thoroughly frightened of revolution and war, they grimly understand our prejudices. Being themselves poor, underfed, ill, and wretched, and consequently interested in revolution and without much to fear from war, they decline to share our prejudices or rally to our military support. The fact is, we do not live in the world that most of the human race inhabits—or at least we have not yet found out that we live in their world.

If, instead of hammering at them to send us more aid in Korea, we had accepted their proposal of an International Development Authority and had placed our fair share of resources at its disposal, to be spent when its own technical personnel were technically prepared to spend it, we would have risked sharing the lot of mankind in the twentieth century and would be able to communicate with the rest of the human race. Finally, even TVA was handicapped by not having heavier capital at the start and by facing the chance of a Congress that would purposely starve it. For an International Development Authority, that danger would be still greater. It should have enough cash at the start and on the barrelhead to guarantee it five years or so of useful life.

Many well-intentioned Americans object at this point that we could not both lead mankind on a crusade for freedom in Korea and join mankind in a common fight on misery. Where would the money come from? Senator Brien McMahon, for example, made his famous proposal that we subscribe ten billions a year as our share of a common fund to get the world's economy on its feet, on February 2, 1950. I was one of the many Americans who wrote to thank him for his courage and realism. But I questioned the wisdom of attaching a string: that we would make our subscription only if we could save the money by a general agreement on scaling down world armaments. Why not offer to do it anyhow, counting on the common attack on world misery to redefine our military problem? But where, many Americans were asking, would the money come from? This question should not be asked out loud, for our neighbors are listening. If they were rude enough, they might answer the question over our back fence: "From wherever you got the ninety-odd billions[15] since then for weapons to defend a status quo, a status quo you are almost alone in wanting to defend."

Russia offers bread and freedom from the day-by-day oppression of landlord, usurer, and colonial rule. Whether Communism can "deliver," or whether it can deliver only at too high a social and moral cost, is not here the issue. It offers to meet the double problem of bread and freedom from existing oppressors. We should offer that and more. We should offer freedom from the kind of dictatorship Russia is under. These people are revolting against things we Americans revolted against when this republic fought for its freedom against misrule from overseas and the British Parliament's refusal to permit the free economic development of our resources in the interests of our own people. We Americans betray our great traditions when we enjoy our own freedom and prosperity and throw our political weight against the effort of other people to win the same things.

The truth is—and it is a most sad truth—that we have allowed Russia to seize the initiative in bringing a new world to birth. When Russia has loudly offered bread to the hungry, we have promised to look into the matter of bread some day provided the hungry will help us contain Russia. To those who have been dying of hunger we have pointed out that law and order must first be guaranteed, and we have sometimes offered in effect to set up a soup kitchen to feed those who would promise in advance to fight on the right side when we had nursed them back into physical condition to fight. That was certainly the essence of what many Americans said in public when India asked for some of the wheat we could not use.

On the colonial problem, Justice William O. Douglas of the U.S. Supreme Court has the advantage over most of us. He took the trouble to travel to many foreign lands, to many poor lands, to rough it, to go among the people and talk with them about the problems they are up against, not the ones the American State Department urges them to be up against. And he reported.[16] In the light of his report, and the reports of others who have sought the answers to the same questions, our foreign policy exhibits tragically what I have called our Fifth False Assumption: "That America can best preserve freedom by backing any anti-Communists she can find anywhere, including reactionaries and even fascists." In so doing, we are identifying ourselves in the minds of men with misery and oppression. Meanwhile, we think we are identifying ourselves in the minds of men with freedom. This misunderstanding of ours is a great tragedy, for us and for all men. It may prove, in retrospect, to be the greatest tragedy of our generation.

During the frustrating years of the cold war, American foreign policy has proceeded on the five false assumptions we have been discussing here. They are negative and sterile assumptions in terms of the real world that confronts us Americans today. They have brought us no nearer to peace than we were when we adopted them. When adults are confronted by this kind of failure, they usually take stock. I submit it is time that we took stock.

At the conclusion of World War II, Russia challenged us. She challenged us by her very existence. In the first place, she emerged as the only other state on earth whose military strength could be compared to ours. Given the anarchical system of nation states under which both we and the Russians are desperately living, this fact and this fact alone would have defined an opposition, regardless of any differences between Communism and capitalism or between self-government and totalitarian government. By her mere existence, Russia therefore challenged us, and military power was the gauntlet she threw down. It is true that by our own mere existence we threw down a gauntlet, too. We challenge each other.

82

But Russia threw down another gauntlet: Communism, which Russia claims is the only way to bring daily bread to the hundreds of millions who now lack bread. We retort that capitalism, which we call free enterprise, will bring it better. Hundreds of millions of people are listening to the argument. And note that, although Communism is many things, it is among other things aggressively dedicated to economic development, and particularly to the development of modern industry in areas that now lack it.

The cold war happened because we picked up one gauntlet and let the other lie. We accepted the challenge of military power and ignored the challenge of economic development. I am aware of all our talk about Point Four. I am aware of our unilateral economic aid to countries we hope to line up against Russia. I am even aware of the pittance we have given the U.N. for the common effort that remains abortive for lack of our support. But, basically, we let the second gauntlet lie. The countries where men and women die because of that decision urge us to pick it up. We cannot hear them: we are gazing obsessively at Russia's military power, and trying to rally all men to our side. They cannot hear us: they are obsessively gazing at Russia's economic development and at their great need of like development.

It is our move, rather than theirs. For they have a better right to their obsession than we have to ours. Hunger is at their gates, and Russia is not at ours. Hunger has invaded their city and slain millions, while no Russian invader has touched foot to American soil. They know the Soviet empire is expanding, or that at the very least the number of Cominform countries is expanding. Many of them are troubled by that expansion. But we cannot ask them to consider Soviet expansion in the same light as famine at home and the disorder famine breeds. Even more important, they know that despite all our cries of "Remember Munich!" it is simply not true that Russian expansion is the same phenomenon that Hitler's was. They know that the Russians never shrink from applying military

83

force, but they know too, that the boast that a master race must rule cannot compete with the Communist promise that all men shall have bread. To us, Russia only looks like tanks. To them, she looks like tractors.

We decry daily Russia's failure to achieve our standard of living, but these people would gladly settle for Russia's standard. And even we have to admit that, whether because of Communism or in spite of it, the Soviet Government achieved a colossal industrial revolution in a third of a century. If they had not, we would not now gaze so obsessively at Russia. We cannot very well tell our starving neighbors that Russian industry is a special kind, powerful for the ends of war but helpless for the ends of peace. They would laugh, if it was the last thing they had the strength to do before dying. We would be wiser to reflect on the speed with which Russia industrialized. We cannot say that the Russians have already reached Seattle, or Baltimore, and that we cannot spare time or money for other things until we have driven the enemy from our soil. A large part of the human race now speaks English; and the word "containment" suggests to them that American policy is not to keep the Russians from crossing our frontiers but from crossing Russia's own. We will not persuade them that military power is as imminent a danger to us as famine and disease are to them. They know from firsthand experience, of a sort we have not had, that the real Communist menace derives from famine, and only very secondarily from Russian arms. They accuse us of trying to shoot Communism, which is a set of ideas and cannot be shot, instead of trying to help solve the real problems of mankind better than Communists can. In short, they are overwhelmingly convinced that the real world crisis is not primarily military, as we insist, but economic. My only reason for repeating these things here is that most Americans are not following the newspapers of foreign countries.

Throughout the cold war a favorite topic of speculation in the

84

American press has been whether America and Communist Russia can coexist. We quote Lenin, or we quote Stalin, to prove that our two countries can coexist peacefully, or that they cannot. Since the works of Lenin and Stalin are rather bulky, the game of quoting shows little signs of ending soon. I should like to suggest that we try to restate the issue, since I believe the very word "coexist" is a dangerously confusing word. It might be a useful word if our generation were living in a period of very gradual social change. It is a static word, useful in a period of status quo. But we happen to be living through a world-wide revolution, and in periods of revolution those who merely try to continue their existence are rarely able to achieve their ambition. If this were a period of history when technology happened to be standing more or less still, when social ideas were more or less fixed and widely accepted, Russia might go on quietly existing in Asia and Eastern Europe; we might go on quietly existing in North America; and never the twain would meet. The other two billion people in the world could go on quietly existing in other parts of the world.

Even the quietest periods history records were not all that quiet. And the mid-twentieth century is by no means one of the quietest periods. It is, in the phrase Arnold Toynbee borrowed from seventeenth-century Russian history, "a time of troubles." In two world wars and a lot of smaller wars, in numerous revolutions, and through far-ranging famine and pestilence, hundreds of millions of people have died, whole populations have been uprooted and deported, millions have known imprisonment and torture, transport and communications have been revolutionized, hideous new weapons have been devised, and the growth of science has advertised the possibility of ending human poverty. Not only have all these things happened; but never has so large a proportion of the human race known so much about the race as a whole. This maelstrom dismays us Americans. Precisely because we have become an extremely rich nation, both in things to enjoy and in tools

with which to multiply such things almost indefinitely, we have
become by all odds the most conservative nation politically of any
of the great industrial powers. Our Paul Bunyan economy is both
flattering to our skill and diligence, and a little terrifying. We
have a ride-'em-cowboy feeling about the powerful productive
machine that carries us forward. It could certainly carry us far,
but it certainly bucks hard. It all makes us a little homesick for
the surrey with the fringe on top.

At the moment, the bronco is carrying us toward World War
III, since war is where arms races commonly carry people. If we
could just get "fool-proof guarantees" that we would not be attacked! Presumably we mean guarantees that would permit us to
act, with impunity, like fools, a rather heavy demand on history.
If we could just persuade our allies and those we hope to make
allies to go slow on change until law and order can be established.
By a cruel irony one of the chief things driving them to change is
the restless American economy. And as for Russia, one of the
possible true descriptions of the Russian Revolution is: the process by which czarist Russia Americanized and rationalized its
production. This description of a thing we hate shocks us, but
the process is undoubtedly one facet of Russian Communism.
And at least technologically, America itself not only is "a permanent revolution"—it is a permanent incitement to revolution for
most of the men and women on this planet today.

Yet, precisely because we have more things to enjoy than any
other people in the world, and more things with which to make
things, we are more distrustful of change, have least to gain from
change, or believe we have least to gain. We are ready to give of
our bounty, provided we do not have to share control of its
sources. Like other human beings, we cherish our special privileges. We want to be let alone by our neighbors, and loudly announce we are ready to let them alone. Freedom, about which we
now talk much more than about justice, means for us: to be let

alone. In domestic affairs, business wants to be let alone, wants to be free.

If we will watch the American domestic scene carefully, we will note that, roughly speaking, it is those Americans with the most things who most dislike change inside America, while those with the least things are the most interested in change. This should help us understand, by a simple analogy, why on the world scene hungry people are less afraid of change than we Americans are. Our reign of law in world affairs frightens them if it means pegging conditions that they find, frankly, a hell. They are determined to change that hell into something less hellish, and our foreign policy will be listened to in proportion to the account it takes of that determination. We have no real need to base our foreign policy on fear—which is precisely what it is based on now. We could base it on hope—and thereby make it the foreign policy of many other peoples. For these hungry peoples are not interested in taking our things away from us; they are merely determined to get things like them. Like us, they get hungry. I am convinced that most Americans want them to eat. Most Americans do not want to go on feasting at a table where most plates are empty and most faces gaunt and most eyes hollow with hunger. But our official foreign policy does not convey American feelings successfully to those who hunger.

Communist Russia is the opposite of conservative. It was born of revolution, and of a recent revolution at that. It is by default the likeliest candidate for the leadership of a world revolution which would rage on even if Russia were destroyed. It does not want merely to exist but to act, and it is acting. If we signed a treaty of "coexistence" with Russia, and continued to evade the problems which world revolution poses, the treaty would soon break down. For while we existed, Russia would go on acting. And to a man who wants peace and quiet, who feels he would be happy if just allowed to exist, an active man always looks aggressive. To a man who wants to stabilize existing conditions, the man who wants to change them must appear a troublemaker and a conspirator. Neither Russia nor we can stop the world revolution. Russia is trying to seize the leadership of the world revolution. From where our neighbors sit, we are trying politically to slow it down and secure the status quo, even while our dynamic American economy exerts irresistible pressures to promote revolution. If we persuade Russia to promise us to coexist, Russia will act, and we shall denounce her aggression. The alternative is for us to act, too, and to seek agreement with Russia not on coexistence, but on coaction.

The problem of the non-Russian, non-American world certainly calls for action if anything ever called for it. If we would take our paralyzed gaze off Russia just long enough to look squarely at that world, we would escape the hypnosis that produced the paralysis in the first place. We would pick up that other gauntlet. We would match the Russian plan with an American plan and submit it to our neighbors. Better still, we would examine with humility and attentiveness the plan our neighbors have already, repeatedly, and thus far in vain, submitted to us. We would examine the plan for an International Development Authority. If we did, we should discover to our amazement that it is an American plan. We should discover that our neighbors, when faced with a life-or-death problem, have more faith in the American way of life than we ourselves have been lately showing.

CHAPTER VI

Two documents appeared in our country in 1951 that should have been read and debated from coast to coast, and that would have been very widely discussed indeed had our political leadership been on its toes instead of totally immersed in cold-war politics abroad and party politics at home. One of these documents was the report of a Presidential commission known as the International Development Advisory Board. It was chaired, appropriately, by Nelson A. Rockefeller, who had already had years of experience in economic development in South America, both on the basis of business profits and on the basis of non-profit enterprise. The report was published, both by the Government Printing Office and by a private publishing firm, under the title *Partners in Progress*. Those who signed it were a number of distinguished Americans, representing many groups in American life.

The other document was a report made not to the head of one government, but to the Secretary-General of the United Nations, Mr. Trygve Lie. It is the work not of a group of Americans, but of five economic experts from five different countries, including our own, and indeed from five different areas of the world: North America, South America, Europe, the Near East, and the Far East. It was distributed by the U.N. through the usual channels— which in our country means through the Columbia University Press—under the title *Measures for the Economic Development of Under-developed Countries.* My guess is that relatively few Americans have ever seen the first report, the American one, and that a much smaller number yet have seen the U.N. report. I repeat, if we Americans were thinking politically about the real world we live in, rather than about one which is in no small measure a figment of our own imagination, these two reports would have been read and argued over from coast to coast.

These two reports are now in your lap and mine whether we bother to pick them up and read them or whether we let them lie there unopened. I shall not attempt to analyze them in detail here. But we ought to compare them briefly; it will help us think about the problem we are discussing. We may call *Partners in Progress* "the U.S. Report" and we may call the report to Trygve Lie "the U.N. Report." Well, the U.N. Report addresses itself professionally and single-mindedly to what most of our neighbors consider the root problem of the human race: the staggering misery of half the planet's inhabitants, a misery that in many places is getting not better, but worse,[17] and a misery that is driving millions toward revolution and war. The U.N. Report is concerned not merely to relieve that human agony but to abolish its causes by the joint action of all peoples or of all peoples willing to act. To win this war against misery, it seizes every available weapon in the arsenal. It demands political and economic reforms in the countries where help is needed, notably land reform. It demands that industrialized countries stop doing some of the things they now do that worsen the problem, and do some other things that would help solve it. It would encourage the flow of private capital. Above all, it demands that the International Bank do a better

90

job than it has done, that an International Development Authority
be set up to help the poorer countries get off dead center, and
that certain other international devices be set up.

The U.S. Report demands very similar things, but with a difference. The U.S. Report was addressed by Americans to Americans,
and particularly to those Americans in Congress and elsewhere
whom the rest of us have chosen to govern and protect America.
The U.S. Report therefore tries to prove that helping the poorer
countries would help us win the cold war and would benefit
American business. It pretty well had to do this, because the
essence of our foreign policy is stopping Russia with weapons
and, perhaps, saving free enterprise from Communism. The U.S.
Report is a product of the cold war, and the U.N. Report is not.
It is true that the U.S. Report also recommends an International
Development Authority—for "the free nations," of course, which is
a distinction the U.N. Report does not make and, given its purposes, had no need to make: for it still rains alike on the just and
the unjust, and hunger feels the same to the free and the unfree
where neither are free to eat. Since the cold war is intensely unpopular throughout most of "the free world," an International
Development Authority proposed as a measure in the cold war
against Russia does not look to the free world quite like an International Development Authority proposed as a measure in mankind's war against hunger and disease. The distinction no doubt
escapes many Americans. It is a distinction which, out of "a decent
respect to the opinion of mankind," we Americans should try hard
to grasp.

These differences adequately explain the striking difference in
style between the two reports. The U.N. Report is heavily factual,
simple and direct, singularly free of rhetorical flourishes; and it
contains passages that must anger some American readers, and
passages, I should say, which must anger for quite different
reasons some readers in every country. The U.S. Report exhibits

91

the slickness of what we Americans call a sales promotion piece. The U.N. Report assumes that all men everywhere have a common interest in getting their now common economy onto its feet and addresses itself to that common interest. The U.S. Report tries to persuade those men who happen to live in America that they have a special American interest, an enlightened self-interest, in helping their neighbors avoid starvation. There is no use blaming the drafters of the U.S. Report for striking a note that must have jarred cruelly on the ears of non-Americans throughout the world. They were, one gathers from their style, "selling" the idea to the Congress. To date, there has been no sale.

There has been no sale because the false assumptions on which the Congress is invited to consider all elements of our foreign policy had the drafters of the U.S. Report boxed, as they have the rest of us Americans boxed. If devices like the International Development Authority are indeed gimmicks in the cold war, then no Congressman in his senses is likely to vote the half-billion the U.S. Report allocates to them. He knows that a half-billion will buy a lot of planes, and he suspects the planes will be needed in a struggle that has, on the whole, steadily gone against our side. Sometimes, after hearing what some of our neighbors in the free world think of the cold war, he wonders whether they are on our side anyhow. If they aren't, why bother with them? He wonders whether the cold war and the world economic development can both be squeezed into the same foreign policy. The bulk of the free world shares his doubts. The free world expresses its doubts by fearing our foreign policy; he expresses his, since he is stuck with our foreign policy, by forgetting about the International Development Authority. Given this deadlock, it is not remarkable that the U.S. Report rang up no sale. As I write, no single major recommendation in it has been adopted by the Congress.[18]

Meanwhile, the underdeveloped countries, in meeting after meeting of the Economic and Social Council of the U.N., appeal for common action to attack the common problem of mankind. Although they deplore the cold war and hope to keep out of our quarrel with Russia, they cannot give top priority to the problem we Americans so anxiously discuss: can the U.S. and the U.S.S.R. coexist peacefully? If Russia abandoned the world revolution and we went on ignoring it, hunger and disease would remain at the top of the agenda for more than a billion people. If, on the other hand, we Americans aggressively joined our neighbors in a common assault on those problems, we would have picked up that second gauntlet, we would have accepted before all the assembled neighbors that one of Russia's two challenges which interests the most people; we would in fact have joined the human race. We would have put an end to our profound isolationism, an isolationism that has shifted from our saying in the twenties that our neighbors could stew in their own juice to our saying in the fifties that we will take part in international affairs if those affairs are run our way. We would be giving the lie to Karl Marx and announcing that the world's economic ills can be cured by the joint action of all classes and all peoples, without violence, without the sacrifice of political freedom where political freedom has been won, and in such a way as to bring political freedom where none now exists. At present we are busy confirming Karl Marx's prediction that those who eat will not help solve the problems of those who do not eat, but will block all change until destroyed by force.

How did we ever let ourselves be maneuvered into such an unimpressive and unneighborly position? How did we ever get from UNRRA to the Truman Doctrine, from international cooperation to the promise of weapons to all who will fight Communism? At bottom by our government assuming that Communism is in essence a military danger, not a system of ideas and a prescription for the actual ills of mankind. Our reply to that prescription has of course been that the prescription will not work.

Sometimes it has been that not even the doctor who wrote it believes it will work. The prescribed medicine, we say, is poison, and the doctor is a quack. But meanwhile the patient is dying, we refuse to examine seriously his case, and it begins to look to him as if only one prescription were available. Some say it cures and some say it kills, and he is dying anyhow. There is really not much choice. That is why, during the cold war, Communism has been spreading rapidly.

Senator McMahon was not the only American statesman to announce, or at least suggest, that if the neighbors will help us stop the quack from practicing, we will be glad to help write a really competent prescription later. But the patient is uncertain that we would prescribe the common world fund for economic development that Senator McMahon mentioned. The prescription the patient hears most about from America is a dash of know-how in a solution of free enterprise with appropriate government guarantees. He claims to have tried this before under an old label: colonialism. He claims it did a lot to bring on his present illness.

The basic cause of this stalemate in the world community is known to countless human beings all over the world. The world economy is one; the world polity is many. Modern technology has united mankind by bonds of steel—and by bonds of manganese, too, and of rubber, and of chromium, tin, zinc, copper, and aluminum. But politically the world community remains unorganized. Instead, several score sections of it are organized, some big, some little, into sovereign states, which know no law above the law they make for their own small communities. Each of these sovereign states theoretically reserves the right to shoot it out if it feels that its vital interests are threatened. In practice, this anarchy partly defeats itself. Even on paper, most of these sovereign communities have signed an intergovernmental agreement known as the United Nations Charter, although it is enlightening that in the very Charter of the U.N. itself their respective sovereignties are guaranteed. Moreover, in fact, many of them are too weak to defend themselves if the storm breaks, so they seek shelter under the wing of a bigger sovereignty. This means that Moscow and Washington make decisions for millions of persons whom they do not officially govern, although both Washington and Moscow have to bribe, browbeat, or cajole their respective allies—or satellites, according to whose team one is discussing. A number of sovereign states are trying to steer clear of both teams, but the suction is terrific.

In this mess the world economy reels along, haunted by our fear of famine in poor countries and fear of unemployment in big ones. When a given country gets in a jam, it tries in the current phrase to "export its misery" by currency devaluation, restrictions on imports, and a dozen other devices, which may help things at home by working incalculable hardship in some distant land. Stock-piling in the U.S. may cause a series of temporary booms in unindustrialized countries and force the price of raw materials to levels where Europe cannot buy what its factories must consume.

But nowhere in this world-wide community is there any agency but the United Nations which even claims as a primary concern the good of this community as a whole. If history means anything, it means that this newly created world community cannot operate except in the most chaotic fashion without a common government. In this respect, it is no different from all the other human communities the world has known.

This has suggested to countless people that what is needed more than anything else is a world government. Scores of statesmen all over the world have publicly declared the need. Popular polls have backed them up. Yet no member government of the United Nations has proposed that the U.N. Charter be rewritten in such fashion as to make the U.N. a government for all peoples who would ratify the new Charter. The most that any member government has done is to speak in double talk about "an international reign of law and order"—and a reign of law is of course terribly hard to get unless you get a government first to make the law and enforce it. Law that is neither made by a government nor enforced by one is not what the ordinary man means by law. And the ordinary man is perhaps not as big a fool as the double-talkers assume he is.

A great many ordinary people, and even more those who profess to speak for ordinary people, look on world government as a crackpot idea anyhow. Sometimes they add that the U.N. could keep the peace if its member states would only use it for that purpose instead of using it as an arena for power politics. That is a little too much like saying that no human community would need government, or law, or the police, if the people in it would just draw up rules and if everybody would voluntarily obey them. I doubt if the town I live in could even handle parking that way, let alone theft and murder. Once my fellow-townsmen lost the protection of the courts and the police, they would start carrying arms to protect themselves. And it should not take more than a year or so to develop a few first-class blood feuds. That is the situation in the world community today, and it is carrying more arms each month that passes.

Those who oppose world government on the grounds that it would be nice but that it is "idealistic" are using a boomerang word. For only the most starry-eyed idealist would expect the new world community which modern technology has created to be so unlike all other human communities in history that it can keep the peace without a common government—can keep it merely by having several dozen fragments living under separate governments, each pledged to protect its citizens, if necessary by force, from the other fragments. Just how romantic such a notion is, two world wars have just demonstrated. We are at the moment busily and expensively preparing for a third, which may convince

96

even our "realists" that the system of nation states can no longer hope to keep a tolerable degree of peace. It may convince even our realists that no national government in the world today can any longer hope to meet effectually the rudimentary obligation to protect the lives and property of its citizens against foreign attack. Increasing millions of people, particularly in small, exposed countries, now know this about their own governments. We and the Russians are relatively so powerful that we are slower to grasp it, but even we may yet grasp it.

It is not merely that science and industry have made modern war incredibly destructive. It is not merely that small professional armies were first succeeded by the conscription of all able-bodied males, and that now these able-bodied males have been supplemented by a "total" war that involves both sexes and all ages. It is not merely, as Arnold Toynbee has eloquently pointed out, that this makes war an impracticable means of settling anything, an impracticable "court of last resort" in which both plaintiff and defendant may be executed before the trial is over. It is also that the present political organization of the new world community into several dozen armed camps not only invites war but comes as near to guaranteeing it as any other device we might hope to invent.

This insane organization of a community has never been so plainly described by any man of my generation, so far as I know, as by a man who described it three hundred years ago. Thomas Hobbes then wrote that "in all times, Kings, and Persons of Soveraigne authority, because of their Independency, are in continuall jealousies, and in the state and posture of Gladiators; having their weapons pointing, and their eyes fixed on one another; that is, their Forts, Garrisons, and Guns upon the Frontiers of their Kingdomes; and continuall Spyes upon their neighbors; which is a posture of War."[19] The same thing holds true of any government of any type which claims sovereignty over one fragment of a human community and accepts responsibility for defending the people in it against all outside attack. If such a government arms, its neighbors shriek that it is planning aggression. Unhappily, this is an awkward charge to answer, because nobody has invented weapons that are an adequate defense and at the same time not useful for aggressive purposes. Indeed, a preventive war, such as a recent member of the American cabinet publicly suggested we fight against Russia, merely points up a fact that every government must face: a neighbor who feels threatened by this government's "defensive" arms may judge it wise to strike first.

Even the question of who struck first is often a hard one to answer. Who "started" the first world war? A mountain of paper and an ocean of ink have been used to measure the relative guilt of those governments whose actions, over many years, helped bring about violence in 1914. The fact is that they had "their weapons pointing, and their eyes fixed on one another" for a good while before the shooting started. Even if we say that Germany started it, and started the second war, too, can we truthfully say she was solely guilty of both? Did not everybody share at least one sin of omission: of not seriously trying to organize Europe politically, including Russia? Of showing no serious concern over the economic suffering and political misrule of the colonial world? Do we not all share now at least the guilt of not seriously trying to organize the world community?

Many Americans will truthfully reply: "I am doing all I can in my small way to explain to my neighbors why the world community must be organized politically if it is not to destroy itself. I am urging that the U.N. Charter be revised to make it the constitution of a true world government, with minimal powers sufficient to guarantee law and order in the international community, leaving all other powers in the hands of the national governments where they are now."

98

Would that be a good thing to do? It would certainly be more reasonable than some of the arguments now being made against doing it. But that is not saying much, or anyhow not enough. Those who still claim that each people is too jealous of its national sovereignty to join other peoples in a common federal government capable of making and enforcing world law have not caught up with history. When a French statesman, Aristide Briand, proposed in the twenties a United States of Europe, he got very little backing, even in France. The French, or many of them, were still under the illusion that they were "victorious"— that they had "won" the first world war. But World War II drove home a lesson that many Frenchmen had learned in the long armistice between the wars: the system of nation states, under which we are all trying to live, had clearly broken down and could only lead from one catastrophe to another until Europe, at least, was destroyed or subjected. For anybody who knew France before 1914, or even in the twenties when so many Americans lived there, a return trip today is highly instructive. The French have become profoundly distrustful of the sovereign state as a means of guaranteeing civilized life. This disillusionment is widely shared in Europe today. What Briand foresaw, many now know: that some common political and economic institutions must be invented, if not for the entire world community, then at least for Europe. It is that sentiment that made the Schuman Plan for regulating the coal and steel industries through a common authority in the interests of Europe as a whole sound realistic. It is true that adoption of the Schuman Plan took plenty of time: in 1912, or even in 1932, it would not have got a hearing. The prestige of national sovereignty has reached an all-time low in Europe. The new constitutions of France and Italy even make provision for surrender of sovereignty. The European has daily proof that no national government can protect the ordinary citizen from either war or inflation or unemployment, and for a simple

99

reason: its jurisdiction is too limited. Yet no international agency, including the United Nations, has as yet been given adequate authority to protect him. In the near panic that has ensued, each national government tends to grow more tyrannical, precisely because it feels its increasing impotence. It exhibits the viciousness of senility. It tries to tax more, to conscript more, to interfere with business more, to interfere with travel more.

Yet an intelligent Frenchman knows that, for all its petty tyranny, it cannot deliver. He knows that what is decided in Washington is likely to affect his life more than what is decided in Paris. And he has no voice in Washington, no representative in the Congress. Precisely because he has won no world citizenship, he has effectually lost his French citizenship, or a large part of it.

But that is France. If we want to see anything like the kind of nationalism France once felt, we must turn to some country in Asia or Africa that once was, or still is, a possession of France, or of Holland, or of Portugal, or Great Britain. There people are not disillusioned with national sovereignty, for they have yet to win it. The problem their attention is focused on is how to chase out those who "possess" them. The centuries of colonial exploitation that made Europe the wealthiest continent on earth for many decades left them with distorted economies, the destruction of their handicraft industries, and a feudal land system. It most often left them too with a burning hatred of the arrogant white man, who had with such gallantry carried the white man's burden—for a service charge that the "native" now considers far too high. We Americans ought to understand: the Boston Tea Party was held to protest that service charge. The "native" wants independence first, the thing we Americans won. When he has won that, he may be ready to examine the inadequacies of sovereignty in a modern world. He is not looking for a common government with Europeans until he can get from under the common government he already has with some European people. And he will naturally want to know just how Jim Crow the proposed government is to be. As one of the "teeming millions" of Asia or the "backward" natives of Africa, he will want to know what the chances of a good life will be for him, under a proposed world government. If it is to be given minimal powers to preserve law and order, he will want to know what order—the present order? He calls that one disorder. He can see why Europeans might want to preserve it, or why Americans would think it quite splendid. But the "backward teemer" dissents.

Why not listen to him carefully? We might learn things that we have to understand before we can build a successful foreign policy. We have had our attention so riveted on Russia that we have been busy saving the free world without listening very much to those we would save. In the process, we have steadily lost moral authority in the free world. That distresses us, and angers us a little. It looks as if nobody appreciates our motives. Probably nobody ever will until we start appreciating his. Of course, if we go on shouting that the enemy is at our gates, that the Red hordes are massing, that the free world must arm to the teeth, that it must meanwhile postpone attacking the problem of when do we eat, why, in that case we shall hardly have time to listen to what the colonial says.

The colonial speaks for the majority of men, women, and children on the planet. We might profitably forget about sovereign governments for a few moments and look at those other, realer beings: men, women, and children. Unlike governments, they have faces, eyes, ears, mouths—and stomachs. And—exciting fact—they have minds. They are, in short, our brothers. And most of them are hungry, or sick, or half-naked, or homeless, and most of them are colored.

They are on the march, in the first world-wide revolution history records. This revolution was made possible by the machines of the white man, and his machines have made it possible in two ways. First, they convinced these outcastes of the world community that their unbelievable misery is unnecessary; competent white economists have shown that machines can bring them the food and clothes and shelter, even the health and education, that they long for. Second, the machines have not only brought them this burning hope, but by tying the whole world tightly into one community they have guaranteed that the revolution shall be world-wide. Nothing can stop this world-wide revolution. It can be guided by Communists—or by us if we can offer a better plan than Communism for getting where these people are determined to get. But shooting Communists will not stop it; destroying Russia will not stop it; destroying Russia plus her satellites will not stop it; nor can we stop it by destroying Russia, her satellites, and every living Communist in the non-Communist world. So it is our move. While moving, we might remember one bitter fact. Since the Communists have loudly and publicly championed this world-wide drive for a decent and human life, every time we attack Communists in the hearing of impoverished subject peoples we risk appearing to attack the world-wide revolution they are committed to.

But if we listen again to our imaginary Frenchman, we shall discover that there is another revolution sweeping the world, also created by the machine and with the machine's help achievable. It is the revolution in men's minds against national sovereignty. For the machine has made nonsense of our frontiers; or, rather, the machine has created a world economy, a world market, and a world struggle for crucial raw materials which is colliding dangerously with the frontiers we inherited from our pre-machine days. This is what the Frenchman has discovered, and a lot of people who are not French. Like Gulliver, tied to the ground by the tiny Lilliputians, the machine technology of a world economy is struggling to loose itself from the frontiers, tariffs, currency re-

strictions, export licenses, and a score of other cords that strain to
hold it back.

As a result the men and women of the world, but particularly
the men and women in the countries with the machines, feel
frustrated and even angered. They know they need international
institutions capable of regulating what are clearly international
problems; and they are beginning to see that those institutions
will have to be responsible to men and women, rather than to
national governments as the United Nations is. They do not want
to do away with their national governments or their national cultures. They merely find increasingly absurd the efforts of their
national governments to handle problems which national governments cannot conceivably handle. And they note with terror that,
apparently, if they cannot make the machines produce world
prosperity, the machines will produce world war. Apparently, the
machine is determined, either as tank or tractor, to cross their
frontiers.

The growing fear of a war between the two giants, the United
States and the U.S.S.R., is therefore Europe's terror; and it forces
her attention upon the second of the two world revolutions we
are talking about here—the revolution against national sovereignty
in a world too small for duels between armed fragments of the
world community. This is why Europe, though less sensitive to
the revolution for equality than Asia is, or Africa, or South
America, is extremely sensitive to the revolution against national
sovereignty. Vested interests and the politics of the parish pump
still hold Europe back, but Europe needs common political institutions and common economic institutions, as well. She will need
them more and more. Meanwhile, visiting Congressmen, although
they have yet to discover that even U.S. sovereignty cannot
achieve the things demanded of it, urge the Europeans to unite,
in order not only to "stop Russia" but also to get their common
economic house in order.

103

In general, those Americans who are aware of the revolution against sovereignty are not aware of the revolution for equality. They therefore demand a world federal government with minimal powers to keep the peace. Since this is the era of cold war, they are inevitably asked: What about Russia? They reply that we ought at least to offer a solution and decide later what to do if no government can be found under which both Russians and Americans will consent to live. Or they reply that we ought to go ahead without Russia, and with whatever nations will join us. But they are seldom aware of the massive distrust of the underdeveloped countries. These countries suspect that a world government with powers only to keep the peace would be a world government to preserve the status quo. It would be a world government to guarantee a white man's world and a rich man's world. It might even tend to guarantee the monopoly of machine production which the white and the rich enjoy. At a minimum, the Asian hears no suggestion that its purpose would be to do something positive about the problems that most concern him. He will be for the revolution against sovereignty, but only if it includes his revolution for equality. If it does not, he will not be against sovereignty, but for it—as soon as he wins it. He is for political sovereignty where it has not yet been won. He is for economic sovereignty, even if political sovereignty has been won. And he wants the new tools that will make his day's labor count.

We sometimes lament that he is so materialistic. It makes him such an easy prey to Communism, which, we have heard, is also materialistic. We cite the Scriptures: "Man shall not live by bread alone." But he cites back: "Give us this day our daily bread." After all, he is not asking for that electric refrigerator our propaganda has so often played up. He has nothing to put in it anyhow. No, he will settle for bread, or, more precisely, for the conditions which will permit him (since we like to cite Scripture) to earn his bread by the sweat of his face. He intends to get them.

104

The passion with which he wants bread comes not only from his belly, or from watching the bellies of his children, but from his mind. For he wants justice. The grievances that caused us Americans to revolt from British rule included some very tangible economic ones. But, I take it, we not only wanted things which they were quite legally taking from us; we wanted the justice of keeping things we believed were justly ours. Since the hungry billion in the world community believe that we can all eat if we set our common house in order, they believe also that it is unjust that some men die because it is too much trouble to arrange for them to live.

CHAPTER VII

If we propose to make connection with the free world we want to lead, we will have to think again about justice. We might reflect that the preamble to our own constitution mentions justice even before it mentions the blessings of liberty. The American Declaration of Independence even mentions that all men are born equal. But our current crusades for freedom do not generally include pronouncements about justice or equality. We have let the Russians copyright those traditional American terms, along with the term peace. We are too busy preparing to fight for freedom to talk about peace, which interests our European neighbors acutely, or about justice and equality, which interest our teeming brethren—if anything—even more. If we ever sit down as equals with our neighbors to discuss the two revolutions that rock our planet on its very axis, we shall have to face up to all these ideas again; we shall even have to make some suggestions about how they may apply in the Mighty Neighborhood we all inhabit; or, even better, we might ask the neighbors what applications they think would make sense.

If we ever do that, I predict that their answers will strike a deep chord in our hearts. We shall suddenly remember that these are no mere neighbors: they are our cousins, and sometimes very close cousins at that. Cold-war words like "un-American" have made us forget so many things. We who came to this land of hope from every continent on earth, and above all from Europe, have cousins everywhere. In the old days before the two great wars, before we shut down on immigration, we used to send them the price of an ocean voyage so they could join us. And in they streamed by the million to help us build the "American way of life." We ought to remember and reflect on the great words of Carl Schurz, that America is a colony of mankind.

If we remembered and reflected, if we sat down with our neighbors to discuss the two world revolutions that can create or can destroy, our poorest neighbors would undoubtedly urge upon us what they have already repeatedly urged in the Economic and Social Council of the U.N.: that it set up an International Development Authority and make a frontal assault on the unspeakable misery of half of mankind. In doing so, they would of course be paying a very high compliment to the American way of life. For the pattern of action which they would be urging was first put into use by the American people through the Tennessee Valley Authority. Among the millions and millions of people who have visited TVA have been many thousands of foreigners. From all over the globe men flocked to see how this job was done. If I were asked to name what thing we Americans have done in our lifetime that is most admired throughout the world community, I should unhesitatingly reply: the TVA. It is most admired for the simple reason that it is the kind of thing which, to paraphrase a great Tennessean, the mostest men mostest need. We just did it fustest.

We have not yet stated in ECOSOC why an International Development Authority cannot be set up to do the job most men most want done. Or, at least, not convincingly enough to keep

108

them from clamoring again to do it. Our principal argument has been that the United States would necessarily be the heaviest contributor, that we need all our resources to defend the free world from Russian aggression, and that until the Russian problem has been solved we must postpone such little matters as a TVA of the world. So the United Nations keeps reporting that the economic condition of large parts of the world is getting worse; Russia keeps on offering Communist revolution as the cure; we keep on looking less and less interested in hunger and more and more interested in war; Communism continues to spread; and the third world war keeps on approaching.

Must we go on shoving our poorer neighbors into Russia's arms, or is there any way of answering them that will not look like stalling? I think that, to a limited extent, there is. I suggest that we might at least throw more light on the problem, rather than just appear to stall, or shrug our shoulders, or sulk. We could at least point out that world economic development is a long-term job, that meanwhile the political system of sovereign states under which we all live furnishes a constant source of friction, that such friction is bound to be at its worst between the two sovereign states which are overwhelmingly stronger than any others, that to that extent we and the Russians are condemned by the system to bear its sins on our shoulders, and that our arms race with Russia is using up not merely our money but also the steel, copper, aluminum, and other raw materials that world economic development would require. Until we "win the peace," how can we participate in the scheme our neighbors propose? How can we pour money into a gigantic development scheme until we can safely stop pouring it into defense? And is not Russia obviously intent on fomenting revolution throughout the non-Communist world and strengthening her grip on the Communist world, rather than on helping establish the stable peace in which economic development could be seriously tackled?

Even if we went whole hog and proposed a revision of the U.N. Charter that would convert the United Nations into a government capable of keeping the peace and making it safe for member nations to disarm, could we convince them? We would certainly be shedding light on the problem. Although the question is somewhat academic, since we clearly are prepared to propose no such thing, we would at least be reminding our neighbors that there are two revolutions on, not one; that the penalty for failing in theirs is indeed starvation; but that the penalty for failing in the one that interests the French is war, one of the greatest causes of starvation.

As for their admiration for our TVA, for the sake of the argument we might swallow our suspicions that, after all, like so many of President Roosevelt's ideas, it was a bit socialistic and to that extent a little too reminiscent of the Russians. In fact, if we are correctly informed by many of those who write our national advertising, it clearly tended to subvert the American way of life. But, setting these misgivings aside, have not our friends from the poorer countries drawn a very imperfect analogy? Could the TVA have worked if Tennessee had been arming against Alabama and trying to persuade Kentucky to shoulder a portion of the burden of common defense? Was not the complete state of peace that reigned between all forty-eight states one of the conditions of success for a project that did in fact promote the economies of seven states quite directly and the economies of forty-one others less directly? Incidentally, it was not the seven governments of seven Southern states that set up the TVA. It was the common government of forty-eight states. Surely, this suggests that you can scarcely hope for a good International Development Authority until there is a good world government to set it up, or anyhow something a lot more like a good world government than the United Nations is today.

There is something in this argument, and it would make a lot

110

more sense to our neighbors than most of the arguments we are offering them today. We would gain much more moral credit by it than we are gaining now by arguing that it is all Russia's fault anyhow and that she alone stands between mankind and peace. There is a good deal in the argument, but not enough.

The Preamble to the U.S. Constitution states that one of the purposes of the American Government shall be to promote the general welfare of the American people; and the TVA is one of a long line of actions through which the American Government has promoted the general welfare of our nation. The government of the State of New York, sitting at Albany, is responsible for the general welfare of the people of New York State but not of the people of the other forty-seven states. One of the chief sources of the mess we are all in now is that, to a considerable extent, the government of the United States has been saddled with the responsibility for the welfare of the whole free world, if not of the whole human race; while the government of the U.S.S.R. has assumed responsibility for the welfare of the whole race too, or anyhow of the working-class majority of the race. This has produced a slight problem of overlapping jurisdictions and is leading all of us straight toward a third world war, and it looks to countless men and women everywhere like a dispute over whether there shall be a world-wide American empire or a world-wide Russian empire.

Most of our neighbors do not want to belong to either empire, and only force can make them belong—force plus, perhaps, a little discreet bribery. But powerful historical forces are pushing both Moscow and Washington to build an empire. We Americans accuse the Politburo of scheming consciously to build one. The Russians accuse "Wall Street" of scheming consciously to build one. But it is not the conscious scheming that is to be feared. It is the decisions which both Moscow and Washington feel forced to make if the peoples they govern are to be secure. This is what makes Russia bully her satellites, and this is what makes us bully our allies. Or, to state it in Russian fashion, this is what makes Russia bully her allies and this is what makes us bully our satellites. Dangerous counterpressures build up: our respective allies (or satellites) balk and stall and sulk. Tito of Yugoslavia breaks loose from Russia's team—and thereby, of course, secures American economic and military aid. France balks at our wanting to arm the Germans, and all our allies balk at the arms burden we urge them to carry. All these matters were carefully described by Thucydides more than two thousand years ago, when the two teams were led by Athens and Sparta respectively.

America does not want war; she wants security. Indeed, Wall Street does not want war, if one may judge from the attitude of the *Wall Street Journal*. Most people in the world outside America believe that Russia does not want war, but only security. Unfortunately, under the existing system of sovereign states there just is not, and cannot be, enough security to go around. For us Americans to feel really secure, we need to carry more weapons than the Russians trust us to carry; and for the Russians to feel really secure, they need to carry more weapons than we Americans trust them to carry. Hence an arms race. It is this vicious circle that has convinced millions of people at home and abroad that the choices before us must ultimately be either war or a common government able to enforce peace in a world in which nation states can safely disarm.

We have heard a lot lately about power vacuums, caused by the collapse in war of such states as Germany and Japan or by the shrinkage in power of states like France and Britain. It is very true that the necessities of military strategy under a system that guarantees international anarchy stimulate governments like Washington and Moscow to move in—if only to stop a dangerous potential enemy from expanding. But the basic vacuum is more than military, and is caused by the absence of a common govern-

112

ment in the world community we have now created. If such a government, or even if such a weak imitation of it as the United Nations is, had handled Europe's economic collapse after World War II we would not have had to move in with the Marshall Plan. Since there was no world government, and since our go-it-alone policy prevented the U.N. from doing the job, the only agency left that could command the resources that would do it was the U.S. Government. This is a pretty example of how the vacuum operates in the economic sphere. The inevitable result has been that Europeans, and not just Communists either, have accused us of building an economic empire; and when we insisted on their signing the Atlantic Pact, the empire did not look too purely economic.

It is these "inexorable forces" that make the average American feel sadly that we have lost control of our destiny, that we are no longer masters of our fate, and that his own power of political choice is gone. This, I suggest, is a cruel illusion. If I do not know that a hot stove will burn my hand, and I "choose" to touch the stove without "choosing" to get burned, I suffer from the same illusion: that in this life there is no way to choose whether or not to get burned, that burns come and go according to some blind fate over which I have no control. But once I get it through my head that to "choose" to touch a hot stove *is* to choose to get burned, I recover my area of choice—simply by understanding the necessary consequences of my own acts. If we once comprehend that "going it alone" in distributing economic aid builds an empire whether we happen to want an empire or not, we shall stop acting bilaterally and join with our neighbors in the common effort which the common task requires.

The story is told that somebody gave an Australian bushman a new boomerang. But it brought him no happiness because he went crazy trying to throw his old one away. Our postwar efforts to get Europe on its feet and then get on with other business

have occasionally threatened to drive us crazy: we seem unable
to throw away our new boomerang of bilateral aid. Our old boomerang, let 'em stew in their own juice, presented no problem to
get rid of: World War II knocked that one out of our hands.

The neighbors are going crazy, too, since they do not want
either an American or a Russian empire, and since they do not
want two young and growing empires, however unplanned, to
collide—or, above all, to collide in their living room. Some of the
colonial peoples, of Asia for example, might not object in theory
to some more white people murdering each other for the third
time in half a century, if it were not that they so desperately
need the economic resources that another white man's brawl
would use up. Most interesting of all, there is no sign that most
men and women, either in Europe or in poorer continents, want
the kind of Communist world the Russians want or the kind of
capitalist world we seem to them to want. To judge by the direction in which they are moving, these men and women of the
middle world want the self-government and civil rights which
we and the West Europeans fought many revolutions to secure,
and the "welfare state" that we Americans now condemn. They
might put it by saying they want both political freedom and economic justice; and they might add that Russia looks to them
short on political freedom and America seems not much concerned about economic justice.

How do we all get out of this hideous mess, which promises
to develop into something a good deal worse than a mess? There
can be no doubt, I think, that the absence of a common government in the long run dooms us. But how do we get a common
government? We Americans learned in the eighteenth century
that no arrangement between sovereign governments, which is
what the United Nations is, can be safely confused with a real
government. A real government for the world community would
not be the creature of the national governments. That is the pat-

114

tern of the thirteen American colonies when they tried to live
under the Articles of Confederation. The colonies hit the same
two snags that we are hitting now: the threat of war between
the various member states, and the threat of economic and financial collapse. A real government for the world community that
actually exists today would be responsible not to national governments, but directly to the men and women who make up the
world community. In such a government the delegates would
be elected by persons, not appointed by national governments.
Such a government would have to levy taxes, not beg for delin-
quent contributions. All this sounds pretty frightening, but things
like that are the price we would have to pay for the right to
live in a governed world community instead of in the anarchy
that automatically breeds war, economic collapse, and famine.

According to Thomas Hobbes, if I may oversimplify his thesis
a little, men obey government because they are too afraid of each
other's violence to face a state of anarchy. This is certainly why
men accept tyranny. It is why many West Europeans who hated
Hitler nevertheless collaborated, on the grounds that the international anarchy which twice tore Europe asunder was in their
judgment an even more intolerable evil that Hitler's New Order
was, or anyhow than what the New Order might conceivably
become.

But most men of our generation, and certainly most Americans,
reject the choice of anarchy or tyranny. They want government
but they do not want tyranny. Perhaps those who have urged
world government for no better reason than the admittedly strong
one that the alternative to government is war, and that total industrialized war is out of the question, have done their argument
a disservice in agreeing with Hobbes that government is based
on fear of something worse. For our own American government
is based not only on fear of anarchy but on hope of a better life
for all. If there is anything in our time that all men hope for, then

115

we might find in that hope the basis of a true community—not just the physical community which planes and radios and an intricate technique of industrial production have made of mankind, but a community of purpose.

The recognition that free government, self-government, as distinguished from dictatorship, needs more common purpose than a common fear of destruction has helped to drive some Americans to another solution: a federal union of all free peoples. Such a "union of the free," they contend, would so outweigh any military force that could be brought against it that we could keep the peace, save our freedom, and outsit the dictators. It is even suggested that we could save capitalism, could save ourselves from socialism, that way. Unfortunately, the capitalism of "the free" rests very largely on what is left of their empires in Asia and Africa. The Atlantic community's economy, as a result of what historians call the expansion of Europe, from the age of the great discoverers on, is in no small measure an imperialistic economy. It is precisely the economy which Asia, the Near East, and Africa are struggling to end. Western Europe depends on its colonial areas in much the same fashion that the states in our American industrial East depend on the agrarian West and South, or as Hitler wanted the Third Reich to depend on an unindustrialized Eastern Europe. A Union of the Free would have to face the problem of the colonial, determined not to be the white man's burden any longer, determined not to face the service charge any longer. A union of the free would look awfully much to Asia and Africa like a union of the rich, and a union of the whites. Is there no solution that takes more account than this one of the economic realities in the world community—and their inevitable political consequences?

Maybe the real difficulty with finding a common purpose for the City of Man, and thereby defining what a common government would be like, was expressed by Plato's remark about the two cities. Any attempt to force the City of the Poor to pretend to be a happy fraction of the City of the Rich runs up against the very trouble Europe's colonial empires are up against. The poor can be kept in the common city in one of two ways. They can be held in, and held down, by force, in a sort of world fascist state. Or they can be led to cherish their citizenship by a determined assault on their poverty. The other possibility is that they overthrow the rich, seize their tools, and build their own city of plenty. This third possibility is precisely the solution the Communists urge. In short, there would seem to be a fascist way, a communist way, and a middle way of doing many things; and the setting up of common government for the world community is no exception. You can impose it from above, impose it from below, or agree on it from both directions at once.

We men and women of the present generation, in all the lands of the world, have not discovered what our common aspirations are. Trading goods with each other has made us dependent on each other and to that extent has given us common interests. Two world wars plus an arms race plus "fantastic weapons" have given, at least to Europe and America, common fears. What we still need to find is our common hope: then we might cease to be merely a community of men chained together by history and tugging in different directions, and might become a community of men all tugging in the same direction because that is where all of us would be wanting to go.

Traditionally, the thing that has most successfully bound men together in a common hope has been a common religion. A world community with a common religion, practiced and not merely professed, would of course face a very much simpler problem than our generation faces. But we are of many faiths or of no faith. And even those men, whether Christian or Moslem or of some other religion, who expect that their faith will ultimately win to itself all mankind have to answer the question

117

whether, even in terms of their own religion, they have left un-
done certain things that ought to be done now. If God exists, it
is certain that religious questions are more important than economic ones. But if He exists, can He tolerate that a man should
turn his back on a neighbor in need, on the grounds that to eat
is less important than to pray? There is an Arab saying: "Better
one act of justice than seven years of prayer." You may not
agree; yet you might still agree that when a man refuses to act
justly, his power to pray withers.

Can it be that those who are too busy praying to perform that
act of justice end up with a knife in a Hindu-Moslem riot or in
an anti-Jewish pogrom or even in a sectarian wrangle between
Catholics and Protestants? If there is anything that Protestant
and Catholic and Jew and Hindu and Moslem ought to be doing
together, even before they learn to pray together, dare they in
the name of religion wait longer before doing it? If that thing
is to build a common government, had they not better get about
building it?

But it may be that, just as our differing religions separate us
and even drive us to kill one another, our differing political
"faiths" do the same thing. It may well be that our confusion of
tongues is even more fatal to immediate common action in the
political sphere than in the religious. For some of us follow
John Locke and some of us follow Karl Marx and many of us are
willing to die for the political principles of one of these thinkers
or the other. Will an American feel morally able to surrender
the freedom that Locke taught him was his? Will a Russian give
up the economic justice which, Marx taught him, measures all
other moral issues? And if neither American nor Russian feels
morally able to surrender, how can they both live under a common government? By consent, that is, and not by force? There
may not be enough political principles on which our generation

118

can agree to permit us to sit down and write a constitution. If so, no common political community can be constituted.

Some of us Americans are replying that surely all men want peace and that therefore all men should be willing to give a common government those minimal powers that will permit it to guarantee peace. But we have already seen that, from where the backward teemers sit, this solution means putting such powers in the hands of those who want only peace because they already have bread. It means a government that has lots of policemen but no obligations to promote the general welfare, a government able to quell a bread riot but not interested in what causes bread riots. The underprivileged suspect that governments are instituted among men not merely to put down bread riots or even to arrest those who stir up bread riots, but to do for those who instituted them what they as individuals cannot do for themselves. We Americans believe—or anyhow our most vocal postwar spokesmen say we believe—that government ought merely to be an umpire and prevent violence. Our spokesmen say that to do more, to bother about "security," is to introduce bread and circuses, and you know what happened to Rome, etc., etc. Yet a well-known American, and a member of the Republican Party at that, once said: "The legitimate object of government is to do for a community of people whatever they need to have done, but cannot do for themselves." But that was Abraham Lincoln; and our postwar Republicans have promised to forget certain views of Mr. Lincoln's in return for the Democrats' forgetting certain views of Mr. Roosevelt's.

We Americans are in no mood to invoke the "general welfare clause" which the Preamble of the American Constitution subversively flaunts. At few times in our recent history has there been less public discussion of the public interest of the American people. As a quite inevitable result, at few times have private interests so successfully used government to their own ends. We have decided that it would be collectivist and socialistic and immoral for us to control the Missouri River by the methods that already control the Tennessee. We want no PWA projects. We want no New Freedoms, New Deals, or Fair Deals. We scarcely want an Even Break. And history's revenge has been to base our economy successively on World War II, on the Marshall Plan, and on rearmament, a triple PWA project of government spending that has already run to nearly half a trillion dollars.[20] By 1951 Roger Babson, the statistician, was rather logically suggesting that we make our arms program a permanent feature of our economy, since the rate of obsolescence in weapons would always justify our melting down old tanks and making new ones and since the rate at which we did so could be gauged to support the economy at maximum efficiency.[21] This is an almost ideal arrangement; it decently veils the fact that our economy now rests on large-scale public investment, and allows our right hand not to know what our left hand is doing. It would protect from the cynic the American myth that the public interest is best served by laissez faire—by allowing every citizen to seek his private interest. In the eighteenth century Adam Smith did say that. We believe also that, except for the police power and national defense, there is precious little else that the government needs to do. This, even in the eighteenth century, Adam Smith did not say.

This right-hand-left-hand method of handling our domestic economy is reflected in our right-hand-left-hand method of handling the world economy—to the extent that we handle it at all. We refuse, year in, year out, to join with our neighbors in investing public capital to get the world economy in motion. We killed Lend-Lease, we killed UNRRA, we refused and continue to refuse to set up an International Development Authority. But we have spent billions aiding our neighbors to become strong enough to resist Communism. We prefer to do this by handing them weapons; but we are willing to finance even their economic development if it can be clearly shown that economic development is the only way they can combat Communism. A convenient example is the Marshall Plan itself, on the whole the best post-war job we have done. When General Marshall proposed it in a speech at Harvard University, nothing he said was anti-Communist. But to get it through Congress, the Administration had to picture it as essentially an anti-Communist move. A second convenient example is the joke I have already repeated about the Asian government's need of a couple of Communists so it could get American economic aid. In short, we have financed part of the economic development the world has needed, not in the name of the public interest of the world community but in the name of our own national defense. Meanwhile, some of us have loudly proclaimed that the public interest of the world community would be best served by turning the problem over to a multitude of private interests, that is to free enterprise. We added, typically, that our government would have to take steps to guarantee the enterprisers against certain kinds of loss.

The American myth has placed a gulf between our thinking in the field of political economy and that of nearly every other people on earth. The word economy, we may recall, originally meant housekeeping. If we Americans did invite the peoples of the earth to set up common political institutions, in brief to set up house together, we should find few who agree with us on housekeeping practices. For the majority agree with Lincoln and Roosevelt and we, for the moment, do not—or at least those of us who are talking the loudest do not. The rest of the world approves, in a sense, of our actions, notably of our government's heavy public investment. They approve of what our left hand is doing; but they are bewildered that our right hand does not yet know about it. They do not accept our account of our own economy, or at least the account they are told is ours.

In these circumstances, for the United States to propose a federal world government with minimal powers to keep the peace would remind the rest of the world of the American delegate's slip of the tongue at Lake Success when he spoke of the United Stations. They do not want to enter a United Stations because it would not have the power to act for the common good which Lincoln and Roosevelt both knew a just government must possess. They do not want a government based only on fear, but one based primarily on hope. It is not merely what the Russians would do, but what the bulk of the human race would do, which might give us pause in seeking to apply the only real political solution there is, a common government.

CHAPTER VIII

Here, then, appear to be the facts that confront us, and that have us boxed. Science and technology have bound mankind together in a world economy. But this new economic community possesses neither common religious beliefs nor even common political views. Therefore, though it has quite enough unity to invite dispute and even warfare, perhaps it has not enough to build peace or to set its common economic household in order. In this sorely divided household are many men and women who believe that the purpose of a good economy is to underwrite a good political society; and many of them even believe that the purpose of a good political society is that men may love God and their neighbors and serve them.

Could it be that, since we men and women of the new world community are not prepared to pray together and apparently not even prepared to vote together, we might try eating together? Could we agree, perhaps for different religious reasons, perhaps even for different political reasons, that all of us who are willing to work should be able to eat—and that we are prepared to take whatever reasonable common action will make it possible for all of us to eat? If we took that common action together, we might slowly get enough mutual respect for each other, and even enough affection, to be able to vote together and, in the end, to pray together too. We might become companions in a common action, remembering the original meaning of companions: persons who break bread together.

When the San Francisco Conference of 1945 drafted the Charter of the United Nations, it was Americans who proposed that the organization should include not only a Security Council to prevent war but an Economic and Social Council to prevent human misery. Between now and then, we Americans have dropped the ball, missed the boat, gone off the track.

By urging that the United Nations apply to a reeling world economy the measures we Americans pioneered in the Tennessee Valley, our neighbors are actually showing us an exit from a rat race that has already cost us more than one hundred thousand casualties, billions of dollars, soaring taxes, inflation, and a kind of wartime hysteria that has endangered our civil rights as they have not been endangered for decades. They know by painful experience that the misery they suffer is the only fundamental cause of the spread of Communism, and that the spread of Communism spurs us on to more weapons, more casualties, more taxes, and more inflation. There is no need for us to pledge this week the money or the steel which their plan would require. Both are in short supply, although not in as short supply as a few first-class ideas in the field of statesmanship. But if we could leave New Jersey to the invading Russian armies long enough to sit down with our neighbors, we would not even have to promise in advance to accept the plan. We would simply be searching with them for a plan that all our governments, and all our peoples, might accept.

Many of our people, who do not want to act like rats in a rat race, running in a down spiral that can lead only to war, are clamoring for disarmament. But by what process do we disarm? The out-and-out pacifist, who represents a very small handful of Americans, would have us disarm first and count on others to do likewise. But the majority of those who want to see the arms race ended and everybody's arms scaled downward want to achieve that result through negotiation. "What is the use?" their neighbors ask, "what is the use of negotiating an agreement on disarmament when the Russians don't keep agreements?" A number of Americans like Grenville Clark have pointed out that what normally preserves agreements between sovereign states is not the love of truth or honor but mutual advantage. The art of negotiation consists in finding a solution which neither party thinks ideal but which both parties prefer to war. So long as the preference lasts on both sides, the agreement will be kept on both sides. When the preference ceases on at least one side, you must either renegotiate or fight, or anyhow get ready to fight if you need to. Meanwhile Mr. Clark is right; our job is to renegotiate arrangements that both Washington and Moscow want for their own good reasons to keep. Unless we quite literally prefer war. Our frequent assertions that Russia wants it have not convinced the peoples we count on as allies.

It is also sometimes suggested that you can negotiate with your friends but scarcely with your enemies. This is to forget what negotiation is for. Most of us feel we do not have to negotiate with our friends. With those who are not our friends we must either negotiate, seek compromises, make settlements, or fight. Mr. Clark has behind him a distinguished career as corporation lawyer, and his professional experience may have impressed on his memory certain things we laymen forget, precisely because we have done less negotiating. But even the laymen have had doubts: an opinion poll has suggested that in the opinion of most Americans our government has not tried hard enough to negotiate with the Russian Government.[22] The State Department has consistently replied that we could negotiate successfully only from "situations of strength"; that the Russians do not respect weakness. But this has raised two difficulties. First, as usual in arms races, our effort to increase our strength could be expected to induce the Russians to increase theirs, since probably they are as much afraid of us as we are of them. Second, our rearmament put such a strain on our allies that, in the words of the British economist G. D. H. Cole, all we were likely to get for our money was "weakness through strength."[23]

In any case, observers like Mr. Clark can with considerable show of reason say to those who demand an International Development Authority: "Isn't there another problem which comes first? Even if we grant that the world community is not sufficiently one to accept common political institutions until a healthy world economy is functioning, we cannot make the world economy function until the arms race has been stopped. So long as that race continues, it will consume the money the other job requires, it will consume the raw materials it requires, it will consume industrial plant and even popular attention. When the arms race has been stopped, we can turn all these resources to the more constructive job of building a going economy for the world community."

It is a tempting argument, but I do not find it wholly convincing. Reducing the issue to a famous Biblical metaphor, our problem is to make fewer swords and start making plowshares; in modern terms it is to make fewer tanks and start making tractors. Until the United Nations or a substantial number of its members have agreed on a joint plowing operation, and maybe until a couple of plows have been made and are plowing, people are not going to make fewer swords. Our plans to prepare for war, incoherent and confused as they have sometimes been, are easier for the imagination to grasp than any plan yet agreed on for a joint operation against economic stagnation and disorder.

It is true that the plans and policies of the North Atlantic Treaty Organization have been too incoherent to catch the imagination of the peoples of Western Europe or to gain their wholehearted participation, which is precisely why General Eisenhower's task in Europe was from the first an impossible assignment.[24] But that was largely because NATO has been from the start an American plan rather than a joint plan. Europe has at least been willing to accept the weapons if we would pay for them, and this dubious "market" for weapons has at least helped support the defense effort in our factories. Constant pronouncements from Washington on the imminent dangers of Russian aggression have given a semblance of purpose to it all.

With the exception of the Marshall Plan, nothing we have done to build a going world economy has been even as understandable as NATO. What we have done has been so obviously in support of our military strategy that the real issues have never been stated to the average American. "Technical assistance" has been so distorted by the cold war as to look like a series of complicated bribes to potential allies. It therefore excites the average American much less now than when President Truman first announced it, although the average American is less ironical about its military purposes than our allies are. Until some such device as an International Development Authority, waiting for funds to get going, to take on personnel, and to place orders, offers the American voter something he can visualize as easily as he can visualize an air force, he will not know what it is all about. Forced to choose between a working military operation and a vague dream stated in technical jargon, he will sadly accept the going operation. Besides, getting ready for a world war is a familiar operation; he has gone through it twice already. It is routine stuff, like a visit to the dentist. He does not like to do either, particularly since they say the third trip to this dentist will make the first two look like fun. But he is being brave about it. His European cousins, who got

127

hurt worse than he did on the second visit, are more anxious to find an alternative. They have lost their faith in this particular dentist; and when they are told to get their things on and get ready to go, they stall.

Over and over, the tender-hearted reader of stock-market news has been shocked to hear that Wall Street was shaking its head for fear "peace might break out." But this remark is less cynical than it sounds. American industry now rests largely on war contracts. If those contracts were canceled, American industry would face catastrophe. The whole American economy would then face catastrophe. And the numerous national economies that depend on ours would face catastrophe. Would that help anybody? If that prospect did not worry Wall Street, would not Wall Street be irresponsible?

This relation between capitalism and war was a favorite point with Karl Marx and was never more clearly exemplified than by the Nazi war economy of the thirties. I repeat here: it is distasteful to us Americans to admit a Marxist point. It is particularly distasteful to admit one that seems to classify us with the Nazis. But those Americans responsible for directing American industry are, on this particular point, excellent Marxists. Perhaps they could paraphrase Prime Minister Churchill's remark in Parliament concerning Aneurin Bevan's position on the arms program in Britain, and admit with wry humor that on this particular point Marx happened to be right—"by accident."

When we Americans reconverted our industrial machine, somewhat too speedily, at the end of World War II, our leading economists confidently predicted a depression. But wartime savings multiplied by consumer needs equaled a boom. When the boom threatened to peter out, the Marshall Plan happened to put a forced draft under industry. And long before the Marshall Plan petered out, the rearmament program put a tremendous draft under it. Instead of the expected deflation, with falling prices

128

and unemployment, we got inflation, with rising profits, rising wages, rising prices, rising taxes, and rising deficits. Temporarily, we are in a strategically good position with respect to our economy. If unemployment looms ahead, we can swap insults with Vyshinsky and speed up war contracts to take up the expected slack. If the rising cost of living hurts too much, we can agree hesitantly with our allies that no Russian invasion of Europe seems imminent, shift our "target" from 1952 to 1954, and delay a few contracts. Since there is basic disagreement on Russia's intentions, and since men in high office admit to doubt as to just how many tanks or planes produce a situation of strength—"Certainly," they generally add, "not as many as the armed forces have asked for"— we have considerable flexibility in regulating the biggest peace-time public enterprise we have ever got hold of. But if we ever shut it down, or taper it off too sharply, we are in for it, unless we can find another PWA project to take its place. If we cannot export tanks, we must find a way to export tractors—or else. To date, no machinery exists for making the shift, except the economic aid to potential allies that can be classified under military preparedness. This means that we cannot export tractors in the amounts required to support our industrial production except as a supplement to tanks. Any peace development that canceled the tanks would almost certainly cancel the tractors.

But we have already seen that this trap catches only those who insist on viewing world economic development as an American job, not as an international one. If we insist on that, then it becomes a part of America's foreign policy, and America's basic foreign policy is to stop Russia. The jaws of the trap then close.

If we sat down with our colleagues in ECOSOC and planned a device for making joint war on the hunger and sickness and ignorance and isolation that are the bottlenecks to breadwinning among most of the human race; if we did this now, with no commitment whatever to adopt the plan until it was complete, a way out of our trap would open. In an expanding world economy, America could safely invest some of the surplus she is now investing in weapons. An expanding world economy would save others, not us, from famine, but it might well save us from the grim alternatives—unemployment or war.

Before we and our neighbors try to find out whether American factories can promote peace better by making more plowshares and fewer swords, maybe we ought to allow the American who is also a democratic socialist to have his say. He might well argue that world economic development and an arms race are not the only two alternatives for disposing of the surplus product of American factories. He might agree that, of course, if we stopped or seriously cut down our arms output, if we canceled all or most of our present war contracts, business would tailspin and unemployment would swell. But this, he would say, is not because the men and women inside the United States cannot make good use of civilian goods. It is solely because most of them have no money with which to buy those goods. And the reason they have no money to buy them with is that the money which factories receive for making things goes only in part to pay wages to those who make them: it goes also in large part to pay dividends to those who own the factories. Furthermore, many of the people who get the profits already have a car and a refrigerator and a stove and as many suits of clothes as they need. So the goods begin to pile up, the factories begin to operate part time or to shut down, workers are thrown out of jobs, even fewer people can then buy goods, so other factories shut down, and you have a typical depression—typical, that is, for a capitalistic society, where only a part of the population owns the machines that produce the goods which most people need. If the whole of society owned the factories, our democratic socialist might continue, and if none of the gross sales prices went into profits, then the people who made the goods could afford to buy the goods and you would get continuous operation. You would be producing "for use, not for profit." And it would be a long time before the poorest workingmen in America had enough of the things they really need. So why dream up ways to get rid of a surplus? Isn't your surplus caused by capitalism, by the bad way your economy is organized?

If the steel manufacturers refuse to run their steel mills at full capacity because they feel they can make more profit running them part time, even though American industry needs steel, then let the government build some steel mills and run them—which is just what President Truman once threatened to do unless the steel men expanded their output. And so on with the other things we Americans need. To devise with other peoples means to get rid of our surplus is merely to pay our neighbors to cart away some of the things we make because we have not enough sense to distribute them at home to whoever will help make them. This may be less murderous than starting a war to use up the surplus. It may even be better than piling the goods up and burning them: at least it would let foreigners use them. But why not socialize our economy and let Americans use them? A lot of Americans certainly need them.

This, in simplified form, is how the democratic socialist proposes to get around the apparent dilemma of arms race or depression. But for several reasons Americans may be more willing to distribute surplus over the planet than they would be to adopt socialism at home. Anybody who has watched closely how the Marshall Plan has operated abroad has been amused at how often its American administrators advised Europeans to take steps which Americans would refuse to take at home for fear of being socialistic. Europeans were sometimes amazed. But our American administrators of the Marshall Plan had to get results for the money the Congress had appropriated, and were in no mood to haggle over political philosophies. If the only way to get a farm population on its feet was to encourage it to form marketing co-ops,

131

then they advised co-ops, even if co-ops at home were being attacked in the Congress as a socialistic device. After all, the whole Marshall Plan operation leaned toward "planned production." As for their praise of American capitalism and American business competition, they had to reserve much of that for news releases to America, partly because European capitalists were even less inclined than many American capitalists to pay high enough wages to let working people buy the goods produced; and partly because Europeans had read the reports of Congressional committees that had investigated monopoly in American business, and they already knew there was less business competition in America and more price-fixing than we Americans were prepared to admit. In any case, the net result of our experience abroad is that we accept "socialistic" practices there which we simply will not accept at home.

Those of us who are not Communists, or even Socialists, might make a counterproposal. We might again observe that most human beings live under a mixed economy, where some economic processes are managed by government as public enterprises and where others are managed by individual citizens or groups of citizens as private enterprises. We probably throw no light on the problem by calling the second kind free enterprise, since the private enterprise we call Standard Oil is no freer of public control than the public enterprise we call TVA is free of private interests. One is free public enterprise and one is free private enterprise. This being the land of the free, both Standard Oil and TVA are to be warmly congratulated on being examples of free enterprise.

Now those of us who are neither Socialists nor Communists—and we greatly outnumber those who are either one or the other—can join Abraham Lincoln and set up a public enterprise any time we feel like it. The present seems like an awfully good time to set one up. Two world wars and preparations for a third have

now taught us Americans that our destinies are finally tied up
with the destinies of the rest of the human race—of which many
of us are proud to be members. And many of us recognize that
the human race needs a common agency through which it can
handle certain economic problems that none of its local national
governments can handle. We recognize also that the government
of the U.S.A. and the government of the U.S.S.R. are trying to
handle some of them, in very different fashions, and that to date
neither government has been conspicuously successful at it. Between them they are heading us Americans and the Russians,
and the two billion people who are neither American nor Russian,
into a third world war. Meanwhile, a billion of our neighbors
are caught in an economic trap and trying to get out.

Acting through their duly accredited delegates in the Economic and Social Council of the United Nations, our neighbors
have been urging a common agency to handle our common problem. We had better examine their proposal more closely, rather
than inform them coldly that we are too busy defending them
against the Russians who may kill them to think about the disease
and famine that really are killing them. If we examine it, we will
discover that what they seem to mean by an International Development Authority is the kind of agency, or else they think it is
the kind of agency, that we Americans set up in the Tennessee
Valley and that has been repeated all over the world—though not
often in America. Since some Americans have never heard of the
TVA, and since most Americans know only dimly how it works,
we might first have a good look at the TVA. We could then ask
ourselves whether our neighbors and cousins in other lands are
right in thinking that this kind of agency is more likely to end the
unspeakable agony of our modern world than are our tanks and
planes and atom bombs.

CHAPTER IX

In the year 1935 about three million human beings lived in the valley of the Tennessee River, a valley that was four-fifths the size of England. Although these human beings were a great deal better off than the Asians and Africans and South Americans we have been talking about, nevertheless their Tennessee Valley was, when compared with the United States as a whole, a typical "underdeveloped country." Their economy was more purely agricultural, which meant that, along with much of the South and much of the West, their relation to the industrial East was essentially the relation of a colony to the country that possesses it. Their economy was a raw-material economy, and that meant that their share of the finished product was low, while the bulk of the profit went to those sections of America that processed the raw materials the Tennessee Valley produced. Moreover, even in their own line, farming, they produced less than half of what the average American farm produced. Educational facilities were low. There was widespread malnutrition. Deaths from such diseases as typhoid and tuberculosis were frequent. Malaria was rampant, and it cut down what the people could produce. Families were big. Since chances to make a good living were poor, there was a steady drift of the able-bodied to other parts of the United States. All in all, this is the familiar picture of the "colonial" economy of an underdeveloped country today.

The Valley was short of capital; it was short of skills; it had had great natural resources, but these resources had been either unused, or destroyed through bad management. Like most American valleys—indeed, like most river valleys throughout the world —the Tennessee Valley had been raped rather than husbanded. The mountains and hillsides from which the River's tributaries fed it had been partly skinned of trees. As an inexorable result, where once a spongy forest floor had absorbed heavy rains and let the accumulated rainfall flow gently, gradually, and regularly to the great River, now the cutover forest lands could neither absorb nor hold those rains, and the water fresheted down to the River, causing flash floods, followed by periods of low water level. To this extent the Tennessee was like a South American arroyo or a North African wadi. Moreover, grassy, spongy hillside pastures had often given way to row crops like corn, which exposed the bare earth to heavy washing. So the streams that fed the River ran red with silt. That rendered them unfit for most of the kinds of fish that once flourished in them. And it silted up the River itself, making it even less fit for navigation. This powerful, plunging River had been harnessed in spots with dams to produce electric power. But the quick oscillations between dangerous floods and sluggish, droughty periods of low water limited the usefulness of the dams, which required a more regular flow if they were to yield maximum power. Finally, many of the rich bottom lands were dangerous to farm because of the sudden freshets, and many of the other areas had been so mined and quarried by single-cropping and lack of fertilizer that the naturally good soil and open climate could not be fully used. As the soil got poorer, many of the people got poorer, and poor people lack the capital, and usually the knowledge, to restore impoverished land. It was this vicious circle that President Roosevelt and the United States Congress determined to break. Furthermore, they assumed that by breaking it they would learn how to break it in other valleys all over the United States.

For decades the problem had been attacked, but always piecemeal. Steps had been taken to render the River more navigable. Dams had been built to help control the devastating floods. During World War I the Federal Government built a damn at Muscle Shoals to produce electric power and nitrates. A number of industrialists, including Henry Ford, tried to get concessions to build more dams, generate power, and manufacture nitrates for fertilizer, but the government refused. Finally the great depression brought a demand for public works to relieve unemployment and stimulate the economy, and in May 1933 the Roosevelt administration and the Congress created the Tennessee Valley Authority. In his message to Congress, Roosevelt suggested that the Authority should be "a corporation clothed with the power of Government but possessed of the flexibility and initiative of a private enterprise. It should be charged with the broadest duty of planning for the proper use, conservation and development of the natural resources of the Tennessee River drainage basin and its adjoining territory for the general social and economic welfare of the Nation. . . .

"This in a true sense is a return to the spirit and vision of the pioneer. If we are successful here, we can march on, step by step, in a like development of other great natural territorial units within our borders."

Now in 1952, nineteen years after the establishment of TVA, it seems clear that the Authority was a very great political invention. Its greatness appears to derive mainly from three interesting ideas. None of these ideas was the massive intervention by government in the economic process of the country. That had many precedents throughout the history of the American Republic. One need only name the land grants to Western railways, or for that matter the homestead acts that gave free land to those who would till it. One might even name the dubious device of the protective tariff to protect "infant industries," which were to become monstrous giants still sucking a milk bottle at public expense, or the freight differentials which did so much to keep the factory a relative monopoly of the rich Eastern states at the expense of the agricultural South and West. No, the anti-Roosevelt cry that we should keep government out of business never came with good grace, because those who uttered it most loudly tended to be those who had made most successful use of government subsidy. Their most recent device has been the tax write-offs for new "defense" plants—write-offs which make mink coats look like chicken feed.

The first of the three interesting ideas back of the Authority was that to get the Tennessee Valley onto its feet you needed a government agency that viewed the problems of the Valley as a whole, that would live in the Valley and work with the people, and that would call on existing government departments for co-operation when needed. To get the economy of the Valley in motion, a lot of things had to be done more or less simultaneously. Some of these things had been done already, over a long period, but never in connected fashion. You could cut down on floods and improve navigation merely by building some dams; but the dams would be hard to pay for unless you let them generate electricity and sold the electricity. But you could not sell very much electricity to the people of the Valley until you helped them learn better farming methods so they could pay for electricity and profit by its use. And they could not profit very much by what you helped them learn until their land stopped washing away. And their land would keep on washing away until something was done to reforest the slopes. Anyhow, until you reforested the slopes, your dams would silt up and ruin your storage capacity, thereby cutting down on your navigation facilities, on your flood control, and on your regular source of power. Besides, without good navigation facilities, you forfeited a potential source of income and a cheap way of getting out the new and bigger crops you counted on to pay for the new electrical appliances that would release man power for local industries to use more electric current—and so it went. No existing government department had authority to tackle all these problems; and to omit one or more of the problems was to do the whole thing the hard way. So an authority was devised that could tackle all the jobs at once.

The second great idea was dictated by the first: it was this business of setting up a "corporation clothed with the power of Government but possessed of the flexibility and initiative of a private enterprise." Congressional debate elaborated this idea: Congress ought "to write a Bill that would establish a Government Corporation on the same basis of operation as the great industrial corporations of America are run—the United States Steel Corporation in its efficiency, for instance. To accomplish that efficiency the captain of the team has to have absolute command. It is the only way in which efficiency can be obtained."

What finally emerged from the hopper was precisely this hybrid thing, something that would act with the efficiency Americans so much admired in the private corporation but something that would be democratically responsible through the Congress to the people of America and not to an unknown group of private investors. It was a hybrid, and it was a monster, a monster that could buy, sell, borrow, sue, be sued, make contracts; make, amend, or repeal its own bylaws; purchase or lease real property, condemn land that it needed; hire and fire its own personnel without regard to Civil Service regulations. It was by no means the first "public corporation" we had experimented with: the Reconstruction Finance Corporation, for example, is several years older. And there are lots of public corporations functioning now, both in America and abroad. But it is doubtful whether in 1933 any existed with such broad purposes and such sweeping powers as the Tennessee Valley Authority.

The first idea, then, back of the TVA was that it should do many things, all connected with each other by the concrete realities of a damaged river valley full of damaged people. The second idea was that, to do all these things well, it had to be a public corporation: public, because it served the public interest, not private interests; a corporation, rather than a government department, so that it could imitate the flexible responsible management of a well-run private corporation. The third big idea behind the TVA was that it should instruct, advise, persuade, and assist other people to help themselves; but not compel, not order people around. It was deeply democratic in its procedures. It would be silly and sentimental, of course, to suppose that it never exercised compulsion. It was an arm of government, like the highway department; like the highway department, it could and did condemn land that was needed for public use. And if your farm, which you inherited from a great-grandfather and love, is taken from you, either by the TVA or the highway department, you feel pretty compelled. "Just compensation," even if fixed by an independent court, is not what you want; because money cannot buy another farm that will mean to you what that farm means. But no society, not even a democratic one, can operate unless through its government it retains the power of eminent domain, the right to take, with adequate compensation, property which the whole society needs for public purposes.

But most of what the TVA accomplished was accomplished not by exercise of this natural and necessary power of government, but by making contracts. Indeed, the TVA today is not merely a network of dams, locks, and canals; it is a network also of legal contracts, contracts which record in legal form the network of

social agreements, small and large, which are one of the hallmarks
of a civilized human community. Just as the dams harness what
was once a raging, senseless torrent of destruction one week, and
a half-dry, sluggish waterway the next, so the contracts and
agreements and understandings that the TVA created harnessed
the economic life of the Valley and converted a boom-and-bust
economy into a vast, harmonious social effort. The river is now
free and powerful, as a result of the dams and canals and catch-
ment basins, and the people too are freer and more powerful as
a result of their contracts and agreements, free to do things together that without the contracts could never be attempted. A
man is not "free" to farm well just by being let alone, if his neighbors up the valley are farming so badly that he cannot hold his
own soil in place. He can win that freedom only by agreeing with
his neighbors to manage well in common the rain that keeps
falling on the just and the unjust, on the wise and the foolish, on
those who plow on the contour and those that plow straight up
and down a hillside and thereby destroy the hillside and let loose
the floods.

So the TVA made contracts: it made contracts with individuals,
with co-operatives, with municipalities, with private corporations,
even with state governments. And in doing so, it imitated the
contract-making world of private business in which it operated,
the world of agreements which so many Americans feel is the
sort of world they want to have survive. In endless conferences,
committees, and public meetings, and on demonstration farms
throughout the Valley, the TVA toilsomely worked out with its
partners, the men and women of the Valley, the understandings
on which the legal contracts must ultimately rest. Many of the
things it did, its engineers could have done faster if the TVA had
not waited for that understanding, if it had treated its partners as
wards. Some of its partners were certainly hillbillies. How could
they understand the problem? Many who were not hillbillies were

illiterate. Why not do the job for them, and count on the next generation to understand? But the directors of the TVA fortunately knew that over-all economic development cannot be done "for" anybody. It has to be done by people for themselves. The great triumph of the TVA was not the building of the great dams. Great dams had been built before. Its greatest triumph was that it not only taught the Valley people but insisted on learning from them too. It placed its vast technical knowledge in the pot with the human wisdom, the local experience, the courage, and the hopes of the Valley people, and sought solutions which neither the Valley folk nor the TVA technicians could ever have found alone. It respected persons.

The TVA therefore came to belong to the Valley people. When they speak today of "our TVA" they are not just sentimentalizing, not just kidding themselves, not just falling for clever public relations. By using the TVA to achieve their own common ends they have actually made it theirs. It was only when some of them, like one of the Senators from Tennessee, tried to misuse it, that is to use a public corporation for private ends, that the TVA balked and refused to play ball. But it played ball with whoever in the Valley was willing to think about the common good of the Valley's people.

It is now nineteen years since the Congress of the United States gave the TVA its assignment: "To improve the navigability and to provide for the flood control of the Tennessee River; to provide for reforestation and the proper use of marginal lands in the Tennessee Valley; to provide for the agricultural and industrial development of said valley; to provide for the national defense by the creation of a corporation for the operation of Government properties at and near Muscle Shoals in the State of Alabama, and for other purposes." That was the assignment. Has it paid off?

The annual reports of the TVA to the Congress and the President tell the exciting story. In the first fifteen years of the TVA, manufacturing enterprises increased in the Valley at nearly double the national rate. Crops went up. Land ceased to wash away. Farm tenancy went down faster than in the rest of the country. Farm real-estate values climbed far beyond the national rate. Per capita income rose from forty per cent of the national rate to sixty per cent. Bank deposits increased about two and a half times as fast as in the nation as a whole. Money for schools soared. Purchases of electric equipment, mostly from Northern and Eastern states, hit the moon: the Valley was becoming a market for the nation. The control of the Tennessee River was saving the nation some eleven millions a year in flood damage, more than half of it downstream on the lower Ohio and Mississippi. A 630-mile channel was added to the nation's inland waterways system. Electric power in the Valley increased tenfold, underwrote an expanding aluminum industry, and sent phosphatic fertilizers all over the country. The average Valley consumer paid about half for his electric current what the average American pays, but used sixty-seven per cent more current. Forests were enormously expanded, sound forest management spread, forest fires diminished. It was possible to accomplish these things precisely because the TVA, alone among either public or private agencies, had taken the whole economic condition of the Valley as its problem. Other agencies were condemned to try to solve a piece of a problem without being able to do much about the other pieces their piece fit into.

This multi-purpose technique is the technique that caught the imagination not merely of America, but of the world. It is this kind of general, basic economic development that the Asians, Africans, and Latin Americans are after. They know that once the spiral starts up, business opportunities open up, and that, above all, the people acquire health, knowledge, skills, energy, ambition, and hope. Above all, because once those qualities have been acquired by the people, the wise and fruitful use of natural resources

143

is well-nigh endless. In the TVA they have the living proof that techniques exist for achieving just those ends. Capital exists too. But most of the capital and most of the techniques do not exist in the countries that most desperately require them, just as in 1933 most of this sort of capital and most of these techniques were available in America but not in the Tennessee Valley.

What the TVA taught the world, and what we Americans have been forgetting since the war, is the massive use of capital and techniques for a twentieth-century kind of pioneering in "colonial" economies. It is the only social technique to date that shows signs of meeting the kind of economic problems which Socialists feel can be met by Socialism alone. And it is available only where there is adequate capital. The history of the Soviet Union is largely the history of a country that undertook to do the job without an adequate supply of capital. It got together what capital it could, through revolutionary confiscation. It defaulted on foreign debts. But, since it could not secure loans from countries that already had a capital accumulation, it accumulated its own from where they had accumulated theirs long before: from human labor. It could do this only by dictatorship, a dictatorship that would force the laborer to produce capital goods rather than the consumer goods he craved. It has been a story of great ruthlessness.

But whoever supposes that Western Europe, or later the United States, accumulated capital without ruthlessness needs badly to read history. The history of the industrial revolution in England in the late eighteenth and early nineteenth centuries is a history of cruelty and compulsion: of Parliamentary land enclosures that ejected the poor from the common land to which they had access and squeezed them onto the new labor market for factories to use; of stringent laws against labor unions that kept wages near subsistence and profits high; of little children working in the factories for twelve or thirteen hours a day; of the military conquest of colonial countries and the exploitation of cheap coolie labor; of the wide use of African slaves. In America, we used African slaves, propertyless immigrants from Europe, and land seized from the conquered natives. In both Europe and America and in their colonial dependencies, at the cost of blood, sweat, toil, and tears, vast stores of capital were accumulated; and that accumulation is what makes the City with the Machines so much more productive today than the City without the Machines. That accumulation is the capital base of Occidental civilization. Much of that capital base came from the labor of the men and women— or the parents or grandparents of the men and women—who today inhabit the City of the Poor and who clamor for the use of that capital. Shall they be allowed to use it, or shall we insist that they reconstruct their City by the Russian method, by dictatorship, and forced labor to produce capital goods? If we do insist, the less wind we waste describing them as "the free world," the better. They will not be listening, or will be listening only with bitterness.

But suppose we recognize their desperate necessity, and suppose we recognize further that our destinies and theirs are now bound up together. We would then stop shutting them up with the remark that Russian aggression has pushed all our resources into defense and should push their resources into defense too. We would accord them the minimal respect of listening carefully to their proposal of an International Development Authority. Surely, the way to show real respect for it would be, not to accept it as blindly as we now discard it, but to ask about it the most critical questions we can think of: and there are several we could certainly think of.

The first obvious question is: How does your proposed International Development Authority differ from the International Bank for Reconstruction and Development, which was set up in 1945 to do precisely this job and which has already lent more than a billion dollars?[25] So far as I understand their criticisms of

the World Bank to date, the governments of underdeveloped
countries object that it does not serve the function they expected
it to serve. Governments submit development projects to the bank
and apply for loans. Since the World Bank is committed to a 4½
per cent interest rate and depends chiefly on the New York money
market, it examines those projects primarily from the point of
view of sound banking principles, not from the point of view
of human need. Like most banks, it is most willing to lend
money to those who least need it. This is not to say that it is
useless; but it is to say that its usefulness cannot reach the areas
of greatest need. It could develop the Indus River Valley, because
in the opinion of such experts as David Lilienthal the Indus River
is a "bankable" river: that is, private banks could profitably
finance its development. But, interestingly enough, the Tennessee
River was not a "bankable" river. This does not mean at all that
the TVA was not a sound public investment. It merely means that
the return on the investment, which has already been heavy, and
will continue indefinitely to be heavy, is not the kind that can be
channeled back through a bank. To get that kind of return, a
bank would have to get a percentage of the raised income of
millions of persons (which in regard to the TVA the Federal
Government, through taxes, could and did do) and the increased
value of millions of acres of real estate (which, again, can be
done through taxes). Banks, in short, are exceedingly useful social
instruments, but not all sound social investments are sound banking investments.

To this sermonette on banks our neighbors might reply that,
even within the restricted area of sound banking practice there
are imaginative bankers and unimaginative ones, and that the
American head of the World Bank clearly falls in the latter
category. Indeed, this precise charge has been repeatedly made.
But if it is justified, is not our problem to get better direction for
the World Bank, rather than another institution to do properly

what the World Bank's disappointed customers say the Bank does improperly? But without knowing—or, indeed, without having even the means of learning—all the ins and outs of each World Bank decision that has rejected a project, we have the right to suspect that the area within which the Bank could move with propriety is still not as great as the area of the problem. In other words, may there not be many projects which should be undertaken if there is to be a healthy world economy capable of supporting free political institutions but which really are beyond the reach of any bank we can set up? It is interesting that the TVA itself was not financed by a bank or even by a consortium of banks.

To this our friends might retort that, although the TVA itself did not go to bank, nevertheless the government that financed it did go quite frequently. All they now ask for is some bank, or anyhow some lending institution, that will lend money to their governments, since their governments lack the credit facilities that the U.S. Government had even in 1933. Let the World Bank go on making loans for bankable projects as long as it likes, but let them have a Development Authority with a more liberal banking policy and more social purpose than the World Bank displays. Such an Authority would lend money to the governments of underdeveloped countries for projects that are socially desirable and perhaps make outright grants where such projects could not be self-liquidating, no matter how necessary to the national, and even the world, economy.

This oft-repeated request makes sense, and certainly makes more sense to more people than our customary replies make. Our replies sound too much like those of a grumbling Santa Claus, who spends 364 days out of every year explaining to the children that Christmas has not come yet—except that we habitually add that it never will until the kids help us make the Russians behave. Meanwhile, the kids suspect that if both they and the Russians behaved well enough, Santa Claus would lose all interest in Christmas anyhow. They have reason to suspect it. When one of our most experienced career diplomats, Mr. Jefferson Caffery, returned recently from the tortured and hungry lands of the Middle East and reporters asked him what we ought to do there, he was quoted as answering: "I think the best thing we can do is try to get these people all over the Middle East to calm down."[26] That must have sounded to the hungry billion like a pretty fair and pretty candid statement of American policy. To those who have seen at first hand the conditions that keep "these people" from "calming down," it is irrelevant to the point of blasphemy.

But, although our neighbors have talked better sense than we have, it might be possible for both of us to talk even better sense than that. The American Government of 1933, which had enough public credit to finance such things as the TVA, was considerably more stable, more experienced, and more powerful than the governments that now seek credit for TVAs of their own. It was also considerably more powerful than the state governments of Tennessee or Alabama or Kentucky. It is interesting that it did not make loans to those state governments to carry out development schemes which they had drawn up to make their respective fractions of the Tennessee River useful to them. Even if we possessed a world government (which would be the natural agency to tackle such jobs for the world community) it is doubtful if it could do the job well by making grants to local, national governments. It could do the job a lot better through an authority that would go at it directly, even though it were required to seek first the permission of those local, national governments within whose jurisdiction or jurisdictions the projected operation lay. A large proportion of the areas where development of natural resources could count heaviest against world famine and world disease resemble the Tennessee Valley in refusing to follow "state lines." We already know from the brilliant work that the specialized

148

agencies of the United Nations have done—the World Health Organization, the Food and Agriculture Organization, the Educational, Scientific and Cultural Organization, for example—that locusts breed in one country and destroy the crops of neighboring countries, that rinderpest develops in the cattle of one country and slays the work oxen in adjacent countries, and that the great rivers are the worst offenders of all in going places without a passport.

We have observed the three big ideas back of the TVA: that it was multi-purpose; that it was a corporation, not a government department; that it worked by consent rather than compulsion. Our afflicted neighbors have given ample proof that they grasp the significance of a multi-purpose agency that can tackle all parts of a human problem rather than one piece of it; and they also show they want consent, not compulsion—if they can get the capital that makes compulsion unnecessary. But I wonder whether they have not missed a trick on the second point, that the agency needs to be a corporation, doing business across political lines. They have certainly not missed that trick entirely: a number of countries have set up public corporations to develop their domestic economies. And they could, of course, remind us that the TVA was purely a domestic corporation.

But a lot has happened to the world economy since 1933. And, I repeat, a lot of resource areas refuse to fall within one national jurisdiction, particularly in the case of countries a great deal smaller than the United States. I propose that with these facts in mind we and our neighbors try to envision a solution for the world's problem areas in terms of the TVA. If we do, we might get something like this: instead of an International Development Authority that would lend money or make grants to national governments to carry out national development schemes, it would make more sense to set up an International Development Authority that would operate as a public corporation, in business—a

149

public cartel, if you like; that would co-operate fully with national governments, just as the TVA co-operates most cordially with state governments here, but that would do the job itself; and that would be responsible, not to governments, but through some ingenious device to the actual men and women who inhabit this planet. The operation that is called for is the proper alternative to the dread Horsemen of the Apocalypse, War, Famine, and Pestilence; and the dread Horsemen have always crossed frontiers: so must the operation we seek to set up now. The Schuman Plan is even now pointing the way by proposing to control those basic necessities, coal and steel, in the interests of all the men and women of several neighboring national states who depend on the Ruhr deposits and the Ruhr industries.

I believe that our neighbors may have set their sights too low. By doing so, they have failed to issue us a challenge we could not refuse. They have asked us in effect to join in setting up a capital fund that would help their governments develop the countries they govern. We have replied that this is the business of the World Bank, that we need all our present resources to defend ourselves and them against Russian aggression, that private capital is a better instrument anyhow. We have now "integrated" economic aid with military aid in such fashion as to arouse the suspicions of the whole world that our only real interest in economic development is to purchase allies and hire mercenaries for a war which, despite our accent on defense, we seem to regard as inevitable. Our replies are not, I admit, very good replies or very relevant to the actual state of the world we are part of. But, without trying to shift from my own country's shoulders a large share of guilt for the present mess we are all in together, I suspect that a different challenge from our neighbors would have brought a different response from us.[27]

If, instead of looking at their own problems nationally—certainly a most understandable mistake for newly formed or economically weak nations—our neighbors had been more insistent on the world-wide and indivisible nature of the problem, they would have put us on a hot spot. They now rightly accuse us of making world economic development an aspect of our national military policy. But some of the requests for World Bank loans have shown the same nearsighted nationalism on their own part. If they reply that they are merely going through the political growing pains that all young nations go through, we can properly reply that growing pains of that type were relevant to an earlier period of history; and that if, as they often and properly urge, it is now too late in history for nations like theirs to get on their feet by their own isolated efforts, it is also too late for them to be got to their feet by an international agency trying to satisfy nationalist plans of development.

They could put us completely on the spot now by demanding not a mere international fund to make loans and grants to national governments for national development projects, but rather an international public corporation answerable to the men and women of the world community for a job in which we all have a common stake—as the TVA is an interstate public corporation answerable, through the Congress and President, to the men and women of the forty-eight states.

Such an Authority would be even more of a monster than TVA was and is, if only because of its size. But the problem we seek to solve is also monstrous—if only because of its size. And the monster we have imagined, in order to solve it, is not half so monstrous as the three Horsemen of the Apocalypse with whom it must now compete. As a matter of fact, it is a nice question whether it is ever power itself that is monstrous. Is it not rather power that is being irresponsibly used?

Many of us Americans wince a little at words like corporation or cartel; and many men in other lands wince even more noticeably. For our giant corporations, both American and foreign, have

151

so often been used for selfish and irresponsible purposes. The fact remains that the modern corporation is increasingly the instrument through which the world's work now gets done. And the great cartels which corporations form in order to divide the world's markets between them have good functions as well as bad ones. Our failure has been to gasp with horror at their size and power instead of insisting on means for their public control. We know that there are business corporations in America that have considerably greater liquid assets than many of the states in the Union. More people are on the payroll of some of these corporations than inhabit some of these states. We know that sometimes these corporations have powerful leverage on state legislators; that to some extent they indirectly make our laws for us. Similarly, the international cartels they form are a great deal more powerful than many of the governments of "sovereign" nation states, and know it.

But the establishment of the TVA has demonstrated that the corporate form can also be made a responsible form. The corporate devices that have been worked out to do things privately for private profit have also been used to do things publicly for public profit. What ought to be done to make the private corporation and the international cartel more responsible to the public interest is itself a fascinating subject about which a considerable literature has grown up. But, whatever ought to be done, there is nothing to prevent our imitating now on an international scale those who sought, in setting up the TVA, to "establish a Government Corporation on the same basis of operation as the great industrial corporations of America are run—the United States Steel Corporation in its efficiency, for instance."

We ought to say to our neighbors: "We are very pleased that you found in an American political invention a device for waging a world war on misery. But we urge you to be bold in your analogies. We can all trim down our plans later if we find there are bugs in them—as there doubtless will be. For the moment, what is clearly wanted is imagination. It has been in short supply ever since the war. For the sake of the argument, we accept your formula of an international agency, public not private, with economic purposes that transcend the cold war, with funds internationally subscribed, and directors internationally chosen. But let us add two new features. This agency should be responsible to the people of this planet, or at the very least, to all those persons who through their governments will contribute to the common fund. Just how that responsibility is to be guaranteed, we do not now know. But, between us all, we ought to be bright enough to devise machinery for it. For in the TVA analogy, something has got to take the place of the Congress of the United States. The General Assembly of the U.N. does that to some degree, but its delegates represent governments, not persons, and that may prove a weakness we must correct somehow in the device we are looking for.

"To the picture you have drawn of a world TVA we would like to add a second feature: it must be a corporation with the ordinary powers of a corporation, and not just a kitty for making grants to governments. As soon as you start using governments you get into politics, which is just where some of the politicians in the Tennessee Valley wanted to get the TVA. And as soon as you start using national governments, legally able to make war on each other, you get into international power politics. You accuse us of letting Point Four do that now. Maybe you are right. Maybe you exaggerate. But, again, for the purposes of this argument, let's say you are right. We notice that our government is not the only one that starts playing power politics when Point Four projects come up. So let's call it quits. Let's admit also that power politics goes on in the United Nations, quite inevitably. Let's insist that our new corporate agency be relieved as much as possible from that kind of pressure. Nothing can relieve it entirely, and you

153

know it. But, if you really think the TVA model is the answer, don't let's stop short with its multi-purpose methods or its action by consent of the community. Let's add what we Americans think is one of its most essential characteristics: its corporate structure, which imitates what some of you seem afraid of but what we Americans have confidence in—that is, what we call business efficiency. Will you go into business with us? Into the big business of really making a frontal assault on the problems of human beings as distinct from satisfying the ambitions of governments?"

CHAPTER X

Should our neighbors admit, purely for the sake of the argument and without committing their governments definitely in any way, that we Americans had improved on their original proposal of an international kitty to help governments that lacked credit, then we would all have reached the most exciting point in history since the United Nations was proposed. It would be literally a pregnant moment of history, for a baby would be about to be born. That means that everybody would be looking forward to new life instead of, as now, to new death. And what a baby this baby would be! A Gargantua of a baby, a monster! We would need the ablest midwives from all over the world to increase the chances of a safe delivery: midwives who were true statesmen in the field of politics, and economists with imagination and not just professional competence. For this monstrous baby would have a great destiny: to create hope in place of fear, reason in place of hate, co-operation in place of stupid rivalry, and constructive work in place of insane destruction and mass suicide. But he would be a monster just the same, and he would therefore take even more watching than most babies.

155

It would be a tough job, but at least it would be a real job, and that would be a welcome change from our recent preoccupations. We Americans would not be left with the present unreal job of trying to figure out how to save the world by destroying it, of how to stop a world revolution without leading it, of how to get starving people to calm down, or at least to starve quietly for a couple of years until we Americans can complete our defense program. It would be a tough job, but at least we would be "on" the job, which is where Americans love to be, and where today we are not.

Our new and more realistic job would have two chief aspects—unless our neighbors could point out even more important aspects which we are not now seeing. This could of course happen: thinking stimulates thinking, just as stubbornness stimulates stubbornness, and recrimination and abuse stimulate recrimination and abuse. One of the aspects of the job is to find workable democratic controls for our International Development Authority, such as the Congress of the United States provided for the TVA. Otherwise it really would be a monster, and no joking. The other aspect is to work out an appropriate corporate charter that would place power and authority where they belong if the job is to be done. Who is most likely to find good solutions for these two problems?

I suggest that delegates of national governments are not the best people to think about such problems. Every national government is a vested interest; and the more impossible a developing world economy makes it for each national government to discharge well the functions for which it was originally instituted, the more rabidly and hysterically "vested" it becomes. The men who try to solve these two problems ought to be men from many lands, it is true, because they ought between them to possess familiarity with many local conditions. But they ought to represent many lands rather than many governments. Before this corporation starts functioning, governments are going to have to consent. Before it has funds to function with, governments are going to have to appropriate. But the governments are much better fitted to decide whether to participate in a corporation ready to roll than they are to plan the corporation. Whatever we do, and however well we do it, there will be plenty of parish-pump politics to contend with later. At least let's not turn over the process of gestation to parish-pump politicians, or the act of birth itself.

I should expect government representatives to think about the problems of the world community even less well than did President Truman's commission when it wrote the report *Partners in Progress*. And I am interested that the international commission of economists which reported to the Secretary-General of the United Nations should have done so much better in their report, *Measures for the Economic Development of Under-developed Countries*. We need somehow to get a group of men like that[28] together, since the members of Mr. Lie's commission were not distracted from thinking clearly about a world problem by the habit of thinking as *nationals* of states that compose the world community.

Here is a pertinent fact. The people who work for the U.N. Secretariat, the executive branch of the United Nations, are required to take the following oath: "I solemnly swear (undertake, affirm, promise) to exercise in all loyalty, discretion and conscience the functions entrusted to me as a member of the international service of the United Nations, to discharge those functions and regulate my conduct with the interests of the United Nations only in view, and not to seek or accept instructions in regard to the performance of my duties from any Government or other authority external to the Organization."

The personnel of the Secretariat are justly proud of their special status, the status of world civil servants. Given the importance of the task we are discussing here, I wonder whether those who are chosen to achieve it should not provisionally join the staff of the U.N. Secretariat and take its oath. Psychologically it would help a lot to be reminded that they are not there to look out for the local interests of their own national state but for the general interests of the men and women who dwell on this planet and of those who will follow them in years to come. The importance of their task would far exceed the importance of any international conference since the United Nations was set up. They ought to remember that, too.

Thus freed from the "practical" considerations that lead straight to defeat and despair, they might re-read the famous passage in the *Histories* of Herodotus which reports that the ancient Persians, when they had to make important plans, imagined them while drunk but decided for or against them only after they had sobered up. I am concerned that our planners also should not be *prematurely* "practical." Their early deliberations should be mainly imaginative and their final ones mainly prudent and coldly reasonable. And there are several obvious things for them to look at while still "drunk."

One thing. Should the International Development Authority, or Corporation, be an agency of the United Nations? If not, who starts it, and who sponsors it? If not, how do you make sure it co-operates with the U.N.? If it is indeed to be responsible to the U.N., to what organs of the U.N.? The Economic and Social Council? To date, that organ has proved not too sensitive to the problem. Nor is it, with its eighteen-state membership, ever likely to be as sensitive to this particular problem as the General Assembly, where every member state has delegates. Perhaps the Authority should be made responsible directly to the General Assembly and the Secretary-General. But the Secretary-General is chosen by the General Assembly, and the delegates to the Assembly are appointed by national governments. Not one soul among them is elected by the ordinary men and women whom this Authority would be set up to serve and who are the ones to judge whether it is serving them. It is this fact that so cripples the U.N. now.

When Representative Warren Austin makes a speech at Lake Success which seems to me and to many of my neighbors clearly absurd, or when he loses his temper, which he apparently does quite often, thereby putting himself at the mercy of a shrewd opponent, there is precious little my neighbors and I can do about it. Mr. Austin is not going to face us at the polls. He is appointed by the President with the consent of the Senate. Of course, we could write our Senators—or the President—what we think. Doubtless, some people have been driven to doing just that. I never have. I never had the heart. It looked to me like a case of remote control. Anyhow, I guessed that Representative Austin might be putting on his act merely to protect the State Department from the next vicious assault from Senator McCarthy. Whereas, if I had helped elect Mr. Austin to his job, neither he nor I would have had to bother very much with Senator McCarthy's antics.

Given the nature of the cold war, I sincerely doubt that the Charter of the United Nations can be so revised as to provide that delegates to the General Assembly shall be popularly elected; and so long as the nine hundred thousand in Costa Rica get the same number of votes as the one-hundred-and-fifty-odd million people in the United States, I doubt if it should be. But, even with the cold war on, I can imagine amending the U.N. Charter to provide for a second chamber, a People's Assembly, in which delegates would be chosen by popular vote and in proportion to population. As a matter of fact, the notion of a People's Assembly has received wide support both in America and in Western Europe, though never—which is not surprising—support from a national government! Moreover, a "People's World Convention" actually met at Geneva, at least in embryo, in 1951.[29] The delegates who met

159

there want to see unofficial elections of delegates from all over the world, at the rate of one delegate per million inhabitants, who would be charged with drafting the constitution for a world government and submitting it to the U.N. and the national governments for ratification. Scores of members of the British Parliament have backed the proposal publicly. The proposal is based on the assumption that if the men and women in the world wait until national governments act, they will never get the common government which the world clearly needs. Incidentally, this scheme for a People's World Convention included, in Britain at least, a world bank and a world food board, which placed it at least nearer to political reality than the proposal of most American Federalists that we establish a world government with minimum powers to guarantee peace.

In 1950 Mr. Walter Reuther's widely discussed pamphlet, *A Total Peace Offensive*, adapted the idea of a People's Assembly of popularly elected delegates from all over the world to supervise the job that we now assign our baby monster, the International Development Authority. Such a People's Assembly, it is safe to bet, would get a lot more eager support from the men and women on the face of our planet than the General Assembly can ever get, for the simple reason that these men and women would have a lot more to say about who should sit in it. It would get a very great deal more support than the Security Council, which now makes the big decisions. For the members of the Council are chosen by the General Assembly, whose members are appointed by governments, which governments are—in varying degrees—chosen by the men and women we are concerned about. That is a pretty thin representation. No wonder many of the men and women in question never heard of the United Nations; and that of those who have, many are hazy about what it is doing.

All this suggests that the directors of our International Development Authority might well be appointed by a People's Assembly, a sort of lower chamber of the U.N., alongside its present upper chamber, the General Assembly. The directors should perhaps remain responsible to the People's Assembly. Appropriations for the corporation should perhaps originate in the People's Assembly and only there, as all appropriations do in the lower house of the U.S. Congress. It would be the business of the General Assembly to accept or reject them.

For the present, of course, since the United Nations lacks the power to tax and hence can do nothing until its members supply it with funds, the People's Assembly would be unlikely to persuade as many governments as should be persuaded to help. Or, if it persuaded them, it would be unlikely to get as much support from them as it needed. But there are several devices for raising the ante.

In the first place, the People's Assembly ought to fight hard from the start to keep in touch with its constituents in a way that the United Nations emphatically does not. When the U.N. was set up at San Francisco in 1945, it was assumed that it would have its own radio facilities, in order that it might report constantly to the people of the world what it was doing and why. It never got those facilities, although they would have paid off many times. The best it could do was lease facilities from—the Voice of America![30] This is calculated to remind our neighbors of the famous accidental title, United Stations. Meanwhile, the average American sees so little about the United Nations in the paper he reads, and sees that little from such a slanted nationalist point of view, that it is small wonder he is not much interested. How can he be interested by any organization which he not only cannot affect except in the most remote fashion, but about which he cannot even learn except in the most remote fashion? And if, as happens to be the case for many hundreds of millions of the U.N.'s "constituents," he does not read a newspaper, or cannot read anything anyhow, he is pretty completely cut off. In these circumstances,

the U.N. stands little chance of rallying world opinion to the purposes for which it was set up. And it does rally very little, as
witness the pittances on which its specialized agencies have had
to work: agencies like the Food and Agriculture Organization and
the World Health Organization. By not enabling it to speak effectively to the men and women it represents, and by not allowing
those men and women in the first place to elect their own representatives, we have effectively hamstrung the organization we set
up with so much blare of trumpets and beating of drums. If, now,
we revised the U.N. Charter to provide a popularly elected People's Assembly, alongside the present General Assembly, with
power to speak directly to the people of the world rather than to
their foreign offices, we would have found perhaps the ideal
device for the democratic control of an agency like our Development Corporation.

Even, however, if all these things were done, there would still
be a problem as to how you and I as individuals could fully support the United Nations. The job before us is a job that calls for
capital, and the bulk of that capital has to be in the form of
money. The fact is that our generation, or at least most of its
members living in the countries with the machines, live in a
money economy. Now, a man can give money to something without giving it his full moral support: in fact, men sometimes use
money to buy their way out of supporting a thing morally. But the
opposite danger is just as real. Men often give their enthusiastic
moral support to something that cannot act without funds and
yet, somehow, they never quite reach down in their pockets to
give their moral support practical meaning. The job this book
talks about will need both kinds of support badly.

The orderly way to get universal support for large-scale action
in the public interest is through taxation. But the United Nations,
not being a government, has no power to tax: it gets what support
it can from governments that have. It is not likely to be given

such power until it has proved its power to cope with those problems like war, famine, and pestilence, that the national governments are now fumbling. The more the national governments fumble, the more they will redouble their efforts and raise their taxes, whether through the tax rate or through inflation will not greatly matter to their victims. That is the jam we are in now. The American and Russian governments, together with the less powerful governments whose policies the nation-state system condemns Washington and Moscow to dominate, are the nearest things to common political institutions mankind can now depend on to get its public business attended to—except for the U.N., which Russo-American rivalry is largely paralyzing. It is most debatable whether this ramshackle, two-headed, loggerheaded, shadowy "world government" can handle the two world revolutions now in progress without producing a first-class explosion.

Doubtless, our paralyzed United Nations will not be given power enough to handle our common problems until it has already handled them much better than it does today. Yet it is hard to see how it can handle them much better while the struggle between the United States and the Soviet Union keeps it paralyzed. It is that vicious circle that makes us feel as if our lives were regulated by a time bomb, and that makes the ticking sound so loud. It is that deadlock that leaves the countries without the machines helpless and unable to get help. We must at all costs break that circle.

There is, happily, a device that might break it and that we have some experience with. One of the agencies of the U.N., the International Children's Emergency Fund, known as UNICEF, crippled in its efforts to save the rising generation from the frightful penalties of war and hunger and disease, took its cause straight to men and women in many countries and thereby supplemented its appropriations from governments. Apparently, one of the few things there seemed a chance of getting everybody to

163

agree to was the proposition that the children of the world should be saved as far as possible from our joint folly. But I am not sure this is the only proposition most persons will agree to, no matter how short a list their governments will agree to. It has become highly desirable that the U.N. have some orderly means of securing direct financial support from the world's people, with or without taxes. Those means would permit it to serve the world's people without depending entirely on its now frustrated member governments.

Now, the two chief means by which we support our governments in making wars are payment of taxes and purchase of bonds, including "baby bonds" that persons with small income can buy. If the United Nations wants to escape from the vicious circle of "no taxes, no accomplishment" and "no accomplishment, no taxes," it would be smart to use the only remaining means of getting direct popular support: issue bonds. It would thereby achieve simultaneously several results that are well worth achieving. It would get funds for self-liquidating projects by an International Development Authority, and it should be able to get them at much lower interest than from the World Bank. In fact, many Americans are proposing that it offer no interest at all— except the interest of the human race in lifting itself by its own bootstraps out of a mess that its various national governments seem unable to lift it out of. There is evidence that if a Development Authority were set up and empowered to make such bond issues millions of people in many lands would welcome a chance to answer the agonizing question now on so many lips: "What can *I* do about it?" Citizens' committees could be formed and bond drives initiated. For this would be a job of ringing doorbells, and so long as one doorbell in town remained unrung the question "What can *I* do about it?" would answer itself. I realize that UNICEF did not use this precise device: it got its support from appropriations by governments and from out-and-out donations

164

by individuals. And it would be foolish not to make suitable provisions for donations to the Development Authority. At a minimum, well-to-do people should be given every opportunity to make free gifts; so should foundations; and in our own country such gifts should be made tax-deductible. But the baby bond, with or without interest, expresses pretty well, I think, the kind of equity the average man or woman needs to have in a joint enterprise of this sort.

The corporation would then be, not a beggar at the door or a servant to be tipped, but a capital fund welcoming additional capital on a responsible basis, a means by which the people of the world could "go into business" together. With hundreds of millions of people lending the corporation money, and with the corporation directly responsible to them through a People's Assembly whose members they had helped elect, and with constant radio reporting from the corporation to people everywhere, there would exist a universal, democratic institution through which men and women everywhere could express their solidarity. That might protect it in part from interference by national governments—might make it less their creature, bound to listen when they cracked the whip.

It would need that moral authority in its day-to-day dealings with governments. Adequate funds alone would bolster such authority, as witness the leverage a private corporation like United Fruit exerted for decades on the governments of the "banana republics" in Central America, if only because its economic decisions were a matter of life and death to so many laboring citizens of those republics. But if, in addition to its funds being large, the Development Authority derived them in large part from ordinary men and women all over the world, it would have a moral authority United Fruit could never enjoy. It so happens that many of the jobs it could and should do can scarcely be done well until social reforms have been undertaken that only

165

government can undertake, whether the government now existing or a new government established for the purpose. The case
most often discussed is land reform in countries with huge feudal
land-holdings. Even the U.S. Government was by 1951 urging
such reform, and the U.S. Government is by all odds the most
conservative of the Big Three. By 1951 the American Government
had had enough experience with the Marshall Plan to know that
making the land more fertile does very little for a population
if only a few own the land. The Development Authority would
be devised to operate in what is a highly revolutionary situation,
and could never do its work by pretending to have only technical
functions. It would aim at bigger crops, but only where bigger
crops would clearly benefit the population as a whole. If the
purpose of the TVA had been the betterment of not the Valley
people as a whole, but only the richest men in the Valley, its
decisions would have had to be very different decisions. It did
of course benefit the rich, and not just the poor, for its job was
not to punish the rich, but to create conditions under which the
poor could become richer.

In many countries, rack-renting by landlords is possible only
because of a shortage of land. Yet in the same countries, in most
cases, new lands could be thrown open if they were first made
fit to cultivate by irrigation or by jungle-clearing. That breaks
the monopoly on land which the landlord class has enjoyed, and
has the same effects economically and politically that opening
free land in the Mississippi Valley had on the social structure
of the older states east of the Appalachian Mountains in the last
century. The answer to monopoly in this country was for decades:
"Go West, young man!" The job of the Development Authority
in many countries would be to create a West to go to. In the
same fashion, usurious rates on farm loans are possible only where
a small group have a monopoly of available credit.

During the great depression, the Farm Security Administration devised a scheme of "supervised credit" which enabled it with fantastically low losses to help the farmer who had no collateral on which to go to bank. In effect the FSA lent him the money on condition that he follow their technical directions until he had paid back the loan. In the process, of course, they taught a lot of farmers how to farm—and how to use credit. A very high proportion of the loans was liquidated. But perhaps their most brilliant achievement was that hundreds of private banks saw the point and installed a similar service. Today this same device is being used by Nelson Rockefeller's American International Association to rescue down-and-out peasant farmers in Venezuela and Brazil.

The Communist formula for breaking a land monopoly is to confiscate the land and distribute it to those who till it. A later stage, of course, is to force the tillers into collective farms. The Communist formula for a monopoly on lendable capital is to confiscate the capital and make it available for economic development by the government. Both kinds of confiscation frequently lead to bloodshed. But these methods are dictated not by the love of bloodshed, but by the lack of capital. A Development Authority with adequate capital can break the monopoly on land in most places simply by opening up new land; and it can break the monopoly on working capital simply by making working capital available at decent rates. In both cases the landlord and the usurer lose out: in the one case, because rents fall and labor becomes dearer; in the other, because interest rates fall and helpless borrowers become fewer. But in the case of Communist revolution the landlord also loses most or all of his land, and perhaps his life: and the usurer most or all of his capital funds, and perhaps his life too. So the Development Authority offers the landlord and usurer a much less painful shift than does Communist revolution; and, since lives are lost on both sides in revolutions, it offers the peasant a less painful shift too. The blood

167

and sweat of those who accumulated the capital in the first place redeems the blood that would have to be spent in revolution by force.

But, make no mistake about it, in both cases the monopolist loses—at a minimum his monopoly. And that is why no International Development Authority could expect much applause from a rack-rent landlord or a usurer. Not unless he were persuaded that the only alternative to an International Development Authority that would break his monopoly was a Communist revolution that would break him too. At present he sees a more attractive alternative: that the most powerful nation on earth will go on vetoing a world development authority and will probably lead an armed crusade against Communism. That combination, he feels, might preserve his monopoly, whether of land or of working capital or both. It is this belief that makes the American Government look to monopolists all over the world like a last best hope. Contrariwise, it looks to their victim, the peasant, like the great barrier to feeding his wife and children.

This simple triangle is quite enough to explain why all over the world, wherever the little people starve, the popularity of America is plummeting. It also explains why all over the world more and more little people are listening to Russia. The more tanks we build, and the more we make our economic aid subserve our appeal to force, the more friends we lose. The more friends we lose, the more tanks we need in case war really comes. This vicious circle might properly be called "the great mid-twentieth-century American rat race," and it is an athletic event which the bulk of mankind is heartily sick of. It has cost countless lives, including the lives of Americans. It is likely to cost more lives unless we call it off.

CHAPTER XI

But calling off the arms race, before a constructive substitute is found, could cost more lives still, even in Korea. Until we have launched the joint war on world misery that our neighbors plead for, when they beg us in vain to set up an International Development Authority, the rat must run. And the tragedy is that we Americans would be the last nation on earth to sanction this rat race if we understood the trap in which we are caught. We do not understand it. Basically, we cannot see the problem because our incredible standard of living has isolated us from the rest of mankind. In our spiritual isolation we assume that if it were not for the Russians everybody would—in Mr. Caffery's words—settle down. Meanwhile, we stagger along under an unprecedented burden of taxation and inflation, bribing governments, cajoling peoples, grumbling that everybody is out of step but us, planning to meet crises wherever one may occur.

We are sick of carrying the rest of the world on our backs, and by March 1951 Senator Connally had to tell the French so in no uncertain terms. "France must do her duty. That is all," remarked the Chairman of the Senate Foreign Relations Committee. This, on the front page of the New York *Times,* plus a characteristic photograph of the Senator—the fat, extended hand clutching the inevitable cigar, the eyes staring into the camera. I have no reason to believe that the French Communist Party paid Senator Connally a single red cent either to make this incredibly insulting remark or to strike that particular pose. But I am confident they would have been happy to pay him a good deal more than a cent for the combined remark and photograph. In France it is easy for Communists armed with such quotes to persuade non-Communists that Washington runs France as its colony. And to have such a remark made by a fat man smoking a cigar—a cliché Communist image for the enemy of the worker and a cliché French image of the American with money to burn—was simply a bonanza. We Americans can of course remind our French friends that at that moment Senator Connally was "talking for the boys in Buncombe County," in this instance the electorate of Texas, where his re-election was endangered by the charge of internationalism. We can say that slapping the French might win him some votes. In fact, the New York *Times* itself offered just this explanation to its readers. The French Communists were unlikely to relay the explanation. The remark, the cigar, the Senator's corpulence, and his key position in the Senate were godsends to the French Communist.

Our policy dooms us to carry the world on our backs, and it dooms the rest of the world to feel just as put on as we do. It almost dooms us to be insulting and the rest of the world to be touchy. Our failure to convince our neighbors that we have a solution to the world's chief problem leaves us with doubtful allies. It therefore drives us to look to our own weapons. It increases our sense of danger, our fear and hatred of Russia, and our deep conviction that a showdown is being forced upon us. Perhaps an American showdown on our own foreign policy would get us more quickly to where we all want to get—to world peace. I suggest we will not find world peace until we join with our neighbors and found it on world prosperity.

If, instead of a showdown with Russia—or China—to see who can murder the most people in the least time, we are to get a showdown in the argument among ourselves on whether to accept our neighbors' challenge and set up an International Development Authority, we shall need now a much clearer picture than most people have of what an authority of this sort could hope to accomplish. If our neighbors retort, "We have already told you it could do for the underdeveloped areas of the world what your TVA did for the Tennessee Valley"—if they retort that way, we should say, "Be patient with us. We Americans have always had short memories for history. The TVA is now in our dim past. Our fear of Russia has made us fear all collective effort except war; has made us think of government not as an instrument for the general welfare but as a policeman to suppress disorder; has made us close our eyes to the government services on which private enterprise daily leans; has convinced us that America's might was built only by love of private profit; has made us see in the most necessary public enterprise a bureaucratic boondoggle supported by tax money torn from the businessman's grasp; has made an ordinary farm co-operative look like 'creeping socialism' and democratic socialism look like Communism the night before. These psychoses, which have served as our defense mechanism against Russia, have indeed cut us off from mankind. They will take time to get rid of. Meanwhile, we insist that the TVA was a product of the American soil, well-watered, it is true, by the bank failures and mass unemployment of the great depression—but American. Is there any proof that the pattern works outside America?"

"Yes," they can reply reassuringly, "there is proof, but most of it is still spotty. Throughout the history of European expansion, of the rise of the great colonial empires, your Christian churches not only tried to spread the Gospel, they also built schools and hospitals and even gave some instruction in agriculture. The investment by your churches in human welfare was, it is true, small when compared with the mammoth wealth extracted by your colonial conquerors, your merchants, and your planters. It was small in quantity but not always in quality. That work continues today. But in addition your foundations, your charitable corporations, your Western governments, and even the minute Technical Assistance Administration of the U.N., have done a good deal, and in any case have accumulated a mass of human experience and a corps of experienced men and women."

Our neighbors are right, of course. This reservoir of relevant experience exists. We are by no means doomed to start from scratch. I count it one of the greatest privileges of my life that I have had since World War II the chance of seeing the process operate in many countries, under many different auspices. I have watched the American International Association at its daily task among the rural population of Venezuela and Brazil. I observed the training of young Latin-American technicians at the Inter-American School of Agricultural Sciences in Costa Rica, conducted by our own and a dozen Latin-American governments. I saw the work of the agricultural school which the United Fruit Company set up in Honduras. I saw in Spain what happens when nobody sets up much of anything, except dictatorship. I marked the spread of French agriculture in Morocco, Algeria, and Tunisia. I talked with the peasants around Thermopylae, where the Greek-Government with American aid was reclaiming a salt marsh to grow much-needed grain. Above all, I saw Palestine. I wandered from Dan to Beersheba—and through the Negeb to the Red Sea. And I understood at last why so many men, more competent than I to judge, look on the State of Israel as the pilot plant for the big job ahead.

172

From each trip, except from Israel, I came back with contradictory feelings. On the one hand I was filled with horror, and on the other I was filled with hope. On the one hand I saw the ocean being bailed out with a thimble, and the prospects looked dim. Could this sea of human misery, of endemic disease, of malnutrition, of fear and distrust, of apathy and despair, be contained by thimbles, no matter how often dipped? On the other hand such small expenditures reaped such incredible results. When you start as close to zero as some of these people were, nearly any constructive step does things by magic.

Those trips are a jumble of images now, of sights, of sounds, and in some places mostly smells, a jumble of horror, a jumble of hope. But I cherish them because I believe they helped me comprehend why other visitors saw in Palestine a land of promise, not merely for the exiled, heartsick Jew, but for the exiled, heartsick human race. The images supply a backdrop against which Operation Promised Land can be grasped in all its high significance.

The eroded mountains of Venezuela. The incredible flowering trees. A government rich on oil royalties. The half-naked children with their swollen bellies and spindle legs. The soldiers. The soldiers everywhere in U.S. Army surplus equipment. No invasion threatened—except perhaps from below. The Caracas shopwindows full of what Main Street balked at buying. High prices. The farm population scattered along the Andean slopes with farm land at $500 to $1,000 an acre; and the vast, empty, fertile valleys below, where everybody had lost someone from malaria. The adobe huts, the earthen floors, innocent of furniture, the thatched roofs. Or the huts built of paper cement bags that the rain had obligingly glued together, the huts surrounded by garden fences of flattened oilcans. The sea of oil in the West, the mountains of iron in the East, the unbelievable agricultural

173

resources, the signs of malnutrition, and sixty per cent of the nation's food arriving from the United States.

The good-natured peasants, sitting on the ground in the Andean twilight while a government truck with a movie projector showed an uproarious Walt Disney movie about a character named Juan who took to the bushes whenever Nature called and was rewarded by the evilest looking collection of intestinal parasites that even a Venezuelan peasant can ever have collected. Child-like laughter from the peasants—and Juan really was funny. Besides, had they not each one a small cement privy distributed by the government? "They keep chickens in them," remarked a government *técnico* acidly. "Will Disney make them use it?" I asked. "Or do they just like funny movies?" "The first time or two, it's just a good comedy," he said. "But they see it three times. Some of them will learn." Each of them had a number stenciled on his mud hut by an official who had sprayed it with DDT. They used the number as a street address, with a good deal of pride. In the city: beautiful homes with no DDT number. But watch out for uncooked vegetables.

The long white curved beaches of Rio de Janeiro, with the post-card scenery all around. The beautiful houses and gardens. Let's climb the picturesque little mountains that surround this gem of a city as those in now distant Venezuela surround lovely Caracas. At home they would be choice suburbs because of the view and the fresh air. But in Rio, as in Caracas, they were without water, except what women carried on their heads; so the poor had been crowded up the slopes. Still, at a distance they were charming. The Franciscan monk from New Jersey guided me. For the first time in my life I stood on a live volcano, with lava running down the steep slopes up which the women plodded. But the lava was human excrement. And the diseased Negroid population clung on, surging down in the morning from their human dunghill to do domestic service along the lovely beach, and surging back at night. The sick faces. The twisted bodies. At the foot of this little mountain, a small polluted stream, where the women washed their clothes.

Bustling São Paulo, with skyscrapers going up everywhere. Beautiful streets and squares. The Communists did well in the last election. Oh, no, there aren't many of them. But people voted for them as a protest against the other parties. "The International Basic Economy Corporation, which Mr. Nelson Rockefeller set up, is determined to prove that business enterprise can earn ten per cent while doing only things that will increase the wealth of the country as a whole. But there is a family in São Paulo that is not satisfied with less than ninety per cent. They think that if a Yankee is foolish enough to take ten, he should be encouraged to do it."

The country back of São Paulo. Santa Rita. Again the American International Association, farm demonstrations, improved farming methods, again supervised credit for small farmers, such as we developed in the Farm Security Administration in the wicked days of Roosevelt and the welfare state. Real excitement among the small farmers. Quick to learn. Less despair than in Venezuela. The active reforestation with eucalyptus trees, and the undertone of excitement about the great valley development of the tumultuous São Francisco River, a development that would exceed anything dreamed of in the Tennessee Valley. But always the dread of famine in the Northeast, of famine that really would break with fury in 1952 and send Brazilian "Okies" fighting their way by truck, by burro, by foot toward fabulous São Paulo.

The really exciting agricultural college in Costa Rica. Preparing youngsters to teach peasants how to make do with little: how to make roof tile in a homemade kiln, with the faithful burro treading out the clay and straw; how to fire brick in it; how to thatch better roofs where the beloved corrugated aluminum roofing is not yet available; how to grow better vegetables and

175

more varieties than the peasants have ever seen; how to set up homemade irrigation works at next to no cost. The man that taught those things is teaching in India now. And, then, my favorite agricultural experiment: to find out whether you can raise a hog exclusively on bananas. If you could, Costa Rica would be sitting pretty. She has lots of bananas. She needs the corn for the people. And the people would like cheap pork. Fine-looking hogs: they ate the whole works, including the peeling and the stems. It turns out that a diet three-quarters composed of bananas does fine.

The exquisitely beautiful agricultural college in Honduras. The prize bulls to raise the level of milk production. "Can near-by farmers use them?" "Oh, yes." "Has it helped their stock?" "Not too much. We know in the States that it's ten per cent the breeding and ninety per cent the feeding. But these peasants, once they breed to our bulls, figure the cow and the calf too can get on without much feed." But the students are learning. Learning all aspects of tropical agriculture.

Chapingo, outside Mexico City, where the Rockefeller Foundation has for several years been helping the Mexican Government develop better seed. Years of patient collecting of strains of Mexican corn. At last the right hybrids. Corn production soared. For the first time in half a century, Mexico had no need to import corn. Passing on now to rice and beans. Not interested in politics. At least, not officially. In the long run, any reasonable political solution would be helped by better seed and more plentiful food in Mexico.

Or North Africa. The exquisite farms, so reminiscent of France. The native Arabs—strangely aloof—in their own costumes, their own diseases, their own squalor. General Juin laying down the law to them in every newspaper. Sullen resistance. American air force officers planning airfields to protect this free world from the Russians. An animal-like misery, combined with the resignation of Islam, and a ruthless fleecing of the tourist visitor from the world of money.

The handsome old mayor of the little Greek village near Thermopylae, with his ferocious mustachios and his cheerful recollections of Oregon. . . . All those who had worked in America and could remember a little English sat around me under the one oil lantern in the café and drank cognac. Those who had never seen America sat in a ring around the wall, without cognac, and admired those who had been to America. We talked farming. I knew, and the Mayor knew I knew, that the reclamation project to get the Mediterranean salt out of the river delta was on, that experts had been brought from Holland to help, and that even while the flooding operation was still in progress they had been shown how to plant their first rice, to make a crop while the technicians toiled to make land for wheat. I said that what they were doing was exciting, that all over the world people were having to be imaginative; and I told about the hogs that ate only bananas. The group laughed, but the Mayor merely said drily: "A year ago we in this village thought rice was made like macaroni." In Greece, too, we are learning.

Nevertheless, said the American administrator in Athens, unless the farmers in Crete learn how to sell their oranges through a co-op, these Athenian merchants will sit out here on the square drinking coffee and getting their crop for one dime on the dollar's worth. I repeated that story a week later in Israel to an ardent pro-Russian, anti-American Marxist. She was incredulous. An American Marshall Planner urging co-operatives instead of bigger profits for middlemen! I tried to explain that many Americans were too busy trying to get results to stop and take their temperature for creeping socialism. This fellow was a farmer type from one of our southern states and did not even know that some Americans considered co-operatives immoral. If co-ops can save an American farmer's skin, why not a farmer's skin in Crete?

177

My American administrator had only so many dollars to work with and was determined to get his money's worth whatever the effect on Greek political thought. It was the American taxpayer's money, wasn't it?

You can see that these impressions really are a jumble. But they fell into place fast enough, once I came to Israel. I suggest that the postwar impressions of the whole human race are pretty much a jumble at the moment, and that a look at Israel might make them fall into place.

CHAPTER XII

Israel is a land of light. There is first the light that bathes the Palestine hills and baffles the expert eye of the painter newly arrived from Europe or America. There is the more mysterious light that is always shed by intelligent human purpose widely shared. And there is the most mysterious light of all, the light that infuses the religious traditions of Jewry, of Christendom, and Islam alike, the light by which Jew, Christian, and Moslem alike see Palestine as holy land. But this really imposing list does not exhaust the kinds of light that the State of Israel sheds for us today. Israel is also, at this momentous hour in human history, a lens and a reflector. It is focusing and reflecting in one tiny State all the problems of mankind. It is as if all the luminous ideas in the world now shone their rays toward Israel and we could see them better there by reflection than in the countries where men first saw them.

Israel is Asia, not only on the maps that little children scan in school, not only on Christmas cards full of wise men and camels, but in hot and dusty fact. Yet Beersheba, with its echoing Biblical past, looks less like Asia than like an American frontier town. Indeed, the whole of Israel is a frontier post, of America even more than of Europe, and in any case of the Occident, of Occidental techniques, and Occidental bustle. It is in many respects a Western colony on the fringe of Asia and on the fringe of Africa. And because the Occidental world so largely grew out of ideas that came from Palestine, Israel is a return, not merely of men and women from the West but of homing ideas, too.

No wonder that when I left Israel I racked my mind in vain for one single important problem in the modern world that I had not seen reflected in that pilot plant for twentieth-century man. I had watched the irrigation pipes of modern Western agriculture thrusting and searching into the soil of a feudal agriculture and even a feudal pastoralism. The swamps had yielded or were yielding to well-drained arable land. The naked, eroded hills were being clothed again in protective forests, tree by painfully planted tree. The orange groves multiplied. The somber Arab costume gave way to European dress—European dress that tended to be frontier dress; mud hut, or black tent of skins, to the concrete house. Food, clothing, and shelter shifted beneath my eyes—along with the body of man himself. From sickly Arab nomad, from the Jew who was twisted, broken, and branded in the Nazi concentration camp, there was emerging a nation of tanned, erect, strong people. Wave after wave, they still poured in, poured home. From Asia, from Africa, from every continent of the world. Forty-seven languages were being spoken until all could learn Hebrew. And frontier bravado still flung out one of Israel's favorite chestnuts: "We are not a melting pot; we are a pressure cooker."

In the first three years of Israel's statehood, the population doubled, chiefly through immigration. Think what that means. Not in our palmiest days of immigration did our country ever absorb immigrants at a rate remotely comparable. And note that these immigrants, though prepared by their common Jewish traditions to be assimilated, ran the complete gamut of health, education, economic resources, customs, and language. Note also that they did not enter a country with vast untapped resources like America before World War I, but a country that even with outside aid could not hope to grow food fast enough, or build houses fast enough, to meet the new strain put on its economy. What had Isaiah cried? "I will bring thy seed from the East and gather Thee from the West; I will say to the North, give up, and to the South, keep not back: bring my sons from far, and my daughters from the end of the earth." And what had the Proclamation of Independence declared? "The State of Israel will be open to the immigration of Jews from all countries of their dispersion."

Each successive wave of immigration is known as an aliyah, a "going up." The present wave, heaviest of all, is the fifth aliyah. Aliyah is a highly resonant word. It is going up to Jerusalem, that holy town in the hills. It is lifting up your hearts. It is lifting your eyes to the everlasting hills. It is rising from deep despair to high hope. It is returning home to God, from whence all things came.

But to all this the Gentile may say: "What is that to me?" And to all this the American or Englishman or Frenchman of Jewish faith or at least of Jewish tradition, no more interested in returning to Zion than a Lutheran in returning to Germany, may say even more loudly: "What is that to me?" If so, they have not caught up with world history in the mid-twentieth century. The Jewish exiles who are going up are indeed escaping from a house of bondage: from lands of horror and persecution and torture and death. But what comfortable American, whether Jew or Gentile, dares ignore longer the hundreds of millions of non-Jews, men, women, and children, who have also been uprooted, have known the Nazi torture chamber, the barbed wire of the

181

concentration camp, forcible deportation and "repatriation," the flight from famine along the road lined with those whose flight is ended, or the frenzied attack of the religious riot in India. We have not caught up with history if we think the twentieth century reserved for the Jew alone hunger, thirst, imprisonment, torture, massacre, and mass deportation. To the hundreds of thousands of persons legally classifiable as D.P.'s—Displaced Persons—must be added the millions of widowed and orphaned, the bombed-out, those who cannot say where their families are, and those whose hearts have been broken and whose reason has been shaken by the vastest human cataclysm in recorded history: the flotsam and jetsam of modern industrialized warfare. There are many and subtle categories of D.P.'s in our world today.

Of all these millions and all these hundreds of millions, less than a million, who happen to be Jewish, have already gone up to a land of promise, a land of hope, a land of building. Can only Jews go up, and of Jews only Zionists intent on emigrating to a particular small country? Have the rest of us no imagination? Can the rest of us not see that in the midst of our darkness here is light? That in the midst of our despair or skepticism or fatalism here is hope? Something a-building in the midst of our plans for destruction?

And can we not do as well as see? Can only Jews demand a better life than the human race now has? Or make sacrifices in order to achieve it? Or submerge their differences on religion, politics, and economics enough to take common action for their common safety? I refuse to believe it. I grant that the Jew, as so often in his history, was a sort of caricature of the rest of us, more wretched, more hunted, and more hated than the other displaced persons of the world; but that most human beings in the world now demand a going up, and even a going up in a hurry, is becoming clearer with each passing month. For they, too, dwell in a house of bondage and are condemned to make bricks without straw, and groan under taxes to build weapons, and watch freedom wither as the decaying system of nation states turns every government into a general staff. They would cross the Red Sea itself and brave the desert to do what the people of Israel are doing now.

If you accept no religious faith, or if yours is that most burning of faiths, dislike of all religion, you may by now be amused or even angered to find me falling into the phrases and images of the Old Testament. But the language of the Old Testament has so much more to do with the actual condition of mankind than has the language of the cold war.

I have tried, and failed, to see how our getting tough, or going it alone, or taking the wraps off the air force, or trying to buy allies, can get the men and women now on this planet anywhere they really want to go. I gather that to more and more governments an anti-Russian alliance wrapped up in Point Four dollars looks less like going up than it does like going along. I fail to see how it could look otherwise. That is why in 1952 government after government balked at accepting American aid on the terms of the Mutual Security Act: Iran, Burma, Afghanistan, Egypt, Iraq, Ireland, Mexico. In power politics all gift horses should be looked in the mouth several times, and there is no use our getting huffy about this ancient and honorable practice. It seems clear to me that Israel is saying more to the human race just now, both spiritually and materially, than we Americans have said since World War II. This may excuse my falling back on Biblical images.

But I have been talking more about Israel's spiritual significance than its material significance, and this book is about the economic and political aspects of our times rather than about its religious aspects. From those points of view, what about Israel?

Well, they are actually doing what most of the rest of us are talking about when we want to win votes or influence allies. They took an underdeveloped country with far fewer natural resources than most underdeveloped countries and turned marsh and desert into cropland, forest, orchard, and garden. They found Near Eastern subsistence farming, with precious little subsistence, and they replaced it with scientific agriculture. They found eroded hills and clothed them with trees. They found a feudal society and built a modern democracy. They made a place for private enterprise, for foreign capital, for powerful co-operatives, for a healthy labor movement, and for Socialist settlements practicing a democratic, voluntary communism that Russia does not claim to have achieved. They took Orthodox Jews, capable of setting fire to the automobiles of those who travel on the Sabbath, Reformed Jews, agnostics, and militant Marxist atheists and are welding them into a common nation, a nation whose constitution guarantees religious freedom. They found a race problem. By February 1952, out of every fifty-nine Israelis seven were Arabs, of whom five were Moslems and two were Christians. Although they have had less success with this race problem than with any other they have tackled, at least they have handled it conspicuously better than we Americans have handled the problem of either the native Indian or the African we brought over in slavery.

Half a century ago the prophet of Zionism, Theodor Herzl, already saw clearly that the most modern technology cannot develop an underdeveloped economy without capital any more than capital can do it without technology. He thus avoided a lot of sentimental nonsense that has afflicted our modern discussion of Point Four, a discussion in which know-how would manage without capital. The Zionists who developed Palestine used both and are still using them. They could, of course, have imitated the pioneers in the film *The Covered Wagon*—a vehicle that was part of the modern technology of its day. Colonizing a twentieth-century planet by nineteenth-century methods is sport for sentimentalists and masochists but need not divert us here. The pio-

184

neers of Israel have made tons of mistakes and are still making them. They learned a lot, for themselves and for us, by making them. But, given the frail instruments through which they had to work, voluntary associations like the Jewish Agency and the Jewish National Fund and the Zionist Organization, it is a wonder they did not make more. They were members of minorities, scattered throughout the world, minorities which were often under severe persecution and nearly always under suspicion and dislike. They had to do it with settlers whose traditions, and often the very laws they lived under, had prevented them from learning the agricultural skills they most needed for the job. To talk as if the Western capital available to the Zionists made it a push-over, not applicable to non-Jews, is to be ignorant of the heroism and anguish of fifty years, fifty years of what the President of Israel called "trial and error."

The real tools they had for the job were human will and human intelligence; and the will came largely, I suspect, from the conviction that there was no real alternative. If any alternative exists for the rest of our generation to doing the same kind of thing in many lands that the Jews have done in Palestine—except the alternative of world-wide violence—it would be most helpful to hear it named. If the world Jewish community could with great effort and much grumbling and quarreling summon enough strength and wisdom to create in the wilderness a home for all Jewish exiles who had had enough, is it certain that the new world community born of the two world wars and of science cannot summon enough strength and wisdom to make a home for the innumerable exiles of every race in its midst? Or must we destroy more cities and waste more farmland before we will believe that modern man is homeless?

I believe the modern going up of Israel can providentially teach us the direction in which we all must move—up, not down to destruction. That going up has furnished a know-how that would give a human context for the scientific know-how we Americans have talked so much about; and this human context would make our know-how relevant to the nations of the earth. Israel could be, if we but looked at it with fresh eyes, not only the bridge it has always been between Asia and Africa, but a bridge between our West and both those continents. The light in Israel could illumine both their problem for us and our problem for them.

Or, if we prefer, we Americans can go on arming for the great showdown, allocating a small fraction of the cost of rearmament to an American Point Four to back up our stock-piling of strategic materials. Foreign governments can keep on going along with us just far enough to keep the dollars coming, and not far enough to be thrown out by their frustrated peoples. In that case, and in the long run, we may look for: a string of revolutions against the present misery of the world; a string of accusations from Washington that these people would have settled down but for Russia; and, in the end, catastrophe. In that catastrophe we may discover on what shifting sands we based our situations of strength, though a rock was there for us to use.

As to the question of putting economics ahead of religion and politics, Israel has made her answer; and by her mere existence demands our answer too. In their Proclamation of Independence, on May 14, 1948, the Israelis declared: "The State of Israel will be open to the immigration of Jews from all countries of their dispersion; will promote the development of the country for the benefit of all its inhabitants; will be based on the principles of liberty, justice and peace as conceived by the prophets of Israel; will uphold the full social and political equality of all its citizens, without distinction of religion, race or sex; will guarantee freedom of religion, conscience, education and culture; will safeguard the Holy Places of all religions; and will loyally uphold the principles of the United Nations Charter."

186

This Israeli Proclamation of Independence is a challenge to our whole generation. For it faces up to the three questions: How can men live a good life together without a common faith in God? How can they live together in peace with conflicting political views and without common government? How can they earn their bread together while divided about God and politics?

You immediately "develop the country" and you consciously develop it "for the benefit of all its inhabitants." If we immediately developed the country men call the earth for the benefit of all its inhabitants, the problem of finding a workable foreign policy would be posing itself positively and not negatively.

You base your development on liberty, which we Americans talk about more and more loudly the more we allow it to diminish. You base it also on justice, which we Americans talk about more and more softly, because we have let the word justice get a Communistic flavor. And you base it on peace, a word which we have practically let the Russians copyright in all countries. For most of mankind are not only hell-bent to develop the country they all inhabit. They also want liberty; and they want both kinds we fought for in the eighteenth century; freedom from foreign domination, and freedom from dictatorial government. But they want justice quite as much as did the men who wrote the Preamble to the American Constitution, which strongly suggests that the first business of government is to establish justice. Nor does most of mankind share the more recent, the current, American view that if you get enough liberty justice will take care of itself. They emphatically reject the view that justice is the automatic result of the sort of capitalism we Americans claim we have, and they cannot imagine its resulting in their countries from the sort of capitalism they believe we really have.

They desperately want "full social and political equality of all— without distinction of religion, race or sex." Indeed, the idea of human equality, on which we Americans were the first to build a government, is moving more millions today than any other idea; and nothing has caused us Americans to lose face in the world community so rapidly as our failure to live up to what was our own idea. Our failure to achieve "full social and political equality—without distinction of . . . race" here in America, combined with our failure to dissociate ourselves more definitely from white European colonialism among the colored peoples of Asia and Africa, has done us great damage.

You may object that the analogy between the people of Israel and the people of the world has already broken down, since it is the Israeli Government that promised to promote the development of the country and to base itself on the political principles of liberty, justice, and equality. Does not this once more suggest that the people of the world cannot develop their great "country" until they have set up a common government? But the exciting thing about Israel is that the Zionists had set up institutions like the Jewish Agency and the Jewish National Fund to develop the country decades before they were able to establish a government. The country's political institutions grew out of the common effort to develop its economy. For decades Zionists in many nations throughout the world toiled at that economic task, confident that out of its partial achievement would grow the appropriate political institutions. This, also, suggests . . .

Out of East European pogroms, out of the milder but painful anti-Semitism of Western Europe, out of the final fury of the Nazi man hunt, they generated a commonwealth, they rebuilt the City. It was a City that would base its government on liberty, justice, and peace, "as conceived by the prophets of Israel." But any city based on the social teachings of those prophets cannot be merely a Jewish city, as Jehovah could not continue to look like a merely Jewish God. Any city based on the teachings of those prophets becomes a City of Man. It becomes a City required by its nature to "safeguard the Holy Places of all religions." It is this appeal to universal principles that convicts of a superficial sense of history both those Jews and those Gentiles who see in the going up to Palestine a purely Jewish event.

And this is true even though it was chiefly that great prophetic tradition that gave the Zionists the guts to develop that naked, treeless, parched, malarial land. It had been a land of milk and honey, and they would make it a land of milk and honey once again. But there have been milk and honey elsewhere. North Africa was a granary of the ancient Romans; Iraq was a fabulous garden that supported many millions in the great days of Babylon; and the ancestors of Hannibal's elephants fed well in a part of what is now the Great Sahara. These too could be restored, not by lonely pioneers armed neither with capital nor technology, nor even by giant business corporations, organized under the law for the profit of those who invested in them, but by corporate effort of quite another kind, designed on purpose to rescue mankind from the famine, pestilence, poverty, and war, which like locusts and rinderpest, know neither Jew nor Gentile, bond nor free, white nor colored, rich nor poor, but threaten all alike. Once we the people of the world recognize the plight that most of us are obviously in and that all of us are actually in, we can learn a lot from the Zionists on how to use corporations, capital, and science not merely to make money but to make men; not merely to get ahead of our neighbors but to join them and go up together to the City that must be rebuilt.

CHAPTER XIII

Many of us believe that the world community has three needs, a common religious faith, common political institutions, and a common opportunity to earn the bread our bodies require; and many would range them, as Toynbee does, in that order of importance. But if we set about the least important task, might we not find our way to the others? If we set about it with agreement only on the goals of the Israeli Proclamation of Independence, would any people anywhere raise an objection to those ideals? As to a common faith—a young American who had read the Israeli philosopher Martin Buber, and who had worked for six weeks in a Marxist collective settlement in Galilee, had a chance to talk with Dr. Buber. "Dare I ask you a personal question?" he said. "In your writings you are deeply religious. You also see hope of regeneration through the collective settlements. But many of the collective settlements are militantly atheistic. Isn't this a kind of paradox?" "I can answer you," replied Dr. Buber, "only by a quotation from the Talmud. 'Would that they had forgotten My name and done that which I commanded of them.'"

Even should you grant me, however, that all I have said about

Israel is true, you might still ask a question that is very dear to those who pride themselves on being practical: Where would the money come from? Where would the money come from to rebuild the world's economy, when the Israelis themselves estimate it costs around $2,500 to bring one Jew to Israel and get him to the point of earning his own way? For fifty years, the question "Where is the money coming from?" brought anguish to the heart of the Zionist. And until Israel's incredible immigration tapers off, it will go on bringing anguish. The Israeli's only defenses against that anguish are hard work and jokes on himself. You may know the one about the Israeli optimist and the Israeli pessimist arguing about the always imminent bankruptcy of the State of Israel. "I have an idea," cried the optimist. "We should declare immediate war on the United States. We will lose it, of course, in twenty-four hours. Then we will be where Germany and Japan are now, and we will be well taken care of." "But," retorted the pessimist glumly, "suppose we win."

What has kept the Zionists going for half a century has never been the ability to answer the question "Where is the money coming from?" What has kept them going is what keeps nations going which enter a war because they can see no alternative. Once you make up your mind to that, it is remarkable how much more money can be found than when you embark on a venture that is one of many alternatives.

Everything suggests that if the world were now spending on economic development, under international auspices, a modest fraction of what it is spending on arms, the whole military problem would be restated by history. How many guns, planes, and tanks does it take to "contain Russia"? It depends on how your allies and the rest of the world view your policies. A sufficiently unpopular policy would make necessary more guns, planes, and tanks than even we Americans could man, or could persuade or hire other people to man. A sufficiently unpopular policy could mean that any guns, tanks, or planes sent abroad would stand an excellent chance of turning up in the hands of our opponents. That is what happened in China, and it could happen even in Europe. A policy that rallied the moral support of most of mankind, and particularly of that portion of mankind to whom the Russians are now talking, would make Russian expansion a most dangerous game, and a game we have—luckily for her—not yet challenged her to play. In the present state of the world, it is not a question of swords or plowshares; it is a question of finding the proper ratio between swords and plowshares in order that the proportion may slowly shift toward more and more plowshares, in order that the world revolution be guided instead of dammed.

I have talked at such length about Zionism and about Israel not for the purpose of examining their books and calculating whether there is enough money in the world to do internationally what they have done in one small country, scarcely larger than the Commonwealth of Massachusetts. My reason was that Zionist purpose and Zionist effort have furnished us with the most eloquent example of what needs doing in underdeveloped countries, and have proved that the kinds of procedures we Americans employed in the Tennessee Valley will work outside America. The Israelis do not make the mistake of supposing that TVA methods cannot be borrowed and adapted; and the rest of us should not make the mistake of supposing that Israel's experience with economic development cannot be borrowed and adapted.

In the spring of 1951 I spent some hours examining a carp-farming operation at a settlement in Galilee. Like most *kibbutzim*, the settlement went in for mixed farming; but, again like most, it had a specialty. It raised fish. The shallow, square ponds lay in neat rows, separated by earth ramparts wide enough for the trucks to travel when they hauled the feed for the fish. "What led you to choose fish-farming as your specialty?" I asked. The *kibbutznik* who was acting as my guide grinned. "Did you see the spring just north of here?" "Yes," I answered, "and it was the finest flow of water I have seen anywhere in the country except the headwaters of the Jordan." "Well," he said, "it's a fine flow all right, but the water contains a mineral that makes it unfit for irrigation. For irrigation, it's bad water. And the land where we stand was, on the whole, bad land. We wondered whether, if you put bad water and bad land together, you might get something good out of them. You do: you get these carp." "And how profitable are the carp?" "We make more money per acre from the bad land covered with bad water than from our good land irrigated with good water."

The conversation remained for me the most deeply typical I had in Israel on the subject of economic development. For everywhere the Israeli, faced with unusually meager resources, is asking himself: "If these two bad things, or these three bad things, should be combined, could one good thing come out of them?" The whole business of economic development will stand or fall largely on how our generation answers that kind of question. In Israel, Necessity is busy again at her old occupation of mothering Invention. The Zionist pioneers had already won half their battle on the day they deliberately married Necessity. Nothing makes her so fertile as to be deliberately chosen in marriage. As to the fertility of her daughter, Invention, she by definition is the one who multiplies exceedingly.

But the successes of Israel are no more instructive than her failures. And in some ways her most disappointing failure has concerned the development of the Jordan River for irrigation and electric power. Much planning has gone into the Jordan Valley Authority. But her Eastern neighbors will not co-operate. Most of the upper Jordan is the boundary between Israel and Syria. The middle reaches, just below the Sea of Galilee, are the boundary between Israel and Transjordan. But the lower stretch, clear to the Dead Sea, runs through Transjordan itself. This fact encouraged Transjordan to announce in 1951 that it wanted to be called Jordan: not all its territory lay "on the other side of Jordan," since the frontier which the military armistice sanctioned left Jordan with a sizable slice of Palestine. Unless Israel can achieve a permanent and genuine peace with both Syria and Jordan, a real JVA cannot be undertaken.

When the Clapp Commission, headed appropriately by the director of the TVA, went to Palestine to see what could be done about the problem of Arab refugees, refugees who during the Arab war had been called out of Israel by the Grand Mufti, the Commission well knew that the proper assault on the problem was a JVA that would open a rich territory to resettlement. But the bad relations between Israel and the Arab states caused the Commission to turn in to the United Nations a timid report, recommending merely the development of some of the small tributaries of the Jordan, since such development could be undertaken without straddling the frontier.

This failure is eloquent. A properly constituted International Development Authority would face no more important problem than securing from sovereign governments the rights and titles that would permit it to tackle those numerous projects that do straddle frontiers. It would possess the enormous advantage of being able to deal directly and separately with governments that for one reason or another would not deal directly with each other. It would be in the happy position of a powerful oil company that needs rights and concessions from two neighboring states if its wells and pipelines are to work with maximum efficiency. But it would have the added advantage that its operations, once it got going, could command far more friendliness and respect from the local inhabitants than a private business corporation could ever hope to command, for the simple reason that those operations would be pointed directly to creating economic opportunity for those inhabitants rather than to creating profits for men in other lands.

195

For the United Nations to attempt a JVA, without a Development Authority to do the actual work, would again require agreements between governments. But if agreements between governments had been possible, work on a JVA would have started long ago without the intervention of the U.N. and without the need of an International Development Authority. If the Authority were merely a kitty from which grants could be made to governments, we would still be stuck. But an Authority that could undertake the job itself, from negotiating with governments in the territory to be worked in, clear through the construction of the dams and canals, to the sale of water and power, would be something else again.

This time the problem cannot be solved either by technical assistance minus capital, since the best sort of technical assistance has already been employed, or even by technical assistance plus capital, since capital could be found if the political problem could be solved. What might very well solve it, though, would be the sort of international public corporation that we have been imagining, which could review the findings of experts, now already available; could dicker with those governments in whose jurisdictions the job lay; could perhaps secure financial contributions from them; could get the thing built; and could operate it for the public good, as the Port of New York Authority operates—not for the benefit of the city or state of New York only, but for the benefit of the millions of people from all over the world who use its roads, bridges, tunnels, and airports.

It is, I suggest, no argument to say that even an International Development Authority might not be able to step into the political cauldron of the Near East, whose ingredients so annoyingly refuse to "settle down," and act constructively for their common benefit. If it found itself stymied in securing the necessary arrangements from the governments involved, it could with dignity render a report to the United Nations, specifying which governments refused to do what, and pointing out without recrimination what could have been done for the men and women who toil for bread in that area if their governments were willing to permit it. It is one thing for a government to exploit popular fear and hatred and all the hysteria of nationalism and to blame the failure of this sort of project on a neighboring government. It would be quite another to deny the verdict of an Authority which would represent most of the peoples of the earth or even a large proportion of them from every continent, an Authority that was not concerned to secure raw materials for America's armed forces or to prevent, by "denial purchasing," the Russians from getting them, an Authority which did not represent the white race alone, fighting to maintain its economic privileges. There are not many governments in existence that could explain away their refusal to co-operate with a properly constituted International Development Authority responsible to most of the peoples of the earth. The feudal government that prefers to keep things feudal and therefore has qualms about economic development and a dynamic economy is usually the very kind of government least able morally to make its political philosophy explicit. Fortunately for such governments, they do not in the present chaos have to make their reasons explicit. They can play billiards indefinitely with the prejudices and passions of their desperate subjects.

The present political anarchy in the world community will always furnish such governments the alibis they need if they are to stay in power. For some of them, an International Development Authority would be as dangerous as Communism. For us Americans, an International Development Authority could guarantee that a hungry world community would stand a real chance of getting both bread and freedom. There is nothing in the American tradition to make us prefer that they get freedom without bread. Our consistent purpose as a nation has been to get both.

Israel throws light, then, both on how to start development

197

without waiting for the ideal political institutions that would make the job easier, and on how limited national governments are, particularly those of small states, in their power to carry out development. It also throws light on how men and women of many political and religious faiths can co-operate for their common economic benefit without stopping the fruitful clash of ideas. That is, it throws light on how fruitful such a clash can be if, instead of planning to settle the argument by force, men state the conflict in the context of a common need and a common effort to meet such need. It suggests how much easier it is to find peace through what I called coaction than by what we now call co-existence.

I found nobody in Israel who wanted to exclude any portion of the population, whether private capitalists, Socialist laborites, card-carrying Communists, or Arab farmers, from the common task. This desire to include on the job, instead of to exclude from any job, one's political, ideological, or religious opponents is what makes it something of an ordeal to return from Israel to the America of the 1950s. Essentially it is to return from hope to fear. My own estimate is that there is more hope, as well as more difficulty, to the square yard in Israel than there now is to the square mile in America. For an American nurtured in our robust tradition of hope and confidence, this confession is hard to make.

The inevitable power struggle between the only two super-great powers left in the world is hideously complicated by the fanatical claims of each that they know how to save the world. The Russian Communist Party spends billions—that ultimately come from the Russian worker and consumer—to persuade mankind that Communism can bring a heaven on earth. American business spends billions—that ultimately come from the American worker and consumer—to persuade Americans that American capitalism can bring a heaven on earth. The Russian Communist Party, by using the Russian government propaganda machine, can

198

finance its fanatical propaganda in large part by taxation. American business, by charging off its propaganda to advertising when March 15 rolls around, can indirectly do the same thing.

Meanwhile Russians who dissent from the Communist view are frequently sent to concentration camps for forced labor. Those Americans who dissent from the American business view and who show, or have shown, an undue interest in Communism are more and more often fired from their jobs and condemned to forced idleness; and the most recent recommendations of the U.S. Chamber of Commerce should, if adopted, considerably increase the number of the condemned.[31]

But whatever the Russian and American may think, there are millions of people who look neither to Russia's Communist paradise nor to the paradise pictured by American writers of advertising. In the economic field they are interested in things considerably less metaphysical than paradise. What they are seeking are institutions that can get the world economy on its feet, so everybody can eat. They are not reassured by this double picture of intolerance. They are not afraid of either private ownership or "the welfare state." They seek a judicious mixture of both. If institutions should be set up that would meet their desperate needs, those institutions would almost inevitably look "capitalistic" and "imperialistic" to the Russian Communist and "Communistic" or at least "Socialistic" to the American businessman or to a lot of American businessmen. Fortunately for us Americans, we have many American businessmen who do not scare that easily and who speak with some acidity of the "line" the N.A.M. and the U.S. Chamber of Commerce indulge in. They can get away with acid remarks a good deal better in America than Russians can in Russia. Which is as it should be.

But we cannot remind ourselves too often that we and the Russians are more passionately ideological than most of the people in the world. The people of the world are for the most part not interested in our ideologies but in getting results, and the need of results strongly suggests to them a mixed economy, particularly since most men, including us Americans, already live under a mixed economy and are concerned with finding the right mixture rather than with eliminating one of its ingredients. They can see why, for historical reasons, we might depend more on private enterprise than they feel they possibly can. We had better learn why they feel they must depend on public enterprise more than we feel is desirable. Finally, those of our businessmen who have not been taken in by the ideology that now fills our advertising matter would do well to ask themselves this question: If American business has everything to gain from political stability in the world, will not our foreign investments be safer in those countries that have made their own adjustment to the world revolution than in those countries where the status quo is being maintained by force? Is not Great Britain a safer field for investment as a result of the peaceful revolution she has been going through than she would be if a "strong" government had prevented her revolution? My guess is that the best foreign fields for American investors are precisely those where the degree of reforms, even of "socialistic" reform, corresponds most closely with the will of the people.

It will take a lot of detached thinking on the part of us Americans to raise us from the function of protecting the status quo, no matter how unjust or unpopular, to the function of co-operating with peoples who are going through a revolution. For the hundreds of thousands of Americans eager to return to the political arrangements of the 1920s, or to the idyllic arrangements that never actually existed even in the 1920s, the readjustment will be painful. Fortunately, there are millions of Americans who regard our own major political changes of the 1930s as both inevitable and desirable adjustments to the rapid changes in our economic system. Those millions are quite ready to understand the problems of other peoples if those problems are fairly presented to them. Once more, the TVA, with all its Lincolnian overtones, is our most usable symbol. If we can remember why we established the TVA, and why even some of our more anti-Roosevelt newspapers eventually praised it, we shall be well on the way to understanding what kind of things most of the people in the world want to see done. If we can grasp that most of the hysterical opposition to "Communism"—which, considering our standard of living and the pitiful showing of the Communist Party in our country, baffles people all over the world—is actually opposition to "the welfare state" and to the position Abraham Lincoln took in the passage I have quoted, we can join our neighbors and hoist ourselves out of the mess their world and ours is in.

We have already seen how the American International Association is using the methods of our Farm Security Administration to .ielp the peasants of Venezuela and Brazil get to their feet. We know how often men have made use of co-operatives to pool their capital resources and to lift themselves out of economic despair into economic opportunity. During the period of the 1930s, following the collapse of our American economy, we Americans evolved dozens of governmental and non-governmental devices to help us get going again. Branding them "creeping socialism" will not make most of us either forget them or regret them. I predict that, if we run into danger of another economic collapse, we shall snatch these devices from the shelf fast enough and imagine some new ones, too. Our present hysterical praise of free enterprise will never successfully prevent us from using free public enterprise whenever or wherever we become sufficiently convinced that it is needed.

If I have chosen the free public enterprise known as the TVA in my hunt for a model for an international institution capable of handling the economic problems of the Mighty Neighborhood we all now live in, it is not because the other devices which men in our country and in many other countries have evolved are useless.

It is because we must find some really powerful human agency better suited than either the American Government or the Russian Government to do the job ahead. If we are clear-eyed enough and brave enough to establish that agency, it would quickly find means of working through all the other sorts of devices that have been found useful. Much of what the TVA did could not have been done if it had not been able to work through co-operatives. There are hundreds of millions of people all over the world, organized in co-operatives of the most diverse types. An intelligently devised International Development Authority would be quick to use them. Much of what the TVA did, it did by working with Farm Security. And one should add that much of what it achieved, it achieved by co-operating with state governments, municipal governments, private business corporations, and banks. But none of these human agencies, whether public or private, is strong enough to take on our problem, while all of them could help Something to solve them. I have been looking for tha Something.

CHAPTER XIV

The course of action I have proposed commonly meets with one, or several, of nine main objections. I believe there are answers to these objections. The objection I hear most often is, in effect, a population theory parading as fact. A little over a century ago an English parson named Thomas Malthus, confronted with the hideous sufferings which the rise of modern machine industry was inflicting on the working class, offered an explanation for the hunger of the poor which has consoled countless well-fed persons ever since. In effect the Reverend Doctor Malthus explained that the poor were hungry because they had so many babies. In effect the neo-Malthusians say now that there is no use helping the Indians or the Chinese increase food production, since they will immediately have even more babies, and you will be back where you started. Therefore, we should refuse to help them until they at least start practicing birth control. One emerges from reading the neo-Malthusian literature with an ominous sense of a limitless horde of unborn babies, limitlessly hungry, and clamoring for a place at our own table. The horrible thing is that most of them are colored. It makes us white people blanch even whiter, as Macbeth blanched at the sight of Ban-quo's descendants. In the loins of the teeming millions alive today we somehow descry teeming billions of hungry, sick, colored, clamorous babies eager to inherit the earth. Why should we go to all the trouble of helping these good folk set up a Development Authority if they insist on multiplying human mouths and human stomachs faster than we can sow rice?

This frightening nightmare was clothed in scientific terms by William Vogt in his best seller *The Road to Survival,* which made thousands shiver. Vogt's book won an honorable place in the apocalyptic literature of the cold war, along with statements pre-dicting that atomic scientists would blow up the earth, or ex-hortations to the U.S. Air Force to set up a space ship between here and the moon from which to dominate the Russians and so bring peace on earth. The Rube Goldberg quality of this litera-ture, all too reminiscent of the fantasies of the Nazi master race, has created by way of antidote a parallel literature. For example, De Castro's *Geography of Hunger* ought to be read by everybody who read Vogt—except for those who just plain like ghost stories and are bored by sunlight. I personally find De Castro a good deal more convincing than Vogt. Where Vogt sees a declining food supply and a multiplying population, De Castro produces some troubling evidence to show that overpopulation is not so much the cause of hunger as its effect. Quite aside from this startling theory, which reviewers seized on and challenged, his book is full of exciting data that makes Vogt's thesis hard to defend.

But scientists' books aside, I am humanly wary of people who tell me there is no use gardening since, if Japanese beetles keep on increasing at their present rate, horticulture is doomed any-how; or that, since the sun is slowly dying, we are more or less through and can spare ourselves the fatigue of a struggle. I am prepared to believe that earth and heaven shall pass away; but it seems to me that to abandon our plans for the coming months or even years on that account is to confuse our human function with the divine function. I detect a growing tendency during these years of low morale to refuse to improve any corner of the universe unless we get advance assurance that the entire universe will be thereby saved. If we Americans were as hungry as the Indians are, we would, I suspect, be glad the Indian Government is busy bringing millions of acres of new land into production and multiplying the yield of millions more, even if they may be destroyed in a few years by megalomaniacs hurling hydrogen bombs from space ships. But I suppose our nightmares suit our American needs. Nobody likes a tale of hideous hardship more than a comfortable, well-fed listener. And it is notorious how courageously men bear the sufferings of others.

I can see a kind of short-range convenience in explaining to the hungry billion that it would do no good to help them raise more food, since the unborn hungry trillion would merely eat it up like locusts. But I think that, though maybe less convenient, it would be much more fun to help them raise the food. On second thought, since large-scale famine can be confidently expected to produce both revolution and war, and since revolutions and wars seem to spread these days, it would even be more convenient to help.

There is strong evidence that, with all our study of population curves, our powers of prediction are still low. This is one of the reasons we had better not try to plan the twenty-first century in too great detail. It is one of the reasons we are apparently not competent to run the universe, either from Washington, Moscow, or a space ship 1,075 miles from the earth's fair surface. We do know that the poorest countries seem to produce the most children. Both Vogt's and De Castro's tables eloquently show that much. We do know, from our own census figures, that the poorer states in the Union produce more children than the richer ones. And most people have discovered by looking around them that the poorest families in any given community seem to produce the most children. Many reasons have been advanced to explain why the poor multiply so greatly, some of them plausible, some less so. The theories advanced to date are a bit awkward to check on, because so few men and women seem to marry in laboratories and have children there under the strict control of scientific observers. Rats have been more obliging; experiments show that malnutrition does seem to increase their fertility. And outside the laboratory, farmers have observed that overfed cattle become less fertile.

As De Castro points out, hunger has been man's most constant practical problem throughout recorded human history; it is overwhelmingly his most urgent problem today; and on the whole, wellfed people do not enjoy discussing it. There has been a kind of taboo on it, like the taboo on sex that Sigmund Freud broke. And it is particularly relevant to this book that hunger causes far more human deaths than war, so there seems little chance that we Americans can persuade our neighbors that law and order are more important than bread. It is true that some of the hunger was caused in part by war. There is no proof whatever that law and order alone can stop hunger.

I have found a handful of Americans who think there are too many Asians now and are willing to have a few millions of them starve, or who are willing to help Asians produce more food provided they promise to have fewer little Asians. But, in general, I find that Americans are horrified by famine anywhere, that they would like to help but don't know how, and that they would rather leave to the Asians the problem of how many children to have.

They are also practical enough to be horrified that hundreds of millions of people should be too sick to do an honest day's work. The mouths and stomachs of these people still crave food, but their hands and arms are not strong enough to grow it. This is a situation which even our "realists" may find it tough to defend. The World Health Organization estimates there are 300,000,000 people suffering from malaria. That is something like one person out of every eight on this planet. They are still consuming, but they cannot produce their share. If they were animals, any intelligent farmer would either get them well enough to work or shoot them. But part of our postwar nightmare is to think about their hungry mouths, and forget about their hands and arms. Yet these people could join the world labor force tomorrow if only we got the malaria out of them. The World Health Organization could have come precious close to getting it out if we had ever given it real money to work with. Considering what has been done to eliminate yellow fever, there is no scientific reason for tolerating malaria any longer.

The drain on the world's productivity from tuberculosis is enormous, and we know a lot about curing tuberculosis that we did not know a few short years ago. One thing we know particularly: the areas of heavy infection are the areas of malnutrition. The great cause of tuberculosis would appear to be hunger—generally "hidden hunger," which results from dietary deficiency, rather than the more obvious kind that results from the total absence of things a man can chew.

The truth of the matter is that in this our first decade of the Era of Hiroshima we still need that good five-cent psychiatrist somebody jokingly prescribed. Vogt's *Road to Survival* became a best seller. Will De Castro's *Geography of Hunger?* I doubt it. Will Brittain's *Let There Be Bread?* I doubt it. Why? Why do we picture India as so overpopulated that soon there will be standing room only? There are many more people per square mile in Britain and Belgium than there are in India. But nobody has asked me tremulously how we can persuade the Belgians to use birth control. It is those Asians that keep teeming. It is true that the British and the Belgians have traditionally been able to make

207

Asians and Africans help support them. On the other hand, no less an authority than Lord Boyd Orr, the first head of the U.N. Food and Agriculture Organization, believes that even Great Britain could produce its own food; that there would be no roast beef but that there would be no malnutrition either. A cloud of witnesses from among the world's leading food experts are convinced that we the people of this earth can feed ourselves, and can feed many more than we now are. But it is the pessimists we are listening to. Why?

The fact is that we have been passing through an extraordinary scientific revolution, and especially an agricultural revolution. Indeed this revolution is the primary cause of the two revolutions this book has been discussing: the economic revolution for equal opportunity, and the political revolution for a common government that can rescue us all from the anarchy of our present system of sovereign nation states. We have scarcely begun to exploit the food resources of the planet we inhabit. But we prefer to shiver. Why?

But, says the neo-Malthusian, you admit that the world's population is increasing rapidly. Is it not a mathematical certainty that if it keeps on increasing, there will literally not be enough dry land left to sit down on? Nothing could be more certain—if. But the practical problem we face is not to find sitting room for our remote descendants, but table room for our descendants' ancestors, namely for our own generation. Why do we prefer to think about our descendants' problem rather than our own? And why in just this way? For we have not only discovered miraculous new food resources, we also have continued to use agricultural practices that are appallingly wasteful, which will not help our descendants very much. If we were thinking about posterity rationally, we would be better stewards of their future inheritance. No, we have curious psychological reasons for thinking about them apocalyptically, almost nihilistically. Why? Might we not cure

208

this psychosis by getting busy on the work at hand, instead of direfully predicting that, in the long run, nothing will come of it anyhow? It is De Castro's great virtue that he relentlessly indicates what the work at hand really is.

The experts do not agree on the curve that population will follow. All we know definitely is that some places now contain relatively few inhabitants and are apparently "overpopulated," and some places contain a great many inhabitants and are not. The evidence is strong that De Castro talks sense when he says famines are man-made, just as a surprising proportion of the earth's deserts is man-made. I suggest that the basic cause of our paralysis and despair may be a simple one. We are at the moment headed for major catastrophe, that is, if we keep on going in the direction we are going. We are moving toward more hunger, more revolution, more war, and conceivably toward world-wide chaos of a sort the human race has not yet endured. Because, through a failure of imagination and of mature political leadership, we Americans have not found anything else to go toward, we find it psychologically comforting to blame fate and not ourselves. It is a very ancient trick: the fault is in our stars. We have not even enough imagination to think of a novel excuse. The Gadarene swine were doomed to leap from a cliff because an evil spirit that had been exorcized from a human being had taken refuge in the swine. But we are human and not swine. We could exorcize ourselves, or put ourselves in a position to be exorcized by God, if we would do the work at hand.

Several decades ago Sir Gilbert Murray coined the phrase "failure of nerve" to name a curious despair and fatigue that have repeatedly paralyzed earlier civilizations once they had matured. The facts at our disposal strongly suggest that our great obstacle to rebuilding the world community is failure of nerve rather than failure of the good earth's resources. It is a failure of nerve that toys with suicide, but does not shrink unduly from the thought of

209

unprecedented devastation by war, and that would instinctively prefer to prevent the birth of a human being rather than devise means to feed him when born. After all, what good would it do him to be born? Or, if it should prove a boon to him, then will it necessarily prove one to his descendants?

It does not follow from anything I have said that there is no population problem. It does follow that there are some other problems that look to most of the human race considerably more urgent and considerably more interesting. Like a square meal, for instance. And at this moment of history, the Russians have in effect challenged us to think about that, not just about birth control or space ships. I am convinced that the overwhelming bulk of Americans would have happily accepted that challenge long ago if our leaders had not focused our attention exclusively on Russia's other challenge, the challenge of rival military power. I am further convinced that despite our leaders American attention is beginning to focus on both challenges and to see both in perspective.

Meanwhile, to those of my countrymen who are troubled by the problem of overpopulation, I earnestly recommend those contemporary writers who have accepted the more interesting challenge of the two. Their writings make you want to pick up that second gauntlet that we watched Russia throw down, the gauntlet of when-do-we-eat. And for that second challenge we ought to be grateful to the Communists. If we are not, hundreds of millions of other men and women are, hundreds of millions who are no more Communists than we are.

The second objection I most often hear to accepting the two world revolutions and guiding them to a successful conclusion is quite different from the first. The first says: "What's the use, since even if we do what you propose the tide of babies will wash away our work?" The second says: "Tide of babies or no tide of babies, we can't do what you propose. Where's the money coming from?"

A more sophisticated version of the second objection says: "Even if you find the money, where's the steel coming from? Or the copper? Or the other raw materials that we are now forced to stock-pile in case of war with Russia?"

Let's take the simpler question, money, first. I am not a very old man, but I can remember the New Economic Era, when the national debt was only $16,185,000,000 and when we were merrily heading for the worst economic disaster in our history. Then, while we dug ourselves out of the debris, the national debt started up. In the digging process we greatly increased our productive powers. But some of my best friends told me that if the debt ever reached forty billions we might as well call it quits. We would be through. If I had been prophet enough to tell them that we would shortly spend a quarter of a trillion dollars on a war, that the war would greatly stimulate our national economy, and that a few years after the massacre had ceased our national income would have risen from $87,355,000,000 in 1929 to $216,831,000,000 in 1949, I would have been locked up, or forced to read a textbook in economics. Even with an inflated dollar, that is a hefty rise.

The economic question I most frequently heard during the years our income climbed was: Where is the money coming from? I heard it less during the war, because victory on the battlefield we accept as a necessity and we are prepared to use anything for money if we have to. But, unlike most people in the world, we have not yet accepted victory over hunger as a necessity. Therefore, when Senator McMahon proposed ten billions a year for five years as America's share alone in financing the war on misery, he conditioned the proposed grant on a corresponding drop in the arms race we had already embarked on. When some of us argued that the proposal should have been made without the condition, that by starting the war on hunger we would so shift the international scenery that the race in armaments could be sensibly discussed again, there came ringing back the triumphant, familiar question: Where's the money coming from? Were we not already straining every sinew to keep up with Russian rearmament? That was in February 1950. Four months later we entered Korea, where we proceeded in the first eighteen to spend over seven billion dollars—besides suffering 102,000 casualties.[32] Where did that money come from? There must have been some sinews we had forgotten to strain when Senator McMahon was making his proposal.

By 1951 we were spending some twenty-five billions a year on achieving a situation of strength from which to negotiate. The situation of strength that we are achieving is a situation in which hundreds of millions of people who now hunger have started asking themselves whether there is any hope of eating until the world has gone Communist. The situation we are not achieving is one in which those millions would see another way of obtaining enough to eat, and one in which America would be participating. At a time when those millions were despairing, we were spending those twenty-five billions a year to contain Russia, and to keep her from helping Communists outside of Russia to help those millions to get food—a description of Communist activity that we do not accept but that, unfortunately, millions of other people do. At a time when those millions had hope, anything like Russian military pressure would be playing with dynamite for the Kremlin. There is no evidence to date that the Russians would be so stupid as to intervene among peoples who had been filled with hope by an aggressive, internationally directed war on hunger. Long before everybody had enough to eat, everybody would know that he, or anyhow his children, were headed toward food. And our entire military problem would have shifted.

The irrationality of our program is, I submit, at the bottom of our current failure even to achieve real arms production. For a free nation to do a job of the size of our arms program, the foreign policy of which it is only a part must be intelligible. And our foreign policy, since we started to go it alone, has never been intelligible. That lack of intelligibility is what let loose the flood of clichés and slogans of which I complained at the beginning of this book. That lack of intelligibility is what has made so many Americans feel that the only sensible thing you could do about rearmament was to get the biggest slice of war contracts you could grab. It is what led the Administration gravely to move "the target" forward from 1952 to 1954, only a few months after the President had repeatedly asserted that this was the gravest hour of peril in our country's history. And this with no adequate explanation of why the Russians had suddenly ceased to be on the verge of assaulting the free world and had decided to give the free world an extra two years to prepare its defenses. It is presumably what led the *United States News* to announce in the issue of March 21, 1952: "Armament is to become more and more a pump-priming project. . . . Armament, as the planners see it, can become the great stabilizer of the future." An armament program that has no intelligible foreign policy to serve turns to serving something else, in this case to stabilizing the national economy. But this involves losing the world to Communism—for want of somewhere else to go for a solution. It involves taxing ourselves half to death. And it ends up, if experience in such matters is a guide, in the war nobody wants—not even those who are making the most money out of war contracts.

The real answer to the objection "Where is the money coming from?" is that it can come from the same place it comes from now. And it would come fast enough if we ever grasped that tractors plus tanks could achieve the sort of world everybody wants a lot faster than tanks alone; also that an international program of tractors, even with national states building tanks too, will get us where we want to get much faster than a program directed from Washington that requires chiefly tanks with only enough tractors to prevent our allies from revolting against our leadership. A real international program of tractors, in which all men and women had a chance to participate as equals, could command financial resources that our present program cannot command. Other peoples would see some reason for helping in a program that made sense to them as well as to Washington. And if every people contributed, in proportion to its national income, it would be less emphatically a dollar operation. Every people should contribute to the Authority in its own currency; and if a people really is unable to contribute even in its own currency, its share should go on the cuff until it can. In a pinch, there is no reason why it should not give the Authority a lien on some of its natural resources. That is quite different from giving a foreign government a lien and quite different from giving a private business corporation a lien. There are few countries indeed who could contribute neither in their own money nor "in kind."

"Where is the money coming from?" would not be asked if ever we saw the necessity of doing this job and if at the same time we saw what a vast source of credit human hope and human labor are when they are mobilized on a world scale. A much realer objection than lack of money is the frightful lack of raw materials like steel, copper, manganese, and the other basic raw materials which the arms race has been devouring. But it may be instructive to note, first that we have begun to suspect over-stock-piling on our own part; second, that when the arms race threatened to smash the economies of our allies, we coolly shifted "the target" by two years; third, that we have never had enough faith in our own program of guns to lay off the butter, although we have pressed some of our allies to do it; and fourth, that we have never reached any agreement on how many guns are necessary anyhow. I have suggested that we cannot make real military estimates simply because we have not previously made real political estimates, while the military problem is merely an aspect of the political problem. The proposal of this book is to shift the political problem, and thereby incidentally to shift the military one. The proposal stands or falls on whether you think our present political and military programs are successful. I have offered evidence that they are not. To date, we have assumed that we could make them successful by increasing our military effort, and by spending enough on bilateral economic aid to solve the political problem—which, from where we sit, is to get other non-Communist nations to increase their military effort too. We are making our political program subserve our military program, and the peoples we seek as allies are equally anxious to make their military program subserve their political program. Our way of ordering our purposes really would make sense if we really were at war with Russia or determined to be at war shortly or resigned to being at war or convinced that Russia wanted war. But our allies believe the Russian challenge is overwhelmingly political and economic and only very secondarily military. That is why my friend, the little old lady from Aberdeen, was confused by New York's bomb shelters in 1952. "Why," she said, "I thought you Americans were so much more efficient and hustling than we British. Yet we got our bomb-shelter signs down years ago and you haven't got yours down seven years after the war."

This book has tried to suggest that, although in a real war we might have to subordinate our foreign policy to a military policy, we have completely failed to win friends abroad by doing so now. In the circumstances, we have two alternatives. On the one hand, we can listen to their views and work out a joint operation that makes sense to them, and I have suggested what such a joint operation might look like. Or, as General MacArthur has suggested, we might inform them they are wrong, and go it alone. In that case, general mobilization is strongly indicated, since the war is likely to be long, and since we are likely to fight it very much alone indeed. Our friends do not think the real problem is the kind you can shoot your way through. If we are sure it is, we had better start shooting pretty soon and we had better not count on them to join the fun. But if we want them to go along, we had better understand why they believe the problem is not what we think it is. And we had better do this, regardless of who is right; for the job, on this second hypothesis, would be to find a common program that was really common.

If we found a common program, the program would dictate how much steel was needed for non-military purposes. I said earlier, and would like to repeat here, that there is no way on earth of knowing whether there is enough steel to cover a joint program of both world reconstruction and reasonable military defense until we get at least an outline of the program. Without such a program, our military needs remain quite indefinite, if not quite infinite. It is therefore premature to say that no program can be even discussed, since there is no steel. And I have already tried to explain how difficult it would be to slow down rearmament drastically so there would be steel just in case we found a program that required steel, for, in the meantime, we might get the gravest sort of dislocation in American industry. A more sensible procedure would be to go on arming while trying, with other peoples, to devise an international program that would redefine our military needs. Obviously, we need not accept the program in advance, before it is formulated. And just as obviously, nothing is going to define our military needs clearly except a clearer political purpose than our present foreign policy presents.

We have already seen how unfair it is to Congress to dump in their laps the reconstruction of the world economy as one item in one nation's military budget. We have already seen how unfair it is to American business to dump in its lap that same problem when it clearly cannot solve it. Well, we have been just as unfair to our military heads in asking them how many tanks, planes, and guns we need, without having a clear enough foreign policy in the political field to give them a sufficient notion of what places we might have to defend and who might be willing to help us defend them. This vacuum has led our military heads to have a go at defining our foreign policy, a tendency which Hanson Baldwin of the New York *Times* quite properly deplores.[33]

These are the reasons why the question "Where would the steel come from?" has precious little meaning if you try to answer it before answering some other questions first. If we were to keep on going in the direction we were going just before we revised our "target"—and I note that we had too much sense to keep on— where would anything come from? If we insist on putting all available steel, except what the consumer insists on using for more sensible purposes and what our allies must have or else wreck their economies, into preparing for a showdown to stop Communism, then obviously there is not one scrap of steel left to make the world a less inviting place for Communists to manipulate.

CHAPTER XV

There is a third objection often made. "Even," people ask, "if you got a foreign policy that would make available some of the money and some of the steel that now go into getting tough and going it alone, what makes you think the Russians would co-operate?" Sometimes the objector holds that the Russians would refuse to do anything and would refuse to allow their satellites to do anything. Sometimes he holds that maybe rather than see our program a success, with America playing a leading role in it, they would start the third world war. Sometimes he holds that the Russians would pretend to co-operate in order to sabotage the program or anyhow to spread Communism. These objections are obviously based on very different assumptions about Russia, but they all stem from one underlying characteristic of our thinking about Russia. That thinking may justify the Russians in calling us reactionary. For, in the quite literal sense of the word, our thinking about Russia really has been reactionary: instead of acting, we have become content merely to react. As Nathaniel Peffer pointed out some years ago, this means our government is Russian-dominated, since one of the deepest forms

219

of domination is never to do anything until you first find out what
the person or group you most fear and hate is going to do. Then
you do the opposite. If we had a positive program today, instead
of this weak and negative one, we would act, not merely react.
If this job is worth doing, it does not matter primarily what
Russia does or what Russia thinks.

Let us examine the three possibilities the objectors entertain.
Russia might indeed refuse to enter an international program in
which Americans would play a leading if not dominant role;
although, interestingly enough, the United Nations program of
technical assistance is one of the few U.N. programs both countries did vote for. It is idle to generalize from Russia's refusal to
enter the Marshall Plan. From the Russian point of view the important thing about the Marshall Plan was that it was essentially
an American program rather than an international program, and
what this book proposes is a program that would be essentially
international rather than American. One of the effects of the
Marshall Plan has been to speed American penetration of Europe's economy. Another effect, connected with that one, has been
to make Europe's economy more dependent on ours. These effects
were not the purposes of Secretary Marshall's original proposal,
but they are nonetheless among its effects. And a third effect has
been that it gave America the power to restrain West Europeans
from trade relations which they have consistently wanted with the
complementary economy of Eastern Europe. The Russians were
not therefore talking complete nonsense when they warned Europe that the Marshall Plan would make Europe even more an
economic colony of ours than she already was. And we are indeed talking nonsense if we cannot see why an international
agency would produce these effects in far smaller degree than a
bilateral program completely dependent on appropriations by the
U.S. Congress. I say in smaller degree, because our productive
might is now so disproportionate as compared with that of other

peoples that there is probably no joint international effort we could participate in that would not be somewhat Americanized. I can offer to seesaw with a child; and I can sit so far forward that I get my thighs pinched. But I weigh a hundred and seventy-five pounds, not counting my good intentions, and I shall always risk leaving him up in the air. Nevertheless, a more equitable seesaw could be built than the Marshall Plan if we really pooled common resources and were really under international management. It simply does not follow from Russia's rejection of the Marshall Plan that she would refuse to enter an International Development Authority. Nor does it follow that, if she did reject it, she would have an easy time explaining her objections to the non-American, non-Russian world.

The second and different assumption, that Russia would fight before she would see world misery diminished or see her chances of exploiting that misery torn from her, is not cogent. Mahatma Gandhi once advised us always to assume in our opponents the highest motives capable of explaining their actions. This was not goody-goody advice but hard political sense. We like to assume that Russia's real motives in spreading Communism are, not to lessen world misery, but to build an empire. Maybe so. Russia likes to assume that our motives in extending Marshall Plan aid to Europe were not to help Europe but to build an economic empire. However, vast numbers of people in the world, while deploring the means Communists use, accept their statement of purpose at face value. Perhaps these people are dupes. There might nevertheless be some sense in our accepting their view as a working assumption when it comes, not to our own military defenses, but to our complicated relations with them and theirs with Russia. There might be point in assuming, in our conversations with them, that Russia's announced purposes are her true purposes.

If, just when we all saw constructive action and hope of food just ahead, Russia should attack, what would happen to her moral position in the world and what would happen to ours? Our neighbors would then be for us, instead of being skeptical of our policies. What risks would we have run by accepting their version of Russia's intentions that we do not already run? Actually, there is no evidence that Russia would do anything so suicidal as to try to break up by force a joint international war on misery. Where now the world doubts if we really care about whether they eat, the same world would then know that Russia did not care. To make such suppositions is to allow our fear of Russia to paralyze our common sense.

But what of the third assumption: "What makes you think the Russians would co-operate?" What of the assumption that the Russians would be right in there pitching—and sabotaging, not co-operating; or at least propagandizing? Does this really hold water? Would Russia gain anything by sabotaging what the world most wanted done? Or would the effect of such sabotage be to consolidate feeling everywhere against Communism, as a false front for Russian imperialism? If the Russians are silly enough to do these things which we out of our abject fear expect them to do, then they are too stupid to be very dangerous either in war or in peace. Russia is indeed sabotaging what Americans think the world most wants: stability, law, and order. But she is not sabotaging what most of the world wants: food and a *new* order—or, anyhow, the world does not agree that she is doing so. As for propagandizing, I take it that, on the one hand, any technician working for an Authority who used his job as a soapbox either for Communism, free enterprise, or any other system, would be fired—not for preferring one of them to the others, but for soapboxing when he had more important duties to perform. If, on the other hand, while obeying the law of the land he happened to be working in, he stated his reasons for preferring Communism to capitalism or capitalism to Communism, are we as Americans seriously opposed to his doing so? I would prefer to follow Israel on this problem and say: "Keep on wrangling, so long as you help us all Go Up." At present, we are all lying in wait for our neighbors, our swords drawn. I would prefer that we were all arguing, while following every man his own plow in the same great common field.

The Pentagon, it is true, ought not to follow Gandhi's advice. They ought to assume the lowest motives in the Russians, and in the British, and in the French. Their business is not to persuade the peoples of the world to take common reasonable action but to defend this country by force when and where reason fails. Meanwhile they are, quite properly, in Thomas Hobbes's words, "in the state and posture of Gladiators; having their weapons pointing, and their eyes fixed on one another; that is, their Forts, Garrisons, and Guns upon . . . their neighbors; which is a posture of War." That is the Pentagon's job; but it is not the job of the State Department or even of Senators. And it is not the job of the rest of us. We can well afford to accept Gandhi's advice and take the Russians at their word: that Communism is a war on hunger and misery. We could then ask Russia—in less belligerent tones, I trust, than we normally employ these days—whether it does not necessarily follow that she must help in the common effort. Better still, some of our and her neighbors could ask her. The world would be listening for her reply (that is the shrewd aspect of Gandhi's advice). She would either come in; or she might answer that economic development is already going forward in the Communist world, and that she has more faith in its being done well on a Marxist basis than on ours. If that is the answer, the rest of us should accept it: the struggle between Communist and non-Communist methods would then be really joined, with the whole world as jury. Many of us Americans believe we could win that contest, and many of us believe that the

223

victory would prove a lot more than would be proved by killing Communists with atomic bombs.

Once we had seized that second gauntlet Russia has thrown at our feet, we could become less psychotic about the first one: the challenge of military might, a challenge which every powerful sovereign state of necessity presents, by its very existence, to every other sovereign state in its neighborhood. Because of the first challenge, we could not dismantle the Pentagon; but, because we had accepted the second challenge, the challenge of world-wide hunger and misery, we would sharply diminish the quota of violence loose in the world today—loose in the colonial areas, loose between East and West, loose between economic groups in the same country, and loose in our own hearts. We could spend less time getting tough and more time getting technical. And the basic problem is technical.

Fourth objection: "Shouldn't we clean house at home first, before trying to straighten up the world?" Is it in our power? My impression is that it is not. I gladly admit that we would be acting more intelligently abroad if we were not caught at home by the worst wave of political reaction in a lifetime. But what chance would that reaction have at home if it were not daily fueled by our quarrel with Russia? The melancholy absurdities of our political witch hunt would, in my judgment, have been long ago hooted off the scene by a disgusted public but for the public's bewilderment about the relations between Liberal and Conservative, the relations between Socialist doctrine and Communist doctrine, the relations between Communist parties everywhere and the Russian Government, and the excessively bad relations between the Russian Government and our own government. The public's bewilderment on these complex issues has furnished a field day for those who are anxious to reverse the four popular verdicts that kept Franklin D. Roosevelt in the White House. It has even furnished a field day for common informers. It has raised the ancient joy of slandering one's neighbors to new heights. But if every Communist state in the world were militarily negligible, do you think this game could be kept going? No doubt the moral state of our domestic politics has poisoned our foreign policy; but it is, I think, our fundamental misunderstandings of our foreign problem that, far more than any other factor, have paralyzed the millions of Americans who would have gotten out their brooms long ago.

The bitter fact is that it is no longer easy to find a purely domestic problem to clean up. Some honest critics urge that we clean up the horrible slums in American cities before we start in on the slums of Asia. I believe their advice is based on two false premises. First, I would expect a cold-war government here to show far more interest in building additional bomb shelters for World War III than in launching housing developments. After all, housing developments have always sounded a little socialistic. The cold war, on the other hand, provides a gigantic PWA project in which all good patriots can rejoice without endangering free enterprise. The second false premise I think I detect in the advice that we clean up our own slums before *we* clean up India is a premise we dealt with many pages back: that if this job is done, it will be done by America, with our exclusive know-how and the only sound money left, our fifty-cent dollars. I have tried throughout this book to say why I cannot conceive of its being done from Washington. I have tried to say that the world wants to do it jointly, with joint funds, under joint management, and with joint know-how. It is not a question of telling our American slum-dwellers to sweat it out until we Americans have provided foreign slum-dwellers with nice houses. It is a question of whether we are willing to join the rest of the human race in a world-wide assault on slum-dwelling. It is not a question of leaving the Missouri River to rage through further catastrophes like the 1951 and 1952 floods while we harness the Indus River and thereby

225

furnish the Indians with cheap power instead of death by drowning. But I sometimes suspect the Missouri will go on drowning people until the people in the Missouri Valley demand the protection that the Indians in the Indus Valley will already be enjoying. Cold-war governments simply do not produce MVA's.

The fact is that we live now on such a dirty street that it is easier to help sponsor a block party to clean it up than it is to keep on sweeping the trash back into the street as fast as it blows in or gets tracked in. The world community has frighteningly contracted; and we don't live in our own little house any more. We live in a rather large apartment house. We do occupy the nicest apartment in it; but the roof leaks, and the outer walls are crumbling, and the floor joists are giving away. Shall we join the neighbors in repairing our now common dwelling; or shall we let her go—and join the neighbors anyhow in a common collapse? We have already noted, that at meeting after meeting of the U.N. Economic and Social Council, they have invited us to join them in doing a job that is to the common interest of us all; and we have already noted that, just as regularly, we tell them to sit down.

I have also had American Socialists ask me whether I thought a capitalist America would ever help? To them, cleaning house meant cleaning out capitalism at home. I can only repeat that I think it would be easier to lead the American people into a third war than into setting up a Socialist government at home. I may, of course, be quite wrong in my estimate. But the problem is a pretty pressing one, and on the hypothesis of my Socialist friends we need to go Socialist awfully fast! I happen to believe that, although very few Americans would vote Socialist, the vast majority would be willing to join the rest of the world in the common task that confronts us—a world, incidentally, which is in large part "socialistic" from the average American's point of view. My impression is that socialism in other countries alarms very

226

few Americans, including those who do not think we need it here. I do find a few Americans, but too few to matter much, who would gladly go to war, or, more accurately, would send other Americans to war, to protect and spread the system of exclusively capitalist production.

Fifth objection. This is an interesting one. Since I get around quite a bit, I not only have friends that are Socialists; I even have friends that are anthropologists. Some of my anthropologist friends suspect I do not know what a ticklish cultural job it would be to shift a primitive agricultural folk into industry, or even mechanized agriculture. They are certainly right; it would be. Anybody familiar with the history of European expansion during the past four and a half centuries knows the profound cultural chaos that changes of this sort bring. Even the American schoolboy knows what happened to the red man when we presented him with rifle and firewater and changed his hunting grounds into plowed land. Or the position of the half-breed, or the squaw-man.

I would be even more worried than I am about these dangers, but for two facts. In the first place, the twentieth century has already refused to leave the "native" in his Eden. And in the second, I think it is high time we recognized that we are all, relatively, "primitive" peoples living in "underdeveloped" countries.

Take Eden first. It was a grave moral responsibility that Europe took when she sent her merchants, flanked by soldiers and missionaries, into every continent on earth. But she sent them. As a result, although the missionaries were not too successful in terms of mass results, and although the soldiers' successes are in our century beginning to boomerang, the job the merchant did has stuck pretty well: only a very modest fraction of the human race remains unaffected by the machine or its products. Again the oilcan and the corrugated roof can serve us as symbols: everywhere the native is accepting the machine, or its products or as many of them as he can get hold of. His handicrafts are decaying. He becomes less and less the isolated self-subsistent peasant with intricate and charming folkways, and more and more the small-town workman who sees movies later than New Yorkers see them. Nobody who traveled in foreign countries before the first war and after the second can fail to be overwhelmed by the speed of this transformation. The "primitive" peoples are less and less outside our history; they are more and more in our economic system; they are merely those who profit least from it, those who buy its leftover junk, and those who do the heavy work of getting out its raw materials. In every continent they are sick of this role of Black Sambo; they are determined to industrialize, and to make the system work for them instead of letting it work them. Folkways and beliefs that made life tolerable for them before Western culture struck them are dead or dying or doomed shortly to start dying. But then, so are ours. One reason for our present deep-rooted hysteria is that we feel our own folkways threatened.

Eric Sevareid, the radio broadcaster, trying to fly the Hump between Burma and China during World War II, reported a significant story. Sevareid's party was rescued from the land of the head-hunters, and his friend St. Clair McKelway hiked into the hills, pack on back, to meet him. The pack was getting pretty heavy when McKelway met a native Naga boy. He resorted to pidgin English: "You coolie. Carry pack. Carry pack. Five mile. Give much rupee—much rupee." He jingled the coins in his pocket. "You help um white man, no?" "No," replied the Naga boy gravely. "I am on my way to the Christian high school and I'm just as fatigued as you are."[34]

All over the world our colored neighbors are just as fatigued as we are and do not wish to carry pack for white man, even for much rupee. All over the world they are learning our folkways. They were touchy about being "backward areas," so we started calling them "underdeveloped countries"; and now they are touchy about that. The story goes that when anthropologists at Columbia University decided to investigate the folkways of Peru, the Peruvians proposed that they come up and investigate the folkways of Columbia. The truth is that we could all stand investigating. Anthropology suggests to most laymen the study of primitive man and his customs; but the word anthropology originally meant the science of man, not just primitive man. A good Development Authority would have to deal with man, including Homo Americanus, not just primitive man. Especially since, in so many ways, primitive man has stopped being primitive. Especially since one of the chief common denominators of men everywhere is that they are all so extraordinarily primitive. Could anything be more lamentably primitive, given the problems we all now face, than the cold war? There is a deep psychological kinship between going it alone in the matter of economic aid, between staking the salvation of the world economy on Congressional grants or even on American business, and assuming that what makes it tough for us Americans to save our neighbors is that they are so confoundedly primitive. But one should be careful, in going slumming, to be polite to the peculiar people who live in slums.

The fear, therefore, of some anthropologists or would-be anthropologists that you cannot change these people anyhow, that East is East and West is West, founders on the same basic and brutal fact: these people are already changing and with fearsome rapidity. So are we. Once again, the trick is not to learn how to coexist with them but how to coact. Whatever else our world is doing culturally, it is at least spinning on its axis. We must learn to roll with the spin. We will not learn by quoting Rudyard Kipling. Somebody has humorously suggested that America is an "overdeveloped country." I suppose all our countries are overdeveloped in some respects and underdeveloped in others. A good Authority should have the planet for its sphere of operation, not a category of countries. For, while it would most likely be more active in a country without machines than in a country with them, for the same reason that the TVA was undertaken in the Tennessee Valley rather than in an industrialized, high-income valley, a good Development Authority ought to be free to operate wherever it can get the quickest leverage on the world economy as a whole. The piecemeal is what it must avoid.

Sixth objection: Even if we admit that the effort we must make must be genuinely international and on a much bigger scale, is not an International Development Authority with billions at its disposal too monstrous in size even for this assignment and too unwieldy to work? The problem differs so greatly in the various parts of the earth. This suggests regional authorities rather than an international one. Moreover, it is not just money that is scarce, or looks scarce; and it is not just steel or other raw materials. It is technically competent men. The U.N. Technical Assistance Administration, operating on a pittance, has genuine difficulties getting competent men to send to the field. And would not the hybrid monster which this book proposes have even more?

No International Development Authority that had more than a dim notion of its function would exist long before it had set up regional offices. But since the problem it must solve has been caused by the growth of a world economy, it is just not practicable to solve it well by separate and unco-ordinated attacks on small pieces of it. A lot of power and a lot of responsibility would have to be devolved, but the co-ordination would have to remain.

As to the scarcity of technicians, they will remain scarce just so long as our efforts remain timid and half-hearted and largely subservient to military policy. It is one thing to ask a soils chemist to leave his present job and his home in order to support an American foreign policy about which he might properly enter‑ tain the gravest doubts. Soils chemists do not like "politics" any-

230

how, at least not in my limited experience. The territorial claims and territorial ambitions that interest them are not the political ones made by jealous states but the ecological ones made by jealous plant species. But even where the present effort is not nationalistic, as for example under the United Nations, is it really reasonable to ask a soils chemist who is working, say, for the U.S. Department of Agriculture, to leave that work and take a job helping the Indonesians when the organizaton he will be working for has a life expectancy that depends on the whimsical appropriations of some sixty governments? It is not a question of selfishness. I am assuming our soils chemist is unselfish, that he wants to be useful to his neighbors, including his non-American neighbors. I shall even assume that he has just declined the offer of a fancy salary from a business firm because he would rather work for the public. But salary aside, he knows the Department of Agriculture is highly likely to outlive him, and this suggests that he will be able to "finish" his professional work. Though not anxious to go to Indonesia, though preferring to live in his own country, as most men do, he might sign up with U.N. Technical Assistance if there were any future in it. Finally, the United Nations—although it has enough money to send some thousand technicians abroad and although it has performed some miracles by doing just that and only that—has not enough money to make the capital investments which technicians frequently find would be necessary if their advice is to count. It is amazing that they are able to get as many good men as they do get.

An International Development Authority would open to a whole group of professions a vast field of permanent employment, employment that would be a greater challenge to those professions than any challenge they have yet received. Professions are callings, and this would be the loudest call yet heard, a call to rescue mankind from a major historical crisis by using our heads instead of our fists. Its service would be an international service to which a man could rightly be proud to belong, a service dedicated to the common good of mankind. There are thousands of agronomists and engineers and doctors and teachers all over the world who would count themselves lucky to be born in an era when such a call was sounded.

We would be making a tremendous mistake to suppose that only famous technical men could be useful in an enterprise of this scope. Neither Washington's Point Four nor the world's United Nations is in a position today to use the services of countless young men and women just coming out of school or college or working at the bench who would be needed quite as much once we took this problem seriously and provided the means for its solution. In thousands of villages all over the world there is a need for work centers where simple industrial techniques can be carried on and taught to others. If the world ever undertakes a joint war on human misery, its army will need noncoms and privates too, not just generals. These youngsters are straining at the leash to do something constructive. Thousands of them believe that this sort of thing is the only real alternative to a third world war, which they, not we older folk, will have to fight, a war in which they simply do not believe. In Europe and America there are thousands of them who see no future ahead. In America, they do not share the fear of "welfare" that some of their elders feel. They think welfare is a good thing. Many of them are veterans who, despite the senseless horror of war, got a thrill out of the teamwork that war sometimes demands. But they want teamwork with a rational purpose. Those that now lack relevant training could be given it, as the "young pioneers" are given it in Europe and America before they are sent out to Israel. Thousands of them would gladly serve an apprenticeship in such a service at pittance pay. I have seen some of them in action: I am not guessing.

Nothing we have done to date has been large enough or enough on the point to justify us in supposing that an International Development Authority could not find adequate personnel to do the job. But if it could not, if it had to grow more slowly than it ought ideally to grow, the international atmosphere would be a good deal less murky once men everywhere knew it was growing. You can hold a lonely ridge at awful sacrifice if you know reserve troops are on the way. What makes the world desperate today is not so much its massive misery as the knowledge that no serious attack on that misery is under way. What makes their misery intolerable is being asked to "settle down." Once the Development Authority started growing, it would open an exciting career for youngsters still in high school, youngsters who would start preparing for that career fast enough. Above all, we should not at this point suffer one of our psychological relapses and suppose that whatever hopes we entertain must be based on Americans. I have been talking partly of young Americans but mostly of the rising generation throughout the world.

CHAPTER XVI

Seventh objection. Even if all this excited talk about youth were true, the whole proposal is idealistic and not realistic, because it is not politically possible.

Our generation of Americans pride themselves on being realistic. They do not shy at sending the human voice for thousands of miles through space, or at setting up a television set and watching a horse race hundreds of miles away, or at adapting the electronic eye to industrial uses, or even at building a space ship; but they often refuse to believe that their next-door neighbors have good sense and are willing to use it to think about the common good of the community they live in. We are too often convinced that most people are dopes—though how we can simultaneously believe they are capable of self-government is not clear. Where our ancestors appealed to the reason of man, we scheme to break down his sales resistance. Almost before we have conceived a plan of action, we hire public relations counsel to describe the baby to the neighbors. Nine months is not too long in our judgment to plan the promotional campaign for his christening gifts. We tend, or our hired advisers tend, to believe that people hate babies and that there will be some high-powered explaining to do when this one arrives and some high-powered salesmanship before people will agree not to cut his little throat for him. We not only hire public relations experts; to a considerable extent we pride ourselves on being pretty good at salesmanship ourselves. And one good swift look around convinces us that, although we ourselves can see the necessity for solving a problem, nobody else on our street can. Each person on the street is convinced of the same thing. You might sell people a third world war if you were clever about it and had some good rousing patriotic songs written. You might sell them inflation, since they are too dumb to know that rising income won't help if prices rise too. But you simply could not sell an alternative to war like this joint drive on human want.

Want to know what people will ask? Why should we Americans go all out to help India, when Nehru won't promise to fight on our side when the showdown comes? Haven't we got to get this Communist business settled before we start scattering big money around the earth? Why should we tax ourselves to industrialize countries that are now agricultural, when all this does is close out markets for our factory products and perhaps cause unemployment here in America? Moreover, why should we industrialize these countries to a point where they may use up their own raw materials, when we depend on their raw materials for our own industry? America is now sititing on top of the world, and although she shows signs of dizziness up there, she is nevertheless sitting precisely where all these other nations would be sitting if they could, and her best game is to sit tight. In this world there is always a top and a bottom, and at the top there is very little room. Given America's position, why, above all, should she enter any international organization she cannot control? What would be the point of putting in the lion's share of the money and then turning the whole kitty over to an international directorate that might, and probably would, outvote us?

236

These arguments are, I think, not too difficult to answer; but we are dealing now with the character who says he knows the answers already, and can understand them, but that "the American people" don't and couldn't. It is pretty certain, I think, that the American people will not understand the answers to those questions in the context of our present foreign policy. But in the context of a reasonable policy I have no fear of their not understanding. To say that they cannot grasp a first-rate idea is to overlook the fact that, since World War II, they have been offered precious few to grasp. They have been hurled into a difficult and complex situation and told stories that a sophisticated child would not swallow. They have been drugged with clichés and bludgeoned into insensibility with slogans. Scarcely a man in public life, except Justice Douglas, has made a consistent effort to acquaint them with the problem in simple, direct, basic terms.

It is obviously not in our power to starve and blackmail Nehru's constituents into promising to shoot Russians if we do, although it is well within our power to make them hate us for refusing to co-operate with the rest of mankind in this hour of man's great need. I have tried to show how unlikely it is that we will settle this "Communist business" while permitting conditions that make most of the human community a happy hunting ground for Communists. Indeed, I would challenge our moral right to settle it while permitting those conditions. And whether I challenge it or not, Asia and Africa do, which is more to the point. I do not believe that trying to maintain a monopoly on the machines which other men need will prove realistic in the long run, and I observe that as a matter of historic fact the great markets for American goods have not been the poor and unindustrialized countries but the rich and highly industrialized. I do not believe that using our power to keep the unindustrialized areas in a weak position economically, so we can force them to let us use their raw materials, will pay off in the long run. Nations do not like to be pushed around by other nations. We cannot defend before world opinion the West's monopolistic position, a part of which we now share with Europe and a part of which we have taken over from Europe.

Many, many years ago an observant analyst wrote: "The world may politically, as well as geographically, be divided into four parts, each having a distinct set of interests. Unhappily for the other three, Europe, by her arms and by her negotiations, by force and by fraud, has, in different degrees, extended her domin-ion over them all. Africa, Asia, and America have successively felt her domination. The superiority she has long maintained has tempted her to plume herself as the Mistress of the World, and to consider the rest of mankind as created for her benefit." Did Karl Marx write those words? No, Alexander Hamilton wrote them, in *The Federalist,* Number 11. He added: "It belongs to us to vindicate the honor of the human race, and to teach that assuming brother, moderation." Hamilton's generation had been taught some practical lessons in the monopoly and exploitation of colonies that would have enabled them to understand, better than we their descendants have been understanding, the com-plaints of Asia and Africa today. If we refuse to do our share in making it possible for the countries without the machines to get them, we shall play "assuming brother"; and history may have to teach us "moderation."

We Americans now make up about one sixteenth of the human race. We own the richest part of a continent that is one of the naturally richest on earth, whether from the point of view of soil to till or ores to mine or seas to fish. Whether in annual income, in machines to produce goods, or in capital available for foreign in-vestment, we stand supreme. Either we can sit on this "top of the world" and try to prevent others from enjoying it (whereas in the nineteenth century we invited them to come on in and develop it with us), or we can help other men get machines like ours (they are not asking for ours) and help them develop their own lands. If we try to monopolize the machine, I predict that we shall fail and that we shall earn only hatred by the attempt. That does not appeal to me as either sensible or "realistic."

If we join with others to develop our common patrimony, the earth, we shall gain neighbors we can depend on and who depend on us. Undoubtedly, if we set up in common an institution that will enable us to do this, we may be outvoted. In the context of a sane and rational foreign policy, we would gladly take that risk. In the context of the immature policy we have been following, our government has quite naturally refused to take it.

For example. The Food and Agriculture Organization of the United Nations (FAO) was organized at Hot Springs, Virginia, in 1943, while World War II was still in progress. Immediately after the war, UNRRA was able to meet, at least in part, the ghastly problem of widespread famine. By May 1946, a special meeting on urgent food problems, held in Washington, directed the Secretary-General of FAO to submit to member governments proposals for coping with the world's grave food problem on a long-term basis.

The Secretary-General was then Sir John Boyd Orr, now Lord Boyd Orr. In September 1946, at a meeting in Copenhagen, he surveyed world food needs and presented his proposal for a World Food Board, which would be endowed with sufficient authority and sufficient funds to stabilize the world market in food. He pointed out that several countries were already doing this for the domestic market, but that the world market was still subject to violent fluctuations. He explained the business operations involved in stabilizing the market. He pointed out why a prosperous and productive agricultural population would not only attack the problem of world hunger but the problem of full industrial output and employment, one of the declared objectives of the U.N. Charter. His proposals met with an enthusiastic recep-

239

tion, even from the U.S. delegate. A preparatory commission was set up, and it met the following month in Washington.

Russia, for reasons unknown, failed to send a representative. It is true she was not a member of FAO, but she had been invited to participate. Great Britain stalled; and the signs indicate that, as a shortage country, she was hoping for a slump in world food prices. But the U.S. delegate did more than stall. His speech is a fascinating study in rhetoric. After making it clear that the United States shared with the rest of the world a determination to solve the problem, the speech shifts key with some difficulty and comes out flatly for leaving the world market to the ordinary processes of trade and to mere consultation between governments. It is an interesting fact that, when the U.S. delegate had joined those of other governments in acclaiming Boyd Orr's proposals the previous month in Copenhagen, Boyd Orr had explicitly rejected this method, which had never met the problem. He had stated the case for a public institution if food to eat, fiber for clothing, and timber for building shelter were to reach those who needed them, at prices that would be fair both to producer and consumer.

But nearly a year earlier, the United States had begun its long and unsuccessful campaign for an International Trade Organization to foster free enterprise in the world market, and was pinning her hopes of prosperity chiefly on that. Our delegate now made this clear. The proposals so enthusiastically hailed at Copenhagen by all, including America, immediately came to grief. The American delegate offered four arguments against the proposed World Food Board. In the context of the Copenhagen meeting, the first three are unconvincing. The fourth is conclusive: "Governments are unlikely to place the large funds needed for financing such a plan in the hands of an international agency over whose operations and price policy they would have little direct control." In short, we do not propose to be outvoted. So long as this remains American policy, and it has to date, there is little likelihood of an International Development Authority with either enough authority or enough funds to work. The power of the richest country to withhold its contribution has hitherto proved to be a most effective veto. Meanwhile we are witnessing a day-to-day demonstration that national institutions cannot handle some of the most urgent problems of a new world community, of which each nation is a mere fraction.

I wonder whether the American people would find it as hard to understand this point as our amateur public relations experts suppose. How many Americans would favor trying to starve the Indians into a military alliance with us? How many would think our present foreign policy was really likely to "settle this Communist business"? How many would want to prevent—or, more accurately, try to prevent—our neighbors without industry from industrializing? How many would want to keep a whip hand over other peoples' raw materials? How many would want to add our country to the long list of countries who at various times throughout recorded history have tried sitting on top of the world? How many could with a straight face agree with the Administration that America must not enter an international agency unless she can keep control of it? As a matter of fact, if we do agree, why does the Administration bother to protest in public that it does not expect to control the international agencies we enter? On the contrary, if the American public knew the extent to which our government had made it impossible to carry out the economic purposes of the United Nations, they would be outraged. The American public has been told over and over again by our government that co-operation with the United Nations is the very basis of our foreign policy and that, had it not been for Russia's refusal to co-operate, the United Nations would now be a strong institution. Americans by and large accept that story as fact.

But is it? On June 12, 1952, the New York *Times* quoted some remarks which Porter McKeever, who should know, made to the U.N. Correspondents' Association. He had served for six years as chief public information officer of the U.S. Delegation to the United Nations. He spoke of our policy as reducing the United Nations to "the size of a pebble." Incidentally, he claimed that the "withering away" of the U.N. would be a tremendous victory for Russia in the cold war. Mr. McKeever urged that U.S. economic aid be brought under the U.N. He pointed out how we had by-passed the U.N. in our 1947 aid to Greece and Turkey, in organizing the Marshall Plan bilaterally, and in setting up the North Atlantic Treaty Organization. Nobody who bothers to read what he then said will be likely to question Mr. McKeever's political morals. He is now executive director of the Chicago Council on Foreign Relations.

An eighth objection to this book's argument is raised by many persons who are neither Socialists nor Communists, although Socialists and Communists would perhaps consider it the most cogent objection of all. These objectors say that since many countries are governed by a small group of powerful feudal landlords and since these landlords not only possess a monopoly of land but often possess considerable hoardings in gold and jewels too, there is nothing we can do while that group retains power. If our government would stop bolstering their power, would not that be about all the help we can give their victims? We cannot make their revolution for them. We in the West overthrew European feudalism, and the feudalism of the Old South in our own country, by violence. Let the wretched people in starving feudal countries overthrow theirs. Then we can help them. Although, once they get land and liquid capital out of the landlords' hands and into their own, they will need a lot less help anyhow.

This objection is not without force. There is certainly not much use helping a "country," if what the word "country" means is the people in it who are already doing nicely. On the other hand, waiting for a revolution to clean out the landlords by force presents a grave problem. The world we live in is now so highly polarized between capitalism and Communism, between civil rights and totalitarianism, and above all between an American military power bloc and a Russian military power bloc that a revolution anywhere always runs the risk of degenerating into the third world war. For every revolution runs the risk of falling into Communist hands, or at least of being accused of being in Communist hands, and Americans quite naturally do not want new governments set up that are Communist and hence almost certainly pro-Russian. It is these facts that make us unhappy about Southeast Asia now.

This book has tried to suggest an alternative revolution, which we Americans could properly back, where revolution there must be, so people can eat. It has suggested that if as many nations as possible pooled their capital and used it to make sure that people everywhere could eat, the monopoly that now keeps them hungry would soon be broken. It has suggested that the capital accumulation in our generation's hands enables us to open up economic opportunity to all men, precisely as free Western lands once opened it to Americans and as the TVA opened it again. We have already noted that this is not an attractive plan for monopolists. But if the weight of America were now thrown against the monopolists everywhere without being thrown in favor of Communist dictatorship, then the hungry billion would have a genuine alternative to Communism and not a mere invitation to help us—on an empty stomach—to destroy the Communists so that we will take their hunger under consideration for possible action some day. It is this limp invitation of ours that is failing them and consequently failing us.

It would be difficult if not impossible for Washington to foster this second, bloodless revolution, even if the American taxpayer would allow the American Congress to put up the sums needed or even if the American investor would allow the American corporation to put up as much as it could of the sums needed. We have already learned from the Marshall Plan just how difficult it is to condition our aid on social reforms. That way, you start off with two strikes against you, as Yankee imperialists interfering with other people's affairs. This has been our problem in South Italy and Sicily. But an international agency could make demands we cannot make. And an international agency that was at the same time a public corporation doing business would not have to put strings on gifts to foreign governments, for the excellent reason that it would not be making gifts to governments. It would be doing business, and doing it in such fashion as to open up opportunity for that stratum of the population that needed it the most. If a local feudal government refused to let it in the country, or refused to let it function properly after it had been let in, the international public corporation would be in a powerful moral position compared with any feudal government now in existence. It is at this point in events that the world would fully grasp just how profoundly revolutionary this new chosen instrument could be. For it is a revolution that neither America nor Russia could oppose without disastrous loss of face. And postwar power politics has taught us at least this: the one thing that Oriental and Occidental governments firmly agree on is that you must not lose face if you can possibly avoid it.

It is precisely this bloodless revolution that Point Four has aimed at—clumsily, falteringly, timidly, but nevertheless aimed. We have enough experience of it now to see when and how it unintentionally condemned itself to clumsiness and faltering and timidity. Point Four condemned itself by assuming that one country, ours, could successfully do what can be done only if many countries band together for the job, as the Charter of the United Nations agreed by implication that its members would do. Point Four condemned itself by trying to do through sovereign governments, struggling to survive in the midst of international anarchy, what can be done only by an international agency as independent as possible of all governments and as dependent as possible on the men and women who dwell together on this steadily shrinking planet. It condemned itself still further by trying to pass the buck to private business corporations, asking them to solve a problem which they were not chartered to solve.

This brings us to the ninth objection and to the last one I shall discuss, not because others may not occur to you, but because these are the most interesting of those actually raised by persons who have written me, or those raised by members of audiences I have talked to in many parts of our country. More than once I have been asked: "Why are you so anxious to avoid the moral issue? You yourself recognize that these appeals to our national self-interest do not actually bring us nearer to solving the problem. Why not invite people to act because it is the right thing to do?" In terms of inciting action, these persons may very well be correct. Where great actions are to be undertaken, it is wise to appeal to the greatness that is in every man, not to the pettiness or selfishness that are also in every man. That is how armies acquire morale in the hour of battle.

I happen to think that we Americans have, among our more easily forgiven weaknesses, a weakness that nevertheless irritates others and blinds us. That weakness is, to use my Australian friend's expression, a readiness to do good against people, which I suppose a psychologist might well term a psychological aggression. At this moment in history, frustrated as we have not previously been during my lifetime, we feel a need for aggression. Some of us quite simply urge that we "drop the bomb and get it over with"—although what the word "it" might conceivably refer to is a fascinating question. But the saner, steadier type of American would rather lead a "war on human misery" than the usual kind. It would still be a war, which would help—one

245

of those moral substitutes for war which a modern philosopher urged us to find. It is interesting that the philosopher should have been an American.

To appeal now to the very moral fervor of the American people, to appeal for a crusade, seems to me to play into the hands of what I shall call the New Isolationism—unless the crusaders made it awfully clear that their goal was to plan *with* our neighbors, not for them. The Old Isolationism led us to tell our neighbors to stew in their own juice, to tell them we would not play the game with them. The New Isolationism, parading as internationalism, leads us to tell them that we most certainly will play the game, that we will even write the rules everybody is to play by, and that we unanimously accept our own nomination of ourselves for the job of umpire. This new isolationism has been in my judgment our outstanding handicap since World War II. It cuts us off more completely than the old one did from the rest of mankind because it cuts us off without our realizing we are cut off, and without our realizing that other people do realize it. General MacArthur has appealed constantly and directly to this new isolationism: we ought to do our duty whether our neighbors agree with us or not. It was in precisely this spirit that we spent 1951 trying to force our neighbors to arm against a Russian invasion they did not believe would happen, and to jeopardize their economies and risk the rise of domestic Communism, which they did believe might easily happen. We did not shift our target from 1952 to 1954 until it had become quite plain that we could not persuade them. A good many Americans concluded that our neighbors refused to see the danger we saw because they were too scared to see straight. A good many Americans refused to consider an alternative possibility: that their view of the nature of the Communist problem was nearer reality than ours.

Too much of the "moral leadership of the world" which we have blushingly accepted has had no more to do with true leadership

246

than Adolf Hitler's "leadership principle" had: it has been plain wrist-twisting. "Is it true," I asked a distinguished American newspaper correspondent, "that we use undue economic pressure on other members of the United Nations to make them vote our way?" The correspondent, whose name for obvious reasons I cannot give, has devoted himself exclusively to the U.N. for many years. I continued: "I've been saying publicly that we twist wrists too much. Do we twist wrists?" To which he replied quietly and deliberately: "You can hear the bones crunch." The American subsidies on which many governments have depended during the economic chaos of the postwar period have given us means for exerting pressure on their foreign policies and on how they vote in the United Nations. The covert allusions in the American press to this pressure have never adequately reflected what has been known to dozens of American newspapermen in the corridors of the United Nations. Anyhow, in view of what the subsidies were doing to our tax load, the average American was not too critical of a little wrist-twisting, where he would not have tolerated our using a military threat. Once we started going it alone in the field of economic aid, and almost completely by-passing the U.N., the wrist-twisting followed as the night the day.

To abandon our isolationism in fact, and not merely to shift it to a subtler form, we would have to abandon bilateral aid and instead, pool not only our resources of money and skills, but our control of our share of them. It is that step that many Americans are not ready to take. They still nurture the illusion that the world economy can be rebuilt by us Americans as one aspect of our defense against Russia. It is true that they simply do not know the facts of our Great Refusal. But in justice to our government, it is also true that a good deal of public education must occur before some Americans will give up the whip hand which our greater wealth gives us over our non-Communist neighbors.

I believe that many more Americans, if they knew the facts,

would not want a whip hand. They would prefer co-operation. If, because of our greater power, our neighbors then wanted us to furnish leadership of the other kind, real leadership, I think these Americans would favor our accepting it. But I think they would want to show more than we have been lately showing what the American Declaration of Independence calls "a decent respect to the opinions of mankind." We were small and weak when we declared our independence, but the words we used then have brought us more real moral leadership than our actions since World War II have brought us. We "lead" governments now; we led peoples then. I like to remember that in making our declaration we showed respect for the opinions of our neighbors. The cynic may reply that we feigned respect because we needed, and finally got, their armed intervention on our side. There is no proof that our motive was that simple. And if the cynic adds that we are now so strong we need not respect our neighbors' opinions, I believe he is fooling himself. If he is correct, I suggest that we spend less money on rounding up military allies and go it alone, militarily as well as economically.

But it would make more sense still to give up an isolationism that has so little relation to the facts of the twentieth century. If we really gave up our isolationism, we should have to surrender our bilateralism, we should have to stop exploiting the misery of the human race as a means of saving it from Russia, we should have to stop treating the men and women of other non-Communist lands like irresponsible children and promising them candy if they behave. We would have to face up to our obligations to the United Nations and use it for what it was built for. We should have to stand ready to put in our fair share of money and skill and scarce raw materials in a common international agency. We should have to help give it a degree of autonomy and a big enough capitalization to protect it as far as possible from power politics. We should have to stop playing Santa Claus or Mr. Big

248

or Lady Bountiful and put our share on the barrelhead. Because we are so much the richest, our share would be the biggest—but we should have to abandon the notion that the biggest contributor has the right to dictate policy. We should have to scrap our policy of not joining international bodies we cannot control. At that point the great myth of isolationism on a crowded planet would be dead, and not merely our vain efforts at physical isolation. For our spiritual isolation would end too, a spiritual isolation that now cuts us off from other men more thoroughly than any ocean can.

Or would it end? Not wholly, one suspects. So long as our material power remains disproportionate, our influence will be disproportionate too. The taxpayers of New York State are accustomed to paying heavier federal taxes than the taxpayers of Mississippi, and do not expect for that reason to hold a veto power over things that less wealthy states vote in Congress to do; but it would be naïve to assume that New York's wealth gives it no influence in the affairs of the nation that Mississippi does not also wield. I must revert to my metaphor of the seesaw: no matter how fair we play, we risk having our bulk and weight sky our neighbors. No matter how wisely we might refrain from the whip-hand career that has already led one empire after another to its downfall, the twentieth century would be in important respects an American century, as in America it is a New York century and not a Mississippi century. But if we shift from whip hand to common consent, it will be an American century with a great difference, and one that in my judgment most Americans would infinitely prefer.

"Point Four" or "technical assistance," no matter by what political tag it goes, is likely to be with us for some time, unless a third world war blots it out and a great many other things with it. We will do wisely not to let politicians bamboozle us into supposing that, by shifting some of our resources from armaments to economic aid, we will meet the problem history has posed for us. It depends on whether the funds for economic aid are turned over to a genuine international agency or whether we go on using them as a weapon, a weapon to strengthen our tanks and guns and planes. Until that happens, we shall go on building an American empire that most Americans do not want, and one that the world most certainly does not want. And this empire could be "sold" so easily to most of us by a judicious mixture of economic aid, strategically placed by Washington, and an appeal to the moral forces of America. It is for this reason that I have my doubts about appealing to those "forces." I would rather appeal to common sense and to the kind of imagination that men must bring to problems of this sort. It would be better if we did not launch a great moral crusade to save the free world against its better judgment. It would be better if we stopped trying to buy friends. It would be better if we sat down with our neighbors and listened attentively to their proposals. It would be better if we pooled our wisdom and experience on how best to pool our money, our tools, our materials, and our skills. It would be better if we made the two great revolutions together, like thoughtful, grown-up people instead of like frightened or angry children.

Then the two revolutions could bring us, one to an expanding world economy that would feed and clothe and house and heal the hungry, ill, desperate peoples of the earth; the other, to evolving the political institutions that would guarantee law and order in a community where all men would then have a stake in order. This is quite different from using American economic aid to strengthen our military program while urging our neighbors to use the United Nations to impose law and order on a world where most men dread the status quo. This second program is to threaten them in the name of freedom with the unspeakable agony through which the Korean people have already been required to pass. We Americans blame the Russians for that agony; and the Russians blame us for it. It might make more sense to the rest of the world if we all recognized it as the inevitable result of not doing what we all should have done: attack our common problem at its root.

More than one hundred and fifty thousand men, women, and children died at Hiroshima and at Nagasaki; but at least, by their death, they taught the rest of us how grotesque an instrument war has now become, how grisly a court of last resort when nations disagree. Millions of Koreans, men, women, and children, have now died; but at least, by their death, they can teach us that the two revolutions are one, and that no institutions yet exist through which they can proceed in an orderly manner; that neither Washington nor Moscow provides those institutions; that they must be invented; and that we should remember that our neighbors have been begging us to sit down with them and invent. and that we have steadily declined.

CHAPTER XVII

I suggest that the sixty-four-dollar question for candidates for national office during recent elections was neither "Do you favor Point Four?" nor yet "Are you opposed to sin?" The sixty-four-dollar question was "Why does our government refuse to permit the establishment of an International Development Authority under the auspices of the United Nations?" And perhaps a second question: "What do you propose to do about it, if you are elected?" Incidentally, the first of the two questions could be usefully asked of newspaper editors as well—and the second question, too, without the political condition. Grants from Washington to potential allies and suppliers of raw materials are vastly different from agreements with our neighbors to contribute our share, and no more, to an international authority capable of lifting this problem out of cold-war politics. Until we Americans can get our eyes off the price tag long enough to see that difference, the appeal to force remains the goal. It is not a goal imposed on us by evil conspirators in Washington, or even in Moscow. It is a goal imposed on us by history, as a penalty for not recognizing our real goal. It will make very little difference to history whether we reach the wrong goal under Democratic auspices or Republican.

These are some of the reasons I have not appealed to the "moral principles" of the American people, but to their common sense. The appeal to moral principles, alas, is being made right and left, for I write these lines in an election year. I hasten to add that I am not opposed to morals! It is surely better to be brave than to be cowardly; better to be self-controlled than greedy; better to be fair than to play dirty. But the virtues of courage, temperance, and justice do not exhaust the list. It is also better to use common sense than to be foolish. Our present foreign policy in respect to the two revolutions spreading through the world is foolish. Can bravery or self-control or fair play flourish long where folly reigns?

I have noted with great interest that wherever the issue has been made clear, Americans have quickly responded. The half-hearted support they have given our foreign policy would have been even more half-hearted if a political opposition had put the facts before them. There has been one fact missing that is the most relevant of all to the destiny of our nation and the destiny of mankind. Washington has repeatedly assured us that our foreign policy is based on working through the United Nations. But on the front where the majority of mankind most want and need co-operation, Washington has steadfastly refused it. That makes Washington's statement of American foreign policy a dangerous piece of hypocrisy. This refusal is the basic fact that most American voters have not possessed.

Orators today are fond of saying that we live in a time of crisis, and this is one of the safest observations they can make since few members of any audience are likely to dispute it. But although the innocent intention of these orators is most often only desire to add to the collection of clichés by which we now guide our lives, they happen to be saying more than they intend. In the contemporary sense the word crisis too often means merely a horrible mess. It might be worth while for us to recall what it meant in ancient Greek before it was borrowed by our English tongue. It meant, among other things, a decision in a law court trial, or the turning point in a disease. This suggests that a crisis is not so much a mess as it is a mess which has reached a point where a decision can be fruitfully made. The mess this book attempts to deal with has now reached that point. So one of our favorite clichés turns out to be more than a cliché—provided, of course, we understand it.

I judge from my recent experience, and particularly from my mail, that once the average American understands, he asks an anguished question: "What can *I* do about it?" For we Americans like to act; and, in the present paralyzed state of our political life, we cannot think of a way to act. I have tried to state in this book why, if we are to act well, we must invent appropriate international institutions through which we and people who are not American can solve our common problems. And why we must persuade our government in Washington to use these institutions, and also to use those—like the United Nations and its specialized agencies—which have already been invented. But this persuasion will take time, since our government has succeeded by its bilateral policy on economic aid in badly confusing the issues. Are we not already spending billions on aid? Etc. Etc.

There are two things we can do in the interval; and fortunately an increasing number of Americans are aggressively doing them. The first is popular political education. In this field the Communists, who offer a rival solution to the problem, have an apparent edge on us Americans. Their governments spend large sums acquainting their peoples both with the problem and with the party-line solution. But I believe this educational campaign suffers from the same weakness as some of our own efforts at "public relations" by government departments. It spends too much time giving the answers and too little time asking good questions. It looks efficient, but is it?

In our own country, we have a grand chance to locate the questions. A rapidly increasing number of voluntary agencies in our country are beginning to locate them. Some of these agencies are organizations primarily interested in foreign affairs, whatever the problem. Some are primarily interested in church missions, which are beginning to see that preaching the Gospel may, in the present circumstances, call for not only medical missionaries but also farm technicians or even engineers. Some are chiefly concerned with the evils of racism, whether in Hitler's Germany, or South Africa, or our own America, and are reviving the American doctrine of the equality of man, regardless of frontiers. Some are labor organizations slowly awakening to the fact that a fair wage is a pressing human problem that knows no frontiers. Some are co-operatives becoming aware of the suddenly heightened relevance of the co-operative to countries where the economy is tribal in nature. These organizations are educating their membership in the problems this book deals with. Point Four conferences are multiplying throughout our country; and the old, easy, patronizing, bilateral solutions arouse increasing opposition.

For example, at a national conference in April 1952, I heard Mr. Eric Johnston, chairman of the President's Advisory Board on International Economic Development, explaining to faint applause why the American government should pick some underdeveloped country as a pilot plant, make suitable treaty arrangements, and invite American business to enter and do its stuff. A cultivated young Negro from Kenya was sitting next to me. "My God," he whispered in horror, "I hope they don't pick Kenya!" But I would judge from the reaction of the audience, representing organizations that totaled millions of Americans living in most of the states of the Union, that Kenya may not be in serious danger. I would judge that to many, if not most, of that audience,

Mr. Johnston's voice came from a great distance, from somewhere in the nineteenth century, and spoke of a world that no longer exists. Mr. Averell Harriman and the Secretary of State also spoke, and the President had expected to speak, until the steel negotiations broke down and he spoke over the radio to the American people instead. Mr. Acheson read his speech for him. There was grumbling that there should be so much talk about Washington, about Point Four, about the cold war, and that so few speakers presented the case for international action by the United Nations. This grumbling is increasing throughout the country. We are discovering the dimensions of the problem.

But Americans are quite characteristically doing something more than reading up on the subject. They are taking direct action. Frustrated by Washington's obsession with the cold war and by its blindness to the two world revolutions now in full progress, many Americans are organizing to act independently of government. A group in Oklahoma has launched a drive for several million dollars to send teams of experts to Indian villages. CARE, which started out as an agency to send food packages to designated or undesignated individuals in postwar Europe, now makes it possible for any American to send a kit of agricultural tools, or a garden plow, to some man in a country where such tools are powerful weapons against hunger. An American industrialist, recognizing that American mass production in the ordinary sense does not touch the needs of most primitive economies, asked himself whether it had some oblique role to play and came up with an interesting answer. He is preparing to apply mass production to the manufacture of small, standardized, "packaged" factories in basic industries, like sawmills or cement factories, and to apply the same mass methods to the instruction of green personnel to run such factories. Other businessmen are organizing lending institutions for self-liquidating enterprises with decent rates of interest. Remembering how Dunkirk, New York, "adopted" Dunkerque, France, after World War II, and remembering that such adoptions became frequent in our country, American towns are again buzzing with plans to adopt towns or villages in under-developed areas. Most exciting of all, a group of young men and women in college communities have organized an "International Development Placement Association" to help place young Americans, either on a salary or on pittance pay or as volunteers, in remote countries where people are asking for them. There are dozens of other private initiatives being launched.

What is interesting about these efforts is not their scale of operation, which is surely too small to accomplish what cries out for accomplishment. What is interesting is that Americans are not only forming study groups to discover the problem their government has failed to locate and to demand a solution of it, but also are acting, and directly. It is not, I think, pure chance that it was an American who coined the phrase: "Learn by doing." If anything will teach most Americans quickly why the world does not want this problem handled bilaterally from Washington as one aspect of one country's foreign policy, and why the world emphatically does want it handled by a genuinely international institution, these efforts to "do something" about the problem should teach them. The men and women who go out on these assignments will be writing home, and their letters will be published, and their home communities will be involved both in terms of money and in terms of human understanding. A peace army is forming. It is true that it is forming only on a guerrilla basis, but guerrillas learn lots of things about the terrain that most great armies can afford to ignore. And the guerrillas in this first engagement will be invaluable to the gigantic effort our people and all peoples will need to make.

Moreover, the effect on opinion and in the end on government could be tremendous. Let us recall that in that terrible June of 1951, when the lives of millions of famine-stricken Indians hung on India's getting access to the wheat that rotted in our granaries, Congress did not act until Americans scattered all over the country had begun to buy wheat on their own and send it to the Indian Embassy in Washington. Private citizens thereby accomplished two things. They did the little they could, while Congress stalled, and they gave the Indian people eloquent evidence that Washington's inaction did not represent the feelings of the American people.

If I have not given the names and addresses of the organizations throughout America which are rising to the challenge our government failed to rise to, it is because most of them are just beginning. But unless I badly miss my guess, nothing can stop them now. And, though all their combined resources can hardly hope to make much of a dent on the problem, the spiritual significance of their effort can scarcely be exaggerated. In many parts of the world, Point Four has become a bad joke. For four weary years our government has made capital of its Bold New Program, and for four weary years so little has been done in Asia, in Africa, or in Latin America. When substantial offers have been made, the offers have been usually so tied in with military assistance against Russia that the hungry billions have felt not like neighbors, but like cannon fodder. It is understandable that they should have come to suspect that the only interest the ordinary American feels in them is the perennial interest of man in cannon fodder. That American volunteers should come to them now as neighbors, that they should detour their cold-war government to join the war on human misery, will be of immense significance to the Asian or African or South American. In proportion to the problem the material help might be meager; but the gift without the giver is bare, and givers willing to share the life of an Indian village or a village in Uganda would be making, without words, a stronger declaration of common humanity than any government can make.

To the degree that such efforts would be American, they would

259

still be bilateral. But half the sting of bilateralism would be gone once the operation was on a man-to-man, instead of a government-to-government, basis. The Americans who joined in this action would, in the nature of the case, go forth primarily as neighbors, not as representatives of their own government's policies. And they would not be long in the field before they would discover why the bilateral method is the wrong method for handling the world's problem. American opinion would be much more sensitive to their judgment than to the judgment of Congressmen. By getting their hands dirty in the actual work that now needs to be done, they would earn a right to speak that Washington spokesmen for Point Four have not earned, and that ghost writers for office seekers have earned even less. The slogan would slowly yield to reality. It is not too much to predict that sanity would creep back again into our foreign policy itself.

We would then have made connection at last with the two world revolutions. We would have turned away from the frustrations and boredom and fear that the cold war has spread like smog over America, and we would participate in the vibrant hope of the "young" societies that ancient peoples would have set up, young societies rejoicing as we once rejoiced in national independence, busy planning their future economic expansion. This is the kind of thing that once took young men West, not merely—as we like currently to believe—in order to make a better living themselves, but also to help build a community. In the long run, this would lead Americans to insist that we resume building our own community, that we brush aside sour warnings of the dreaded "welfare state," and that we concern ourselves with the general welfare of the American people, now inextricably interwoven with the general welfare of mankind.

We should remember, too, in assessing the value of these spontaneous efforts of the American people, not only that their government has earned wide distrust among the poorer nations of

the earth, but also that the "United Stations" has inevitably met
with increasing distrust. These peoples feel that the United Nations is in large measure Washington's false face; and, although
they have gratefully co-operated with the really heroic work of
its specialized agencies to wipe out famine and disease and help
them make the first halting steps toward getting machines to hew
their wood and draw their water, they can hardly believe for the
moment that Washington and its industrialized allies, clutching
their shrinking colonial empires, will ever help them set up the
International Development Authority they have been clamoring
for. A spontaneous movement from the men and women who live
in America would rekindle their hope of escaping from these years
of parochial power politics into a period of world statesmanship,
from the "realism" that leads straight to world war and ruin for
us all into a common-sense attack on the problems of the whole
world community. In the long run the smog would be lifted from
America. A different kind of smog might even be lifted from
Russia.

But should the cold war continue to paralyze statesmanship
and prevent the establishment of a development authority able to
release the energies of mankind and restore to the United Nations
one of the basic functions originally assigned it, then the many
private initiatives might at least federate themselves and even set
up a development authority of their own that would raise a
standard for the millions of men and women in this and other
lands to rally to. Perhaps, since a real development authority
would by its nature be essentially a revolutionary institution, invented to meet what is essentially a revolutionary situation, this
volunteer institution is the one that the twentieth century is
actually big with and struggling to give birth to. But whether the
volunteer agencies are destined to be catalysts for the United
Nations or to tackle the job themselves, the problem is theirs at
the moment. If they act and act well, no future history can wipe

261

out the significance of the Act. For the Act is what has been missing, all these weary postwar years.

This book may have sounded at times angry and bitter and pessimistic. I admit I have been angry with the American Government for not meeting a high challenge, and angry with myself as one of the voters responsible for that government. I admit I cannot help sharing some of the bitterness felt by millions of my fellow-men in my own country and abroad as futility followed futility, and as opportunity after opportunity slipped through our fingers, and as Washington alternated between hypocritical assurances about Point Four and the United Nations and successful efforts to prevent our neighbors from setting up some device proportioned to the problem that faces us. But I do not admit for a moment to pessimism. When in the summer of 1950 I wrote the pamphlet which I quoted earlier, I did feel pessimistic. What made me pessimistic was not our worsening relations with Russia, which I had assumed during World War II would be bad when the war was over—and which Thomas Hobbes had taught me would almost certainly be very bad indeed. What made me pessimistic was not the nation-wide attack on civil rights and the growing hatred of ideas of any sort. What made me pessimistic was the widening gap between us Americans and the two billion people who are neither American nor Russian. It was the spiritual loneliness we seemed determined to condemn ourselves to. It was the phantasmagoric world we in this country had created out of our own imaginations, a world that resembled so little the real world in which we were dwelling.

But a great deal has happened since the summer of 1950, and I am ashamed now of the pessimism I then felt. There has been a massive shift in public opinion since 1950. Some of us may have felt that the speed of the shift was almost glacial. But that may have been in part precisely because glaciers are large things to shift. Our relations with Russia remain bad, as was to be expected.

But what with our allies dragging their feet, what with the colonial peoples putting Washington on the spot about colonial misrule, what with their patiently maneuvering the development problem from the relative obscurity of the U.N. Economic and Social Council into the General Assembly, and what with the American people's growing skepticism about our efforts to make "those people settle down" and to try to cure a world revolution with increased armaments, there is every reason to be cheerful.

I am most grateful for the widespread discontent among the hungry people of the earth. That human beings should starve is indeed bad news, terrible news. But that human beings should insist that something be done about it is magnificent news.

I am tremendously heartened by the speed with which the technological revolution continues, almost unnoticed in 1950 in the ecstacies of the cold war and the fine indignation of teaching the Russians a lesson, but increasingly noticed now. The summary account of that revolution which Robert Brittain gives in his book, *Let There Be Bread*, is enough to cheer any generation, and enough to make anybody proud to belong to the human race.

I am delighted that Communist propaganda forces the rest of us to remember the hungry billion every time we try to think of something more pleasant. Of course it would be even more thrilling if we remembered them out of love of our neighbors. But it is something to remember them at all, even if only from fear the Communists will stir them to revolt and end by making them their military allies in a power struggle against America. For once we start helping our neighbors on a scale commensurate with their needs, or even start helping them out of our own pockets and with our own energies on a scale commensurate with our individual private means, we shall learn to love them and to accept their friendship in return.

I am grateful for the many Americans who have refused to allow the cold-war fanatics either to flatter their prejudices or to

263

insult their intelligences and have gone on quietly insisting on their own rights of free speech and on the right of men in distant lands to eat. I am grateful for all those Americans who, instead of looking under the bed at night for Communists, or helping to slander their neighbors, have looked into their own hearts to see if evil might be there too and have determined to use their heads on problems that will not yield to guns. I have become slowly convinced that such Americans are far more numerous than either our press or our radio had led me to suspect.

I am proud to number among my friends Americans in distant unblessed lands, Americans who have rolled up their sleeves and worked beside farmers whose language they could barely speak but whose plants and animals apparently understand good American slang. I am proudest of them because they belong to the human race, to which I, too, belong; but, heaven help me, I am a little proud that they sprang from the same American earth that I sprang from, that they belong to the same "colony of mankind" that I belong to, a colony to which all continents have contributed their labor and their love.

I am grateful, in short, that I live in a time of crisis, a time when real decisions can be made because real issues have emerged that the human mind can grasp, and real problems have been located that human will and human reason can solve. I am grateful for, if still I am a little frightened by, the Mighty Neighborhood I live in, a neighborhood which no ancestor of mine ever inhabited. I would rather explore it than take a space ship and explore the moon. I prefer the light in it to moonshine. I am exhilarated by the enormous growth in human wisdom that its many diverse cultures can stimulate.

Far from being pessimistic, I am filled with hope. I have lived through two world wars which have all but destroyed a civilization I hold dear. There is blood on my hands, as there is blood on the hands of every man who has not protested clearly or firmly

enough against the sins of omission and commission, against the
folly and greed that produced those wars, and that laid so many
fine men low. There is indeed blood on my hands, but I am beginning to see a way to wash it off, and I find that many of my
neighbors have seen the same way. It will require me to stretch
my imagination beyond its usual limits, to think more clearly
about complex problems that I would like to leave to others,
perhaps to work harder and to go without. The temptation to get
tough instead is strong. But it is fleeting, because it is based more
on bad habits than on anything I really want out of life, or anything I believe anybody else really wants.

Make no mistake: I see no millennium in the offing. Even if we
keep our wits about us, even if we accept history's orders to share
our neighbors' lot, and even if we act with the most commendable
good will, there will be ample opportunity for impatience, grumbling, and mutual recrimination. We are still the same human
race that fought the two world wars and we are not easy to get
on with. But any man who has ever known the keen joy of working with his friends for a common end need not draw back now.

EPILOGUE 1955

I wrote this book as a member of the human race, of American background and citizenship, caught in the practical problems of the twentieth century and faced with certain political choices—in short, as one who is himself heavily engaged. But I happen to be by profession an historian, and I would like to comment on what I have written, from the more detached point of view of an historian.

By the year 1950 nearly two centuries of science and the machine had concentrated material power first in the hands of Europeans and more recently in the hands of Americans. America was mankind's El Dorado. America was also mankind's biggest capital investment in large-scale economic development. There was not only the money capital that had poured from Europe into the United States during the nineteenth century. There was the even more mammoth investment of human labor. From all over the world came the men and women who developed the American economy. In the seventeenth, eighteenth, and early nineteenth centuries they swarmed in from Europe and from Africa, too. But in the second half of the nineteenth, and up to World War I, they

267

poured in smaller streams from Asia and Latin America as well. The other countries had borne the expense of raising them to manhood and womanhood in most cases, and sometimes of teaching them valuable skills, and America took their labor to build a continental empire. Nobody ever calculated the value of this last investment.

The other continents poured in not only money and skill and muscle for investment. They poured in also the hopes of mankind. Those persons who were doing nicely stayed, naturally, where they were. Those who profited by social injustices often had little motive to sail for El Dorado. But those who were discontented came by the million. They came, either to worship God in their own way, or to escape war and military service, or to live under republican government, or to find land to till or other work to do. Hope for bettering man's lot here below beckoned him Westward. What Americans would call the American Dream was essentially mankind's dream, although to some extent it was realized only on American soil. The human family grubstaked millions of its relatives; and, as a result, Americans were the successful relatives of most of the human family.

Naturally, they were a debtor nation, and remained a debtor until World War I. Dividends from the world's biggest capital investment in large-scale economic development poured back to Europe. But dividends poured back also in private letters, to cousins in Sweden and Sicily and wherever the home folk awaited news. Long before the war debts of World War I or Lend-Lease or World War II, the little remittances, with news for the family, had blazed the trail. And since at least some of man's political hopes were realized too, the United States by its mere existence shook the faith of people everywhere in the thesis that men must be governed despotically because they have neither the will nor the wit to govern themselves. The investment in hope, too, was paying dividends. Washington and Jefferson and Lincoln became symbols not just in America, but wherever men groaned under oppression or suffered humiliation or sought in vain their daily bread.

From at least the 1920s on, the rest of the world began to undergo a process of Americanization. They began to imitate their successful relatives. Coca-Cola in Burgundy, Hollywood films in Athens, Negro jazz everywhere—all were part of the story. But, above all were the assembly line and the economy of mass production, which dictated mass consumption. Undoubtedly, much of this Americanization meant vulgarization, sometimes of the most distressing kind. But the word vulgarization came from the Latin word *vulgus,* and *vulgus* meant crowd, and the assembly line was a device for making things for the human crowd. It inexorably imposed economic democracy, and spread middle-class standards of living to an ever increasing multitude. Since a part of the world's revolution for equality was precisely the world's determination to secure just those standards, the Americanization of the world was not merely a push from America but a pull from the rest of mankind. It represented, if you like, a kind of imperialism; and successful imperialisms are two-way propositions.

Moreover, as the course of empire had taken its course Westward, the two-way nature of imperialism seemed to have increased. The Assyrian Empire had been military, and ferocious to the point of sadism. The Roman Empire, though it had used its legions ruthlessly, had brought law to a Mediterranean world that would not perhaps have submitted so soon had it not craved and needed law so much. The British Empire, though its development contained dark chapters, had certainly displayed a smaller measure of force and won a larger measure of consent than either of these predecessors. Yet now, in 1950, no imperial people in the world was more aware than the British that empire building in the nineteenth-century sense was finished. Whoever built the next empire would have to base it so much on consent, and on consent of such a twentieth-century sort, that the unimaginative would refuse to call it an empire. Regardless of the precise political devices employed, it would have to rest on the consent of the governed: it would have to "represent" their will to a degree that nobody had guessed when the Americans had revolted against empire nearly two centuries before. The shift of name from "British Empire" to "Commonwealth of Nations" was recording the changed conditions for imperialism.

Was this, then, indeed the American Century? Yes and no. Americans had once declared that it was their Manifest Destiny to move West. All signs indicated by 1950 that their Manifest Destiny was to Americanize the planet. Or, if you prefer, it was now the Manifest Destiny of mankind to be Americanized. In the process, if Americans were wise and reasonably modest, they would learn quite as much from the rest of mankind as others would learn from them. Meanwhile, history required the rest of mankind to note that, just as there was no chance of Americanizing them by force but only of assisting them to complete their new process of Americanization, so also they would be committing an anachronism if they reacted to the coming American "empire" as if it were imperialism of the old type. Even so, this reciprocal process could not complete itself without rancor or without mutual recrimination. Moreover, America's position of power, which her own vast economic development had given her, had undoubtedly begun to corrupt her, since power over others normally corrupts. How much she would be corrupted, how much disliked, how much the rest of the world would feel dominated and oppressed, would depend not merely on individual insight and wisdom but primarily on whether the Americans and their neighbors could between them devise the human institutions they needed to bear the load that history had placed on a whole generation of men.

Leadership in the twentieth century still sought the terms, and the institutions, on which and through which it could operate. By 1950, the Americans were saying to their fellow-members in the United Nations: "If America must assume the primary responsibility of keeping the world fit to live in, then help us put down military aggression, whether in Korea or anywhere else." To which their fellow-members in the United Nations replied in effect: "Not until you recognize your full share of responsibility for the economic objectives of the Charter you and we signed—not until then will we enforce with you wholeheartedly that Charter's military objectives. Not until you recognize the general welfare and the sanctity of common consent will we acknowledge the necessity in the resultant community for some sort of police force." To which the Americans answered: "We have no money for really attending to the general welfare, because our money all goes to paying the police, which you refuse to support except by token contributions." That was the point at which the discussion had by 1950 bogged down. Both America and the world felt frustrated.

It was clear that the deadlock might prove final, that a generation might accept the vast irrationality of a third world war rather than a rational solution of their joint problems. But the approach of 1955, when the Tenth General Assembly of the United Nations would be obligated by the U.N. Charter to explore the desirability of revising that Charter, strongly suggested that both the Americans and their neighbors had a 1955 rendezvous with Manifest Destiny. As 1955 and Charter revision approached, more and more Americans were learning that their efforts to solve the world's problems singlehandedly were foredoomed to failure. They were learning that the task of economic development could be carried on better under U.N. auspices than under U.S. auspices, though even the United Nations would probably continue to look like the "United Stations." In the 1950s the first task for Americans, as indeed it is always the first task of any true leader, was to listen. The immediate and dangerous alternative was to go on talking to themselves. Their second task was to work out with their neighbors amendments to the U.N. Charter, so the United Nations could do through appropriate public corporations the work it had been set up to do.

NOTES

Note 1—In his address to the joint meeting of Congress on April 19, 1951.

Note 2—As reported by the Associated Press in the New York *Times*, Nov. 6, 1950, p. 1.

Note 3—Senator Flanders' comments appear in the *Congressional Record*, Dec. 2, 1950.

Note 4—According to Jean-Jacques Servan-Schreiber (of *Le Monde*, Paris), in "Europe's View of the Crisis," New York *Herald Tribune*, Dec. 6, 1950. At the time the author was in the United States, on a State Department fellowship.

Note 5—The population figure has been compiled from data appearing in the May 1952 issue of the *Monthly Bulletin of Statistics*, Statistical Office of the United Nations. According to the same source, "The 65 per cent of the peoples of the world living in Asia, Africa and Latin America mustered only 17 per cent of the income of the globe." Even that ghastly figure gives a false picture, since much of this income derives from extractive industries like petroleum and rarely has much effect on the population as a whole.

Note 6—*United States News and World Report*, Aug. 31, 1951, p. 36.

Note 7—Technically some Lend-Lease continued, notably in considerable quantities to China. But the suddenness of the shift from
wartime Lend-Lease gravely disorganized the planning of many
governments.

Note 8—This phrase is quoted from the *Yearbook of the United Nations 1946–47*, by John MacLaurin in his *United Nations and
Power Politics*, p. 90.

Note 9—In general the American position has consistently favored
private enterprise, private investment, the International Bank,
and the Export-Import Bank, as adequate to the problem. In
general the Russian position has been based on two considerations which have lent it a certain ambiguity. First, as Marxists,
they are convinced that the fundamental problems of the underdeveloped areas are insoluble without a change in class
structure. Secondly, they have naturally wished to avoid the
appearance of indifference to the sufferings of the poorer classes.

Note 10—In this negative vote, Russia and America have been consistently followed by the other industrialized countries on all committees that happened to be involved in the problem of whether
an Authority should be established.

Note 11—The relevant—the unrestricted—official documents of the
Economic and Social Council of the United Nations trace an
intricate parliamentary path for the proposed International Development Authority.

Note 12—Henry Steele Commager, "Appraisal of the Welfare State,"
in the New York *Times*, May 15, 1949, Section VI, p. 10.

Note 13—The budget figures have been rounded on the basis of their
more exact quotation in the New York *Times*, June 11, 1952,
p. 1. Our last budget appropriated $8,171,000 for the "United
Nations Expanded Program of Technical Assistance" for economic development. This was in addition to the "regular program," to which the United States contributes a little over half
a million. We will also contribute several millions to specialized
agencies like the World Health Organization and the Food and
Agriculture Organization. In 1952 our contributions to the
specialized agencies were somewhat over $9,000,000, perhaps

half of which was spent for technical assistance. It may be worth noting what the United Nations and the major specialized agencies cost America per capita. The U.N. costs each of us approximately a dime; UNESCO, about two cents; WHO, two cents; ILO and FAO, one cent apiece. These institutions are regularly heralded by our political leaders as the cornerstone of our foreign policy.

Note 14—The U.S. contribution has never accounted for more than two fifths of the total budget of the United Nations. But there can be little doubt that, had the U.S. urged placing adequate funds in the hands of the U.N., other member nations could have been rallied.

Note 15—This estimate is based on Congressional appropriations for our own armed forces and for purely military subsidies to our allies since the late Senator McMahon's speech; but it does not include technical assistance, even though one of the avowed motives of such assistance has been to preserve the capitalist system.

Note 16—William O. Douglas, *Strange Lands and Friendly People.* Harper, 1951.

Note 17—On the progress of poverty in the underdeveloped countries see the speech of Sir Herbert Broadley of the U.N. Food and Agriculture Organization delivered before the National Commission for UNESCO (quoted in the New York *Herald Tribune,* April 16, 1950); Trygve Lie's address to the twelfth session of the Economic and Social Council on Feb. 20, 1950 (quoted in *United Nations Bulletin,* March 1, 1951, p. 208); and Michael L. Hoffman's article "Rearming Helps the 'Haves' at Expense of 'Have-Nots'" in the New York *Times,* Feb. 11, 1952.

Note 18—Mr. Nelson Rockefeller made this clear on April 7, 1952, when he addressed the First National Conference on International Economic and Social Development, Washington, D.C.

Note 19—Thomas Hobbes, *Leviathan* (Oxford University Press, 1929), Part 1, Chapter 13, p. 98.

Note 20—I have accepted estimates of the cost of World War II at $330,031,000,000; of the Marshall Plan at $9,865,000,000; and of rearmament at $106,000,000,000; giving a total of only $445,896,000,000. Actually this leaves us over 12 per cent short of my "half a trillion." At the present rate we should make good on this deficiency very soon.

Note 21—See Mr. Babson's syndicated column of April 20, 1951.

Note 22—The results of a Gallup poll, released December 19, 1951, showed 70 per cent answering "Yes" to the question, "Would you like to see Truman and Churchill meet with Stalin to try to settle the differences between their countries?" And yet by this date the American people had been subjected to a merciless barrage of propaganda to prove that it would be quite useless to negotiate with the Russians. Indeed, Mr. Truman had publicly stated that the only place he would meet Stalin was Washington.

Note 23—The quotation is the title of a pamphlet, *Weakness through Strength*, by G. D. H. Cole, published by the Union of Democratic Control, London, 1951.

Note 24—By June 1952, after great difficulty, Secretary Acheson had persuaded both the French and German governments to add another signed document to the collection we have been making, this time a document providing for West German rearmament. As of this date it is far from certain that either the German or French parliaments will ratify it. If they do, it is still farther from certain that the agreement will get the popular support without which it is worth very little indeed. In general our government since the war has shown more skill at getting other governments to agree to our military plans, than the peoples they govern. It should be added that some of these governments could hardly hope to stay in power without subsidies from Washington.

Note 25—To be more precise, $1,097,000,000, after cancellations, according to the Sixth Annual Report of the International Bank for Reconstruction and Development.

Note 26—As reported in *Time*, Dec. 31, 1951, p. 15.

Note 27—It is true that a number of underdeveloped countries, led by Señor Santa Cruz of Chile, waged a valiant battle at the thirteenth session of ECOSOC for a real operating authority. They abandoned that objective for that of a mere development fund only after being defeated by a narrow margin at the sixth General Assembly in January 1952.

Note 28—The members of this group are listed at the end of the Bibliographical Notice.

Note 29—The Convention opened on December 30, 1950. One state in the American Union, Tennessee, actually sent delegates. Tennessee had authorized the election in August 1950 of such delegates. Three delegates were elected, of whom two attended the Convention. Attendance was very incomplete and plans were made to try for fuller attendance in some future year.

Note 30—Naturally U.N. broadcasts are frequently confused with U.S. propaganda and jammed accordingly. This situation would be comic if it were not tragic. Not all U.N. officials would welcome a real solution of the problem at this stage: they object that, unless and until the United Nations can liberate itself from the disproportionate pressures of Washington, its voice had best remain weak!

Note 31—The recommendations can be found in a report of the Committee on Communism; *Communism: Where Do We Stand Today?*, Chamber of Commerce, U.S.A., 1952. To date the Chamber has had very good luck in persuading the Congress to translate its recommendations into legislation.

Note 32—Appropriations for the Korean War have totaled about five billions a year.

Note 33—Hanson W. Baldwin wrote two articles entitled "Military in Politics," which appeared on April 1 and 2, 1952, in the New York *Times*.

Note 34—Eric Sevareid, *Not So Wild a Dream*, 1946, p. 298.

BIBLIOGRAPHICAL NOTICE

Although this book is not a scholarly work and is primarily an interpretation of events recorded in the press, recent experience has taught me that many individuals and study groups seek advice on the best things to read for persons who want to investigate further the matters I have discussed. Hence this notice.

For what I have written, I have drawn heavily on the daily and periodical press here at home and in a number of foreign countries, particularly in Europe. During the cold war it has been unusually necessary to read the foreign press, because of the wide gap between the way that press interprets current events and the way the American press interprets them. This gap has happily narrowed in the past year or two; or at least the better American newspapers, beginning with the New York *Times,* have done a better job of letting their readers know how we look to our neighbors.

I have obtained invaluable information from the official documents of the United Nations, information which was rarely published in our press. I have fortunately been able to discuss it with

a number of United Nations officials. It has also been my good
fortune to travel rather widely in Europe, North Africa, the Near
East, and Latin America since World War II—on the problem this
book discusses, prewar travel hardly counts; things are changing
so fast. Moreover, I traveled not as a tourist, but with the problem of economic development in mind; and I was able to discuss
that problem with many experts at their work, in the field. Finally,
I have been able to secure abundant advice, both written and
oral, from various experts who have served as consultants to the
Foundation for World Government, which for several years I
have directed.

For those who cannot give full time to the problem but want to
know more about it, a steadily increasing literature is available. I
list a few books; and, to facilitate purchase, I also list publishers
and generally the publication dates. On what I have called the
first revolution, the revolution against national sovereignty, an
ancient Greek classic, Thucydides' *History of the Peloponnesian
War* (Everyman), is more illuminating than any modern work I
know. It is a profound analysis of the struggle of two power blocs
in a system of sovereign states and in a community whose needs
demand a common government. I can understand why General
George Marshall finds it to the point today. I would put beside it
Hobbes's *Leviathan* (Oxford Press), particularly the portion beginning with Book Two, Chapter 13, and running through Book
Three; and that great American classic, *The Federalist*, by Alexander Hamilton, John Jay, and James Madison (Modern Library).

The problems Thucydides and Hobbes located are studied in
the context of today's events by a number of writers. For example,
Union Now, by Clarence Streit (Harper, 1940), proposes a federal government for fifteen Western democracies. *The Anatomy
of Peace* by Emery Reves (Harper, 1946), is a popular statement
of why the modern world needs a common government. Arnold
Toynbee's *War and Civilization* (Oxford, 1950) throws light on

the same problem. In addition to these popular works, P. E. Corbett's *Law and Society* (Harcourt, Brace, 1951) and Gerard J. Mangone's *The Idea and Practice of World Government* (Columbia, 1951) are first-rate. Professor Corbett examines the emergence of law in the world community; Professor Mangone is particularly felicitous in dealing with the kinds of understanding a democratic world government would require. A third well-documented and eminently readable work is *The United Nations and Power Politics,* by John McLaurin (Harper, 1951), which gives the American reader a view of our role in the United Nations which he is unlikely to have gotten from our daily press. Finally, the reader's imagination may be fruitfully stirred by *Preliminary Draft of a World Constitution,* by the Committee to Frame a World Constitution (University of Chicago Press, 1948). He should of course be familiar with the Charter of the United Nations, which is available in any good almanac. And the *Monthly Bulletin of Statistics* can be secured from the Statistical Office of the United Nations in New York.

On what I have called the second revolution, the world-wide revolution against hunger, misery, and foreign exploitation, the reader might best begin with *The Geography of Hunger,* by Josué de Castro (Little, Brown, 1952). Dr. De Castro is a Brazilian nutritionist, with experience in the Food and Agriculture Organization of the United Nations. His book gives a moving account of the role of famine in the world, yesterday and today. Robert Brittain's *Let There Be Bread* (Simon and Schuster, 1952) summarizes the extraordinary means which modern science has placed in our hands for attacking world misery, means which most of us have been too busy with the cold war to keep up with. His book makes exciting reading.

On the subject of imperialism, the contemporary American reader needs most to know how imperialism looks from underneath, not from on top—that is, to "the natives," not the empire

281

builders. In this category, the classic work from the liberal point of view is still J. A. Hobson's *Imperialism: A Study* (George Allen & Unwin, Ltd., 1948). The standard Communist analysis—and it is desperately important to our country that Americans should know the Communist analysis—is Lenin's *Imperialism: The Highest Stage of Capitalism* (International Publishers, 1939). A second Marxist analysis, but this time by a contemporary and a democratic socialist, is Fritz Sternberg's *Capitalism and Socialism On Trial* (John Day, 1952). No comparable work that I know of has been produced, unfortunately, from the point of view of present-day American capitalism. But a journalistic effort in that direction is the February 1950 issue of *Fortune* magazine, exclusively devoted to the economic development of under-developed countries.

The briefest statement of the problem this book deals with is a pamphlet, *Let's Join the Human Race,* by the author (University of Chicago Press, 1950). A longer survey of the whole problem is a set of eight pamphlets under the general title *The Bold New Program Series,* written by a group of experts and published by the Public Affairs Institute in 1950. The pamphlets are inevitably uneven, but they are well worth study and, because of the bibliographical material they contain, they make a particularly good starting point for a study group. They show, I think, an insufficient awareness of a question that has, since their publication, grown steadily more insistent: Is this job of economic development an American job, or a United Nations job? Two other American proposals on problems of economic development are well worth reading. They are: *A Total Peace Offensive,* by Walter Reuther (UAW-CIO, Detroit, Michigan); and *Point Four,* by James P. Warburg (Current Affairs Press, New York).

For a look at various segments of the postwar world as they actually exist, there are several good books. *The State of Europe,* by Howard K. Smith (Alfred Knopf, 1949), is more worth reading on Europe than anything I have seen since. It would, I think, have become a famous book if it had not been thrust aside by the psychoses of the cold war. It is the work of America's ablest foreign correspondent in radio. *The Situation in Asia,* by Owen Lattimore (Little, Brown, 1949), remains essential on Asia. Professor Lattimore had won his spurs as a careful scholar and an authority on China before most of his Congressional tormentors were ever heard of. Harold R. Isaacs and Emory Ross have dealt with postwar Africa in the Headline Series of the Foreign Policy Association. See their *Africa: New Crisis in the Making* (January–February, 1952). For South and Central America one might well begin with a recently published book, *The State of Latin America,* by Germán Arciniegas (Alfred Knopf, 1952). Justice William O. Douglas's *Strange Lands and Friendly People* (Harper, 1951) presents moving sketches of Asians as they live and think today. And Clare and Harris Wofford, Jr., do a fresh and vigorous job of interpretive reporting in *India Afire* (John Day, 1951). Needless to say, these books about the present condition of mankind in four of our continents have been chosen rather than others because of the way they throw light on those aspects of man's condition with which the present volume is concerned.

Last year Aneurin Bevan and his supporters published *One Way Only* (Tribune Publications, Ltd., 1951), pointing out the folly of Great Britain's attempt to meet the arms "target" which American statesmen had set for her. It was a good, clear, and remarkably moderate statement. It was immediately denounced by the Conservative press in Great Britain; and Bevan himself was denounced as a Huey Long by the press in our country. The pamphlet was not published in America, so the American voter never heard a case he badly needed to hear if there was to be real understanding between us and our chief military ally. All the American voter got was a passage or two quoted without context. A few months later Churchill was forced by events to vindicate Bevan's view on the rate of rearmament. That Bevan's pamphlet never appeared in this country was a publishing scandal, partially redressed when Simon and Schuster in 1952 published his new book, *In Place of Fear*. Three other pamphlets published in Britain should have been available to the American people: *Weakness Through Strength*, by the well-known British economist, G. D. H. Cole (Union of Democratic Control, 1951); *Tanks Into Tractors*, by Sir Richard Acland (The Association for World Peace, London, 1951); and *War on Want: A Plan for World Development*, by a committee which the Rt. Hon. Harold Wilson, M.P., a "Bevanite," headed (The Association for World Peace, London, 1952). I have cited these titles, not merely because they deal either with the theme of this book or with related themes, but because they are such beautiful illustrations of how cut off from world opinion, and even from important streams of opinion among our closest allies, we Americans have been during our cold-war leadership.

Newcomers to the "trials and errors" of contemporary Palestine might well start with Walter C. Lowdermilk's *Palestine, Land of Promise* (Harper, 1944), and *Palestine: Problem and Promise*, by Nathan, Gass, and Creamer (Public Affairs Press, 1946). Though Palestine moves fast these days, from triumph to triumph and from crisis to crisis, these two books are still good primers.

The student of the TVA can begin with David Lilienthal's *TVA: Democracy on the March* (Harper, 1945) and follow through with the *Annual Report of the Tennessee Valley Authority* for successive years. This can of course be secured from the Superintendent of Documents, U.S. Government Printing Office. He might then read Herman Finer's *The TVA: Lessons for International Application* (International Labor Office, Montreal, 1944). Whereupon he will be ready for two books which I discuss in the text: *Partners in Progress* (Simon and Schuster, 1951; or U.S. Government Printing Office), and *Measures for the Economic Development of Under-developed Countries* (U.N. Department of

Economic Affairs, 1951). The former report was written by a Presidential commission headed by Nelson A. Rockefeller. The latter is the work of a group of five experts, appointed by the Secretary-General of the United Nations. They are Alberto Baltra Cortez, Professor of Economics, National University of Chile; D. R. Cadgil, Director, Gokhale Institute of Politics and Economics, Poona, India; George Hakim, Counselor, Legation of Lebanon, Washington, D.C.; W. Arthur Lewis, Professor of Political Economy, University of Manchester, England; and Theodore W. Schultz, Chairman, Department of Economics, University of Chicago. This report, like most U.N. documents that are not "restricted" and that have been printed, can be obtained from the International Documents Service, Columbia University Press.